Saggistica 36

D1296857

Espresso

To Andrea, for whom my love
is stronger than espresso

ESPRESSO

THE ART AND SOUL OF ITALY

Sally c Wolf,
Hope you enjoy the book!

Wendy Pojmann

Wendy Pojmann

BORDIGHERA PRESS

© 2021, Wendy Pojmann
Index by Jac Nelson of Nelson Indexing

Library of Congress Cataloging-in-Publication Data

Names: Pojmann, Wendy A. (Wendy Ann) author.
Title: Espresso : the art and soul of Italy / Wendy Pojmann.
Description: New York, NY : Bordighera Press, [2021] | Series: Saggistica; Volume 36 | Includes bibliographical references and index. | Summary: "The clamor of the cups hitting the saucers, the sounds of the coffee grinder, the machine and the steamer, the smells of coffee and fresh pastries, the counter filling with customers making a million different requests the "baristi" had no trouble remembering, the ordered chaos of people finishing their items and then moving along as the next group arrived, chatting, laughing, enjoying their short time together at the bar. Every espresso bar had its own characteristics, and some I sought purposely looking for a certain atmosphere or because I especially liked their "crema di caffè." Others I happened into because they caught my eye while I was heading somewhere else. When out and about with family and friends, there was never a question of if we would "prendere un caffè" but there was usually some discussion about where. ESPRESSO explores the art and soul of Italy through the production, popular imagery, and ritual of coffee"-- Provided by publisher.
Identifiers: LCCN 2020050100 | ISBN 9781599541686 (trade paperback)
Subjects: LCSH: Coffee--Italy--Social aspects. | Espresso--Italy--History. | Coffee brewing--Italy--History. | Drinking customs--Italy.
Classification: LCC GT2919.I8 P65 2021 | DDC 394.1/20945--dc23
LC record available at https://lccn.loc.gov/2020050100

Printed in the United States.

Published by
BORDIGHERA PRESS
John D. Calandra Italian American Institute
25 W. 43rd Street, 17th Floor
New York, NY 10036

Saggistica 36
ISBN 978-1-59954-168-6

TABLE OF CONTENTS

FOREWORD

ESPRESSO IS EVERYTHING!

"Espresso is indeed everything," is a thought that entered my head one busy morning while having an espresso on my way to the national archives in Rome. "I should be writing about espresso," I then said to myself as I scurried into the shelves seeking information on another topic. I am not entirely sure how many espresso beverages I have consumed over my years of conducting research in Italy. There's usually a cappuccino in the morning, a caffè macchiato for my mid-morning break, an espresso normale after lunch, then perhaps another one later or an espresso shakerato on a warm afternoon or a marocchino on a cool one.[1] I drink five espressos a day on average. At home in the United States, I have not owned an American filter coffee machine for many years. When I earned tenure, I bought myself a capsule espresso machine for my office. My colleagues joke that if they need espresso, they know where to go. A few of them have purchased similar machines now.

My espresso passion developed when I was a graduate student finishing my Ph.D. It has held on ever since, but other than for a few conversations here and there with chatty Italian baristi interested in explaining to me why I preferred espresso to American coffee or even to an americano, I had not really given that much thought to what goes into making un buon caffè [a good coffee]. I just knew that American coffee gave me the jitters and often seemed just really, really bitter. I was happy to learn that I was actually taking in half as much caffeine by drinking espresso and I was certainly spending less. But, on that particular summer day, I realized as I looked around, that the espresso bar was one the main things I love about Italy. The clamor of the cups hitting the saucers, the sounds of the coffee grinder, the machine and the steamer, the smells of coffee and fresh pastries, the counter filling

---

1   In Italian terms, a cappuccino is a shot of espresso with steamed milk in a large mug, a caffè macchiato is a shot of espresso with a little steamed milk in an espresso cup, a shakerato is espresso shaken with ice and served cold with the ice removed, a marocchino (or mocaccino) is chocolate, espresso and a little steamed milk.

with customers making a million different requests the baristi had no trouble remembering, the ordered chaos of people finishing their items and then moving along as the next group arrived, chatting, laughing, enjoying their short time together at the bar. Every espresso bar had its own characteristics, and some I sought on purpose looking for a certain atmosphere or because I especially liked their crema di caffè.[2] Others I happened into because they caught my eye while I was heading somewhere else. When out and about with family and friends, there was never a question of *if* we would *prendere un caffe*[3] but there was usually some discussion about *where*.

It was all so far from my American coffee drinking experiences, which started with a mug of Joe at an Iowa Perkins with high school friends and eventually turned into grabbing a latte at Starbucks on my way to a college class or a temp job while in graduate school. Most of my Starbucks experiences made me miss Italy and allowed snarky thoughts to enter my mind. Why was the line always so long? Why did they write my order and name on the paper cup and then usually get something wrong anyway? Why did it take 10 minutes to get the wrong order? Why did the coffee taste burnt? Most importantly, why did I keep paying more than $4 for coffee I didn't even love? It wasn't for the setting. If I requested a ceramic cup and stayed, the anonymous corporate environment didn't stimulate me at all.

The first time I took a group of American college students to Italy, I was careful to explain how the Italian bar works. They were, after all, used to another routine. I told them they would need to pay in advance of ordering and place their receipt on the bar counter. A small tip of 10 or 20 cents would be appreciated and might get them served ahead of someone else, or it might not. If they wanted to sit and have their espresso, they would have to order from a server and pay more because the tip was included. If they wanted to sit and admire a beautiful view, such as in Piazza Navona in Rome, they would pay a lot more because they were paying for the table and the view. Some of the students were visibly anxious about having to recall these details.

---

2   A crema di caffè, cream coffee, is a mini espresso-based milkshake.

3   To get a coffee.

None of them had trouble adapting, but all of them said I had ruined coffee for them because the Italian espresso bars could not be fully replicated, not even in New York City, where many of them lived.

The idea of writing about espresso continued to linger and became more than a whimsical notion. I began to read about the history of coffee, pay more attention to the people in the bars where I went, and ask more questions of the baristi. At first, I thought about writing about the bars in Rome because it was the city I knew the best. I had first studied there as an undergraduate at Loyola University's Rome Center and then had returned while a graduate student at Boston College and stayed for several years. Most of my research had been based there and I went to Italy at least once a year, sometimes more, for work and family. Soon, however, I began to expand my scope and decided to write a book that would encompass cities beyond Rome. It seemed worth pointing out, especially after I had completed a National Endowment for the Humanities Seminar on the unification of Italy, that the emergence of espresso seemed to run parallel to the modernization of the new Italian state. Espresso was a unifying tradition or habit that developed along with the process of "making Italians," yet each region retained its own special way of preparing and drinking it. I wanted to know why and how that happened. Moreover, during the time I had started going to Italy, espresso had become globalized. Granted, I was not the only one who wanted to drink good espresso when I was not in Italy but when did the Italians decide to take it abroad? In other words, what was so special about "made in Italy" when applied to coffee? This book attempts to explain the history of espresso and espresso culture in Italy by looking at it as modern, unifying, and universalizing while at the same time showing how it is local, historical, and sociological.

My research is based on the studies of scholars and journalists who have been working on this topic for many years. To their work, I have added interviews I conducted with many owners, managers, and employees of espresso bars and espresso producers. Newspaper and magazine articles, web sites, and informal conversation have been important to piecing together my perspective as well. In no way are the places I feature comprehensive. There are more than 100,000 independent espresso bars and more than 1000 espresso producers in Italy today. I have chosen a few that reveal something about changes over time, local and regional traditions, and shared forms of identity. Those focal points are the work of a historian. I have not written a guide to espresso bars or manufacturers. Of course, cooperation has also been key to my work, and I must extend my thanks and appreciation to all the people who responded to my e-mails and calls, agreed to talk with me, shared materials with me, and helped me to complete my picture of what espresso means in modern and contemporary Italy. Of course, any errors or misjudgments remain my own.

CHAPTER ONE

ESPRESSO IN MODERN ITALY

Espresso today is a global phenomenon. It is now possible to order
an espresso beverage from New York, NY to Shanghai, China and
from Bettendorf, Iowa to Spiddal, Ireland. Starbucks, the world's
largest chain that produces and serves espresso, especially to the
middle classes, is ubiquitous with approximately 23,000 locations
worldwide. Nespresso, part of the Nestlé corporation, is gaining
ground with its capsule delivery system and more than 450 upscale
boutiques in major world cities. Coffee, of course, has been around
since the Middle Ages and consumed in various fashions according to
national histories, traditions and tastes. The Turks boil their roast into
a thick, dark liquid. The French press steeped grounds to the bottom
of a pot of boiling water. Americans watch it drip from a paper filter
that water passes through slowly. But espresso is an Italian obsession
born of the twentieth century that has now traveled the globe. But
why? What factors came together to make espresso the leading coffee
drink in Italy? And how did espresso come to surpass other forms of
coffee in the global marketplace and become known for its higher
quality and chicness? Without a doubt, national coffee-drinking
preferences reveal variations in technology and culture as much as
among individual palates. They also tell us a great deal about modern
historical developments.

   The history of espresso parallels the transformation of Italy from
a largely agrarian conglomerate of states and principalities loosely tied
together to a unified industrialized nation. It is my contention that the
"made in Italy" phenomenon that has made the Italians world famous for
good taste in food, design and fashion is closely tied to espresso culture.
As will be discussed in detail in later chapters, artists and anarchists,
feminists and students, politicians and athletes have all congregated in
and around particular bars in cities such as Turin, Rome, and Naples.
Moreover, tourism and globalization can be seen in the production
and distribution of Italian espresso, the subject of chapter two, with
more than 1000 small producers sharing the marketplace with large

companies such as Lavazza and Illy while successfully keeping out multinational rivals such as Starbucks. The first Starbucks, a Roastery in the tradition of the Seattle flagship store, opened just in September 2018 in Milan. The history of espresso reveals the complex flavors of a modern state with strong local and regional roots, a complex national narrative punctuated by fascism, democracy, and populism and ties to colonialism, capitalist growth, and migrations. The dark liquid served up in so many different ways is worth further scrutiny because it is located at the center of Italian historical identity and placed in the European and global landscapes. This chapter offers an overview of the history of espresso in Italy and its penetration of the global marketplace. It also seeks to explain the significance of espresso as a key part of the process of the modernization and Italianization of the peninsula and its islands. Multiple, related factors converged to make contemporary Italy the center of the espresso-drinking world. As will become clear, it did not occur by mere accident or serendipity.

Because of legends dating to the tenth and eleventh centuries, we know that coffee plants were found on the plateaus of Abyssinia. Inhabitants used it to make a sort of tea infusion from the leaves and flowers. It was in the Muslim world in the fifteenth century, however, that the beans were collected, toasted and extracted to make coffee. The spread of the Ottoman Empire brought coffee to Syria, Egypt, and the Maghreb region and grew in popularity in part because of a religious prohibition on alcohol. In fact, when coffee appeared at the gateway to Europe through Constantinople at the beginning of the 1500s, some commenters deemed it the "wine of Islam."[4] The first coffeehouse opened in the Ottoman city in 1554 as a cultural center and news of the Turkish hot beverage traveled back to Europe with visitors. It was not until the end of the 1500s, though, that coffee arrived in the Venetian Republic, its first appearance in Italy. By 1693, the first coffeehouse opened there and by 1763, Venice counted over 200 establishments that served coffee.[5] Coffee spread across the European continent during the same period with colonialism

---

4   Edmondo Capecelatro, *L'arte del caffè* (Naples: Rogiosi, 2014), 15.

5   Ibid., 18.

and slavery contributing to the spread of its reach. Although some Europeans were suspicious about the Islamic origins of coffee and others had concerns about its effects, linking caffeine-induced behaviors to the devil, it began to spread among the elite classes. Pope Clement VIII's (1536-1605) full absolution for coffee and his own enjoyment of it contributed to coffee's acceptance in the Catholic world. France quickly became the world's largest coffee producer and the Parisian and Viennese aristocracy delighted in adding coffee to their selection of other preferred hot drinks, namely tea and chocolate. Stories about Louis XIV (1638-1715) describe the King regularly making coffee for himself and his guests. Increased cultivation and the upset of the social class system ushered in by the Enlightenment and French Revolution meant that between the eighteenth and twentieth centuries coffee drinking in the West became more commonplace, with tens of thousands of coffeehouses extending across the continent. Most of the coffee consumed in them was prepared using the Turkish (boiled) and French (steeped) methods.

Although there is some disagreement as to the official moment in which espresso was born and whether the Italians or French are to be credited with its invention, most accounts trace it to the appearance of the first steam coffee machine, in reality a sort of percolator. The Frenchman Eduard Loysel de Santais debuted his two-espresso machine at the 1855 Paris Exhibition. His prototype brought water to a boil at 100 degrees Celsius inside a chamber and allowed for an equal mix of water and steam to pass through a connecting pipe that ended with an arm holding a filter and the finely ground coffee beans. The extraction of the coffee could be termed "espresso" in the sense that it was produced by high steam pressure and was therefore more rapid than other methods. The fact that the water had to reach and sustain a high temperature, however, meant that the coffee tasted burnt. Roasting the beans a little less before they were ground helped to correct the flavor, but accounts suggest it was woody nonetheless as well as hard on the stomach because it retained impurities and had a high caffeine content. Over the next several decades, a number of designers re-modeled the original prototype. In 1885, Angelo Moriondo of Turin registered a patent in France for a steam pressurized machine, which heated water to 1.5 BARs of pressure, that is, of the Earth's atmospheric pressure known as barometric pressure. Then in 1901, the Milanese engineer Luigi Bezzera registered the first patent for a true espresso machine in Italy. It was a cylindrical standup model that inspired other makers, including two French companies and seven Italian ones, such as Gaggia, Faema, and Arduino. Pier Teresio Arduino, in particular, implemented technical modifications that made the machines more efficient and allowed for their regular use in existing tea rooms. Desidero Pavoni exhibited a machine called the Ideale at the 1906 World Fair in Milan that featured a pressure release valve. The valve prevented hot coffee from spilling all over the preparer and further sped up the preparation process. The machine became very popular in the cafes. In addition to their functionality, the style of the machines was also important. They entered the elegant world of the late Victorian and Art Nouveau eras in which clients valued high design features. Many of the early coffee makers were large and elaborately decorated with floral or sculptural elements or crafted with bronze and ceramic pieces; they attracted visitors in their own right.

The taste of the coffee was still on the bitter side, however, because of the necessity of boiling the water at a high temperature to produce the necessary steam to press it through the chamber over a period of about 45 seconds. In 1935, Francesco Illy substituted steam pressure for pressure based on compressed air to create the first automatic machine. By the end of the 1940s, manufacturers had developed a piston machine that made the pressure even faster and led to the appearance of a creamy top layer on the espresso, termed crema caffè, and a better taste. Achille Gaggia is credited with transforming perceptions of the light foam from "scum" to "cream" and a feature of the best quality espresso. Moreover, Gaggia's lever piston machines increased steam pressure from 1.5 to 8-10 BARs; today most machines operate at 9 BARs. Water no longer had to boil inside a large chamber. It was reduced to just an ounce, which became the standard measure of an espresso. The lever, moreover, made "pulling an espresso" a craft and the link between man and machine more visceral. Coffee roasters also realized that the more finely ground the beans, the better the final flavor of the espresso. As Francesco and Riccardo Illy explain, "Thanks to the high pressure of the water that passes through the grounds you can, really you must, grind the coffee finely, thus increasing the surface contact with water to the maximum and favoring the extraction of the soluble substances that are mostly responsible for the taste."[6] Not only did the new methods improve flavor, they also made fast pressure-produced espresso the healthiest form of coffee. The quicker the water passes through the powder, the fewer the impurities, especially excess oils, are able to reach the final liquid. Less caffeine arrives in the drink as well. By comparison, French press coffee contains the greatest quantity of undesirable substances and a regular size mug of American filtered coffee has twice the amount of caffeine of an espresso. Many people believe espresso to be "stronger," but in actuality it is the taste that is purer.

Despite its earlier origins in express mail and express trains, the term "espresso" first appeared in the Italian dictionary in the 1920s. It was under the influence of modernist aesthetics and philosophy, especially that of Futurism, that an espresso culture and economy began to flourish. The Futurists, mostly a group of young men who embraced nationalism, new technologies, and speed, and expressed themselves through poetry and art, found espresso to be not only a tasty drink but also a symbol of progress and Italian identity. It freed modern man from the past. It could be consumed on the go and used to re-energize. Futurism's founder Filippo Tommaso Marinetti declared himself to be "the caffeine of Europe," suggesting that he, followed by other caffeine charged young men, was at the forefront of a movement that would leave behind the dusty old vestiges of romantic decay in favor of science, industry, and strength. The new streamlined designs of coffee machines by La Pavoni, Arduino and other manufacturers stimulated the eyes as did coffee posters by futurist artists such as Fortunato Depero who used thick lines and bold colors to advertise growing brands. The posters Leonetto Cappiello created for Arduino during the 1920s are especially masterful representations of modernity. In one image, a man dressed in an overcoat leans from a train car to fill his cup with espresso from a large cylindrical metal machine with gauges on the side, multiple spouts extending from the

6   Francesco and Riccardo Illy, *Dal caffè all'espresso* (Milan: Arnoldo Mondadori, 1989), 166. All translations are mine unless otherwise noted.

front and adorned on top with an imposing metal finial. Steaming cups of espresso fill the foreground. Trains and espresso machines are linked through materials, design, and speed; they are the future of Italy. As historian Claudia Baldoli has noted, the Futurists moreover put forward "a patriotic message: an exotic product, coffee, was Italianized, that is, transformed into espresso, made modern."[7] In other words, the origins of the beans and the fact that coffee had spread across much of Europe mattered less than did this new way of preparing and drinking it. Espresso could claim to be distinctly Italian.

Despite the breakthroughs in technology and general enthusiasm for espresso during the 1910s and 1920s, coffee consumption was relatively low. Most Italians, and mostly men at that, enjoyed one espresso per week in a public establishment. During World War I Italian soldiers received a daily coffee ration, but it was a sort of green coffee or orzo. In fact, many more Italians were familiar with drinking coffee made from orzo, a barley, than from coffee plants. The grains were roasted, ground and prepared in the same way as regular espresso. Orzo is cultivated in Italy, which made it less expensive and easier to obtain and the taste comes very close to regular coffee. Caffè d'orzo has remained a popular decaffeinated alternative to espresso even today but was and is considered an inferior product even in the early decades of espresso. In October 1935, after the League of Nations had sanctioned the Italians for their invasion of Ethiopia, Mussolini's government extended its policies favoring the domestic production of all possible goods to a ban on the importation of coffee. Caffè d'orzo was supposed to serve as a substitute but public outcry led to a lifting of the embargo after just seven months. The Italians wanted the real thing even if they were not drinking much of it yet.

Nevertheless, fascist politics influenced the terminology and economics of espresso drinking in several ways. First, barista is the Italianized version of barman, a term taken from the Americans but modified to sound more Italian. Because of the rapidity of serving espresso, many tea and coffee houses added a counter space where customers could order and drink their espresso while standing (not

---

7   Claudia Baldoli, "L'espresso, modernità e tradizione nell'Italia del caffè," *Memoria e ricerca* 23 (September 2006): 14.

generally, as in American bars, seated on bar stools). Customers began to refer to the espresso server behind the counter as the barman until official fascist policy dictated the use of barista to replace the foreign word. The term held on although barman again appeared in the postwar era. Barista, in the meantime, has been adopted by the English and Americans to distinguish those who serve coffee from those who serve alcohol. Second, the corporatism of fascist economics extended policies put in place in the 1910s, when local governments established caps for the prices of some beverages, including coffee. Family-run businesses became prevalent as a result and operated on low margins, another espresso tradition that has remained intact. In fact, American travelers to Italy are pleasantly surprised to find that a cappuccino averages about 1 Euro and 20 cents, compared to about 3 dollars at several U.S. chains. They are generally not aware, however, that the absence of a large markup is historically based. Finally, the fascists encouraged the use of aluminum, claiming it advanced the cause of Italian nationalism because it was readily available and easily adaptable to the aesthetics of Italian design.[8] In fact, it was during the prewar years of fascism that Alfonso Bialetti invented and began to produce the iconic Moka Express, a stove top brewing pot, using aluminum. Bialetti combined the knowledge he acquired working in the aluminum industry in France with his observations about how center-pipe washing machines operated to create the prototype in 1933. His goal was to deliver an espresso-like experience in the home. Between 1936 and 1940 Bialetti sold only about 10,000 mokas per year, mostly because of his limited marketing efforts. Nonetheless, he began to plant the idea of having an espresso at home that was as good as at the bar and reached a larger segment of the population, especially women, who were less likely to drink their espresso in public establishments. Aluminum was widely adopted by other espresso machine manufacturers as well and the new streamlined aesthetics of the art deco period fit well with Italian tastes.

The fascists advanced several coffee-friendly policies that became long-term traditions, but during World War II and the immediate

---

8   Jeffrey T. Schnapp, "The Romance of Caffeine and Aluminum," *Critical Inquiry* 28, no. 1 (Autumn 2001): 244-69.

postwar years coffee consumption suffered. Espresso was still a luxury good. During periods of economic strife and rationing few people could afford coffee and it was not considered an essential dietary need. Fighting in northern Africa and the Asian theatre reduced coffee production and exports. Italian coffee imports from Africa were interrupted periodically after 1941 and not always adequately met by the substitution of Brazilian coffee. Moreover, many dedicated fascists held on to the ideal of Italian autarchy. Espresso was being Italianized but coffee beans still pointed to foreign dependence. It was better to attribute a renunciation of espresso drinking to patriotism rather to any failure of the state. Committed anti-fascists also drank less coffee. Since their activities were being monitored, many of them stopped meeting regularly in their preferred coffee houses. Public assembly became too risky and Bialetti's moka was not yet common in most homes. Coffee shortages continued even after the war, but by 1953, about 70% of Italians reported drinking espresso at least occasionally – about 50% of men drank it outside the home compared to just about 14% of women. Middle-class men consumed more than laborers, who still favored wine with their lunchtime meal.[9] Over the next several years, espresso became increasingly popular until it reached a major explosion in the late 1950s.

Starting in about 1958, Italy entered a period of economic boom. Postwar growth had been slower than in some countries, such as Germany and the United States, but new economic policies and greater political stability helped usher in expansion in industry, housing, and the service sector. Per capita income growth in Italy outpaced that in Great Britain and France by the end of the 1960s. More men and women joined the work force and enjoyed their discretionary spending. They also began to change their coffee drinking habits. Espresso had been established as Italian and modern during the first half of the twentieth century, but it was still relatively limited in reach. During the second half of the century, it became a way of life for the vast majority of the population. Between 1956 and 1971 the number of bars in Italy

9   Jonathan Morris, "Making Italian Espresso, Making Espresso Italian," *Food & History* 8, no. 2 (2010): 173.

grew from just over 84,000 to more than 118,000.[10] Today there are more than 150,000 independent espresso bars. Several factors are responsible for the expansion and democratization of espresso. Many of the centrally located tea and coffeehouses of the eighteenth and nineteenth century elite morphed into espresso bars for the intellectuals and artists of the new upper classes, who gathered to discuss ideas and projects in the still elegant atmospheres of the well-established spaces. Coffeehouses were not new but the arrival of espresso in Italy changed them. Before espresso, clients normally gathered at tables and ordered from a waiter, just as in a restaurant. They drank tea, hot chocolate, alcoholic beverages, and some coffee. Pastry eating and tobacco smoking also outpaced coffee drinking in most of the Italian establishments. The elaborate new espresso machines and the new figure of the barista, joining that of the waiter, contributed to the increase in espresso consumption in the older coffeehouses. Reading newspapers and plotting revolutions retained their roles even among coffeehouse regulars newly caffeinated with espresso, but the boom atmosphere transformed them from remnants of a past associated with aristocratic origins to a present populated by young, glamorous go-getters. In fact, many of the coffeehouses associated with the *dolce vita* generation of the 1960s are the same ones in which the leaders of Italian unification met a century earlier.

Independent, often family-run, bars remained the standard in the postwar era. Italians embraced many aspects of American culture, but the anti-consumerist policies of both the Catholic Church and the Italian Communist Party favored an economic model that kept the development of chains and franchises at bay. Even highly successful bars today rarely expand into another neighborhood though in many cases their espresso blend does.[11] And while the idea of "express" consumption appears to have offered fast food companies an opportunity to turn bars into burger joints, the Italian marketplace was not ripe for such a transformation. Bars certainly served some food items, but they were

---

10   Jonathan Morris, "Why Espresso? Explaining Changes in European Coffee Preference from a Production of Culture Perspective," *European Review of History* 20, no. 5 (2013): 885.

11   Coffee production is the subject of Chapter Two.

not seen as substitutes for a home prepared meal, especially not in the 1950s and 1960s. For a period in the 1980s, however, some conservative family groups argued that the bar was a threat to the stability of the family since fathers and children more frequently left home in the morning without eating breakfast together with the declaration that they would pick up a cappuccino and pastry at the bar on the way to work or school.[12] Whether true or not, such a sentiment was indicative of the growing numbers and role of bars in the neighborhoods. Some of the new bars attracted clients with their modern, chic décor and became trendy gathering spots. However, it was mostly the growing government and service sectors that contributed to the development of espresso culture during the years of the economic miracle. Middle-class workers in these office jobs took pauses during the workday and went out into the city centers to have an espresso together. They favored counter service over the sit-down model since they were on short breaks. Women, too, joined in the ritual with co-workers and housewives would meet friends for a quick coffee while out shopping or after walking the children to school. Espresso drinking was also a symbol of adulthood; students flocked to bars to spend time being cool with their friends and to charge up for late nights of studying. In addition to the bars of the city centers, milk shops in the periphery turned into espresso bars for migrant workers from the south and rural areas seeking work in the cities. Housing conditions for workers were often less than ideal, which meant that socializing tended to occur in public spaces. More latterie, milk shops, offered espresso and many became bar dello sport, that is espresso bars where men would go to bet on Totocalcio, read the *Gazzetta dello Sport* and *Tutto Sport*, the daily sports newspapers, and discuss sports and other events of the day.

In all of these cases, espresso was the focal point of the bars. Low prices, in part a result of earlier price setting in Italy and in part a result of market prices established by the European Common Market, and improvements in the quality of the coffee, because of better roasting and preparation techniques, factored into Italians' preference for bar espresso even as the Bialetti moka became a staple in most Italian homes. The crema caffè could not be achieved using the stovetop

---

12   Baldoni, "L'espresso," 16.

maker regardless of the type of coffee used. Aluminum, foam rubber, and plastics had led to design changes in espresso machines used in bars that resulted in consistently good espresso when used by even a minimally trained barista. La Pavoni created a horizontal boiler, which took the machines from being tall to being wide and allowing for more espressos to be produced at once. The machines also moved behind the counter. Appearances still mattered but in relation to function rather than pure novelty or artistry. The Pitagora machine, for example, designed by the Castiglioni brothers for La Cimbali in 1962 won the Compasso d'oro, an industrial design award, and became an industry standard because maintenance was easier on a high production output. And production continued to grow over the following decades. Most Italians began to consume coffee on a daily basis and, by the late 1980s, coffee drinking habits on the national level had been well established. A Nielsen study revealed that 64% of respondents drank coffee both at home and in bars, 32% only at home, and just 3% only at a bar. A little over 28% of the bars' total revenue was based on coffee with 60% of all coffee consumed being served as simple espresso. Bars prepared about 50% of their daily coffee before lunch, 30% in the afternoon, and 20% in the evening.[13] This translates into a large number of espresso drinkers stopping at a bar for their morning coffee, then returning for a mid-morning break and an after-lunch espresso and then sometimes for a late afternoon break. Fewer clients come in after dinner either because of wanting to avoid caffeine to facilitate sleeping or because they have a late coffee in a restaurant or at home. In fact, fewer bars remain open into the evening unless they have another specialty, such as cocktails or ice cream.

The extension of bar espresso to most of the population – today more than 13 billion espressos slide across Italian bar counters each year – meant that the role of the barista was professionalized after the 1960s. In fact, another change to postwar coffee culture was that the witty, quick barista became more of an attraction than the espresso machine. Clients searched for bars that suited their coffee palate but also looked for places in which they could develop a rapport with the

---

13   Giulia Settimo, *Un caffè per favore, L'espresso al bar in Italia. Una straordinaria ricerca su tutto il territorio nazionale* (Milan: Pubblistampa, 1989).

barista. Baristi in Italy often undergo extensive training to learn how to operate and maintain the machines and how to prepare different kinds of coffee drinks. They must also possess certain characteristics since the job requires physical stamina, efficiency, sharpness, and patience. Being a barista in Italy is generally not a short-term commitment for high school or college students, as it often is in the United States. It is a long-term vocation. In fact, a survey of baristi found that more than 60% had been at their job for 10 or more years and that 67% of them were very satisfied with their work. Baristi typically love espresso and enjoy contact with the public. Like bartenders or barbers, baristi are often attentive, but discreet, listeners. More importantly, however, clients count on them to deliver a good espresso or other coffee drink. There are even competitions among the top baristi. The Istituto Nazionale Espresso Italiano, for example, awards an annual prize to the barista who can prepare the most perfect four espressos and two cappuccinos in just 11 minutes for a jury. Both the taste and the appearance of the coffees are factored into the scores. Although most of the winners have been Italian, the 2016 prize went to a Greek barista and recent finalists have come from China, Korea and Germany.[14] And, of course, the arrival of millions of foreign migrants to Italy has contributed to greater numbers of non-Italian baristi. It is increasingly common to be served by men and women of various origins and some bars are now owned by immigrants, especially in neighborhoods with large numbers of foreign residents.

The extension of bar culture throughout Italy that began with the economic miracle did not curtail espresso drinking at home. The crema caffè may not have been possible to achieve with a moka, but Bialetti and the manufacturers who copied him, made the home preparation of caffè an important activity in postwar daily life. The Neapolitan cuccumella, a seventeenth century invention, worked on a similar principle of boiling water on a stovetop, but it was more complicated to use because it was slower and required good timing to be able to flip the pot at the correct moment. Bialetti's coffee maker requires the user to simply add water, slip in the filter, add coffee, close it up,

---

14 See the Istituto Nazionale Espresso Italiano's website: http://www. espressoitaliano.org/it/Espresso-Italiano-Champion-2016.html.

put it on the stove, and wait for the coffee to emerge from the top, a process that takes just a few minutes; it is express. In fact, the 1930s design of the Moka Express had changed very little by the late 1950s. But, the return of Alfonso's son Renato from a German POW camp pushed the company in innovative directions, especially in terms of production and marketing. Bialetti focused almost exclusively on the Moka Express and was soon turning out about 1000 units per day. At the same time, the company began major advertising campaigns by buying massive billboards, placing ads in leading publications, and filling large spaces at the trade fairs held in Milan. The ads generally featured images of the Moka Express and a caricature of Bialetti's founder, the *omino con i baffi* [the little mustached man], whom the public found irresistible. Bialetti promised to deliver "a caffè at home just like at a bar" and to make it within everyone's reach. Housewives, of course, appreciated being able to have a good coffee themselves as well as to make it for family and friends, but men were not excluded from the equation. Some ads featured dads using the Moka Express while moms were off having fun. The strategies paid off. Today, Bialetti produces about 14,000 mokas each day for worldwide distribution.[15]

Desire for the crema caffè of bar espresso did not disappear because of the Moka Express, however. The creation and distribution of home pump espresso machines is the most recent development in the industry to try to match the experience of the bar. According to one source, in the early 1980s, the founder of Nespresso was having a coffee at the famous Caffè Sant'Eustachio in Rome when the idea for a new kind of machine came to him. He asked a barista if making a good espresso was very difficult and received the half-joking response of "no, you just push a button."[16] He, too, wanted to be able to just push a button and have a tasty espresso whenever and wherever he wanted, not only while on holiday in Rome, and so worked with a team at Nestlé to design a small pump machine that worked with pre-prepared capsules. Nespresso released the first two machines, the C100 and C1100, and

---

15 Schnapp's article is an excellent source on the history of the Bialetti Moka Express.

16 Interview by Author with Raimondo Ricci, Bar Sant'Eustachio, Rome, June 23, 2015.

the first varieties of its capsules in 1986 in Switzerland, its home base, France, and Italy. Growth has been remarkable. As of 2020, Nespresso is available in 84 countries and employs more than 14,000 people worldwide. In 2000, the company had just over 300 employees. Several factors can be attributed to Nespresso's success, among them its high-end design appeal and slick advertising campaigns. But, it is the public's craving for an authentic bar quality espresso that has defined this new niche market in which all the large espresso machine and espresso coffee manufacturers compete both with traditional espresso blends and capsules. The high end "Made in Italy" phenomenon that factors into perceptions of quality in the fashion, automotive, and building sectors is also key to the demand for espresso. Taste is surely important but historian Jonathan Morris attributes the success of espresso across Europe partially to "the repositioning and presentation of Italian coffee as a lifestyle product within which both drink-in and take-away culture could be presented as 'cool'."[17] Coolness in turn has become a justification for large markups on coffee beverages outside Italy.

Over the course of the twentieth century, no single type of coffee preparation has completely disappeared from the Italian peninsula. There are still percolators and the cuccumella. Most people in Italy own at least one moka and many are buying the new pump capsule machines as well because of their convenience. The preferred method of preparation is individual and personal. Espresso at home is part of the intimacy of sharing life with family and friends and can also be consumed alone. Yet, the bar has not disappeared. There are espresso lovers who claim simply that bar espresso is different and, at times, the only way to find satisfaction. Others value the sociability of the bar and the role it plays in their daily lives. Going to the bar to *prendere un caffè* is an important collective habit. Espresso and the bars that serve it are interwoven into modern Italian identity. It is no wonder that this made-in-Italy experience is being sought around the world but rarely achieved. Approximation has its limits. Italians often lament the lack of availability of good coffee while they travel. They sometimes even admit to having to resort to Starbucks or Dunkin' Donuts. Tourists returning to their home countries are sometimes sorry that they now

---

17   Morris, "Why Espresso," 893.

know the difference of the Italian espresso experience because it so difficult to replicate at home. Even a *New York Times* journalist was dismayed to find he was unable to enjoy an espresso in Manhattan that came close to his Roman experiences and suggested that "when the need for real espresso becomes overpowering, buy a ticket for Rome."[18] Clearly, *un buon caffè*[19] is more than the beans, the machine, and the water. It is people, history and culture.

18　William Grimes, "Critics Notebook; New York's Best Espresso?" *The New York Times*, May 15, 2002.　http://www.nytimes.com/2002/05/15/dining/critic-s-notebook-new-york-s-best-espresso.html.

19　A good coffee.

CHAPTER TWO

ESPRESSO PRODUCTION AND PRODUCERS

"Made in Italy" has become synonymous with high quality artisanal goods whether produced in small numbers or on an industrial scale. During the second half of the twentieth century, especially after the economic boom that began around 1958, the Italians expanded their historic leadership in artistic craftmanship and applied it to the manufacturing sector. From automobiles and interior design to high fashion and food products, Italian creativity, aesthetic sensitivities, and outstanding quality became universally recognized. Italian food and beverages are an integral part of the worldwide appreciation for excellence. People around the globe adore Italian pizza, pasta, and wine, for example, even as they transform it into local cultures. Authentic Italian taste is often sought even if it is not fully achieved. In recent decades, Italian espresso has extended beyond its national borders and is, in many places, considered exemplary coffee. As pointed out in the first chapter, however, coffee has been around since long before the invention of espresso. And coffee is not native to Italy. How then did espresso production emerge over the course of the twentieth century? Why is Italian espresso an industry standard even though coffee drinking takes many forms around the world? This chapter explores the significance of the Italian historical traditions of artisanal production and generational continuity in espresso production and shows how roasters and distributors are positioning themselves for the future. Italian companies, in general, have followed well-established patterns that value the avant-garde so long as is it rooted in the past. Espresso producers are part of this heritage and are benefiting from continued expansion in a competitive multibillion-dollar marketplace. More than 1000 small to large espresso roasters in Italy are currently serving national and international clients in the espresso bar, home, restaurant, and office sectors.

The longest continually operating coffee and espresso makers trace their histories to the end of the nineteenth century, before what is now known as espresso had even been invented.[20] Three of the earliest of these include two Piedmontese producers, Caffè Vergnano (1882) and Lavazza (1895), and the Trombetta (1890) company of Lazio. Lavazza is currently Italy's largest espresso producer with approximately 25% of the national market and leads the Italian companies in international exports.[21] Vergnano and Trombetta are large regional producers that distribute in Italy and numerous foreign markets. Both Piedmontese firms began as apothecaries, however, not as coffee roasters. Beginning in the 1600s, coffee was prescribed in Italian pharmacies because it was believed to be good for digestion and for the liver. It continued to be used for medicinal purposes into the nineteenth and twentieth centuries. In 1895, Luigi Lavazza opened a pharmacy on the Via San Tommaso in Turin, which today houses the company's espresso bar and restaurant. He surrounded himself with bags of raw coffee beans and became interested in creating his own special blends, an interest that then led him to travel to Brazil and other parts of South America to learn about different types of coffee plants and the flavors they could give to roasted beans. Domenico Vergnano began making coffee in 1882 with a sort of traveling apothecary based in the small town of Chieri, just outside Turin. Also fascinated by the healing elements of coffee, Vergnano set up a small shop and began to focus especially on mastering the techniques of roasting beans and making blends. His interest in flavors and the enjoyment of coffee soon came to outweigh his focus on its curative properties, however. Around the same period, but in Rome, Vittorio Trombetta opened a small roaster near the Termini train station where travelers could stop for a coffee at the beginning or end of a trip and purchase freshly roasted coffee to take to friends and family. In these early years, coffee was usually prepared with a percolator and was not widely consumed. However, with the invention of the first espresso machines in Italy and new knowledge about coffee beans and roasting techniques, the Italians were well positioned to develop their own approaches to espresso preparation

---

20 The company Web sites, interviews by the Author, and materials given to me are the main sources on the espresso producers.

21 Lavazza, *Annual Report 2016*, available for download at http://m.lavazza.com/default/.content/document/pdf/LAVAZZA_2016_ANNUAL_REPORT.pdf

and distribution. Lavazza, Vergnano and Trombetta were soon joined by a number of other visionaries, one of whom was Francesco Illy, who learned about the coffee and chocolate trades in Vienna before settling in Trieste and, in 1933, co-opening a firm there called Illy-Hausbrandt.

During the early years of fascism, especially before the outbreak of World War II, the espresso trade began to flourish. In 1927, Luigi Lavazza opened his family coffee business—his wife and sons were listed as partners—on the Corso Giulio Cesare in Turin, and with 1.5 million lire in capital expanded across the region. The opening of the Fiat Lingotto plant nearby aided in Lavazza's growth since the company was able to benefit from the use of automobiles and an extensive sales network. Luigi Lavazza's new double-parchment paper packaging allowed the company to distribute freshly roasted and ground espresso within the region and was a first step in preparing espresso for travel. Francesco Illy's development of the vacuum sealed can in 1934 further advanced the ability of espresso to be transported, and his 1935 creation of the first high pressure machine based on compressed air, the Illetta, modernized coffee brewing. Technical advances were enhanced by knowledge of coffee growing as well. For instance, in 1930, Domenico Vergnano's passion for understanding the coffee plant led him to purchase a coffee plantation in Kenya and gave him the opportunity to follow the full production process from beginning to end. Knowledge of the intricacies of coffee growing, technological improvements, improved transportation networks, and entrepreneurial vision allowed these first espresso producers to survive the years of wartime shortages and Benito Mussolini's autarchy. Although still consuming espresso on a rather limited basis, the Italians had developed a taste for the warm brown liquid that extended into the postwar years and attracted other roasters and brewers into the trade.

In fact, several other coffee manufacturers began doing business in the period at the end of and just after the conclusion of World War II. In 1944, Tazza d'Oro in Rome opened its doors near the Pantheon as a roaster and two years later expanded to include an espresso bar, in which clients could taste the freshly roasted and ground beans prepared by professional bar machines. Immediately popular among Romans and tourists, the Tazza D'Oro quickly established a reputation for high quality espresso. In Turin in 1949, Leonardo Venezia founded the Mokadoro roaster on a similar model—a small roaster of exceptional quality with an internal espresso bar and packaged coffee available for sale. Neighborhood residents and workers connected to the multitude of automobile manufacturing and related businesses enjoyed the freshness of the espresso in the small store and bar. Both Tazza d'Oro and Mokadoro have been housed in the same locations since the 1940s, continuing to serve generations of locals and passers-by. Some espresso makers of this era got their start as mobile operations, however, as was the case for the Neapolitan producer, Passalacqua, whose business began on wheels in 1948. Founder Samuele knew that there were not many jobs available after the war, and he recognized the people's desire to focus again on the small pleasures in life, such as espresso. He bought a fire roaster that could handle up to 5 kilograms in 20-minute roasts. Rather than taking on the expenses of a storefront, however, Samuele took his beans into the neighborhoods of Naples on a cart. The aroma emanating from his cart in the narrow city streets did the rest, attracting clients excited to try his fresh coffee.

During these first years after the war, local tastes became more defined as well, with a preference for stronger flavors in the south and sweeter flavors in the north. Nevertheless, Lavazza and Illy, having survived the war years and the temporary ban on imported coffee imposed by Mussolini, looked to ways to expand their reach beyond their immediate regional surroundings. Both companies focused on improving technologies while experimenting with new combinations of coffee beans. Francesco's son Ernesto obtained the *laurea*, a university degree, in chemistry and worked with his father to find ways to improve the shipping of coffee to southern regions, where demand was growing rapidly. Often times because of delays on train lines, roasted coffee would sit in less than ideal conditions for up to a month and end up losing much of its flavor or spoiling by the time it reached its destination. The Illys developed a pressurized packing system by sending nitrogen into the cans to slow oxidation, a method the company perfected and then used for cans they produced themselves for transport by 1957. Lavazza, too, was undergoing a similar process. Luigi's sons joined the family business and worked on branding and packaging, also using pressurized cans and creating the famous logo with the larger A at the center, LavAzza, that was added to the packaging labels. By 1950, the company was shipping vacuum sealed cans for the home market throughout Italy.

During the late 1950s and into the 1960s, consumer consumption accompanied Italy's economic boom. After the years of fascism, war, and general deprivation, the Italians were able to return to focusing on beauty and craftmanship in their work. They sought new entertainments and enjoyed leisure time in the company of family and friends. Espresso became integrated into daily life for most Italians rather than being a luxury item, or anyway a beverage for just occasional drinking, such as some liquors. Lavazza capitalized on the expansion of the middle-class, took advantage of new means of advertising, introducing for example, the "paradise in a cup" campaign, and opened a new vertical production facility on the Corso Novara in Turin. By 1957, Lavazza had become the largest espresso company in Italy, making 40,000 kilograms of espresso per day and, by 1965, had opened the largest factory in Europe at Settimo Torinese, a facility still in operation today. The Illy family turned its attention to expansion into Europe and opened offices in the Netherlands in 1962. The company then created a new international development office in Trieste in 1965.

New regional producers emerged during these boom years as well. In 1963 in Naples, what is now known as Kimbo got its start as Café do Brasil, founded by the Rubino brothers who had been working in a bakery with their father but wanted to grow the business through espresso roasting. The idea of a breakfast enjoyed with a warm *sfogliatella*, a ricotta-filled pastry, accompanied by excellent freshly roasted coffee was popularized and people from neighborhoods throughout Naples came to the Rubino bakery to try both. Traveling to the people remained a part of the Neapolitan tradition as well. The Moreno company began through distribution networks in the areas in and around Naples with founding father, Fernando Percuoco, delivering roasted beans to clients. Images of the family patriarch and his delivery van are now proudly displayed in the Moreno tasting room as is a photo of the multiple generations of family members who have continued the early traditions. Family, old methods, and the artistry of espresso are stressed by all the Italian producers. However, the Neapolitans tended to emphasize the pleasure of espresso, whereas the northern companies capitalized on the idea of the fast pace brought about by the boom and the swiftness of drinking espresso.

In the mid-1970s, a crisis in the espresso and coffee industry threatened the entire global market. It required that the Italian companies seek new sources for coffee beans and develop creative strategies to persevere through the worst of the disaster. In 1975, terrible frosts in Brazil, the largest coffee growing country and main source of Italian espresso, killed most of the coffee plants and sent raw bean prices soaring into the highest figures ever known. As the Italian newspaper *La Stampa* reported in 1977, never had espresso drinking been so threatened. High prices and lower quality may "lead consumers to do what not even the war succeeded at imposing, giving up coffee, eliminating it from our routines." Moreover, Ernesto Illy, who had taken over leadership of the company in 1962, pointed out that the consequences extended far beyond consumer prices and, in fact, "could affect entire populations and lead to hunger in half the world."[22] Illy focused on design and packaging during the crisis and looked more to the restaurant and bar markets rather than expanding in home consumption where the higher prices were more difficult to absorb. The special espresso cups the company designed became collectibles and even the cans themselves were heralded as objets d'art. Ernesto's son Francesco ensured the high-style, northern design elements the Italians seemed to appreciate would endure once the crisis had passed. Lavazza continued across all markets and in high volume and ramped up advertising with celebrity testimonials by actors such as Nino Manfredi, who remained with the espresso company for sixteen years. Lavazza and Illy also invested more money in research and development. All the companies looked to other coffee producing countries to ensure the supply of raw beans. Although they favored a high percentage of arabica from Brazil, Colombia, and other South American producers, the espresso manufacturers recognized the importance of the role of high quality robusta from countries such as Vietnam, Sri Lanka,

---

22   Sandro Doglio, "Mezzo mondo rischia la fame se scende il consumo del caffè," *La Stampa*, June 5, 1977, 21.

and Uganda. In the lower cost markets, however, lesser quality beans temporarily met needs while the Brazilian crops recovered. Some companies substituted coffee with hickory, a strategy that was not popular with consumers, however. Once the crisis passed by the end of the 1970s, Italian per capita coffee consumption reached 3.5 kilograms and Italy became the fourth largest green coffee importer.[23] Considering that the average dose of espresso is only 7 grams, this put Italy near the top of coffee loving European countries along with Germany, France and the United Kingdom, and among the largest consumers worldwide with the United States and Brazil.

As domestic and foreign espresso consumption grew during the 1980s and 1990s, the historic coffee producers that had secured their continuity further developed their brands to succeed in an increasingly large and competitive marketplace. Lavazza and Illy looked toward the export market while underscoring their value as Italian companies. According to Lavazza, espresso was an Italian invention and Lavazza was the most beloved of Italian espresso brands. By 1988, that claim seemed to be bearing out as the company reached 40% of Italian households and had grown by 40% in exports. In 1990, the company created an association in Great Britain to help promote Italian espresso and secure the market there. Back in Italy, the newspaper *La Stampa* reported that 7 in 10 households purchased Lavazza espresso for daily use in 1992. In 1980, Illy became the first espresso company to enter the United States market and, by the early 1990s, the company had developed direct purchasing from Brazil. The larger producers also continued to work on technological improvements to meet growing demand. Illy put its digital bean sorter to use starting in 1982, and the other companies mechanized parts of the production process. Kimbo, which had gotten a late start compared to the other large companies, moved into second place in the domestic market by 1990, in part because of its reach in southern Italy, but also because it found a market elsewhere in Italy, even in Turin, the home of the giant Lavazza. As a *La Stampa* journalist pointed out, "the highly aromatic espresso 'made

---

23   Vincenzo Sandali, "Italy," in *Coffee: A Comprehensive Guide to the Bean, the Beverage, and the Industry*, edited by Robert W. Thurston, Jonathan Morris, and Shawn Steiman (New York: Rowman & Littlefield, 2013), 184.

in Naples' departed for a conquest of the north. It invaded the bars of Turin enjoying a flattering success and putting an annoying splinter in the side of Lavazza, the leading company in the sector."[24] The smaller regional producers, such as Passalacqua, Moreno, Vergnano, and Trombetta were not left behind during the growth years, however. Rather than looking to industrial scale production, they focused on the high quality of their products that retained artisanal traditions, especially during the sorting and roasting processes, catered to regional tastes, and emphasized personalized, family-based service. The still smaller roasters/bars, such as Tazza d'Oro and Mokadoro counted on local niche markets in which new blends could be tried out on a loyal clientele or where tourists were willing to pay more for exotic or specially prepared coffees.

Since 2000, the Italian espresso makers have set standards for sustainability, fair trade and service systems while the industry continues to grow. In 2015, per capita consumption reached 5.6 kilograms.[25] The Italians imported just over 7.6 million 60-kilogram sacks of raw coffee and exported almost 2.5 million sacks of roasted beans.[26] Recognizing the impact of the industry on the environment and economic systems, most espresso companies now devote research and development to reducing emissions, ensuring the long-term health of the environment and the plants that keep it going, and paying farmers and workers equitably while providing a good working environment. Several certification schemes and consumer labels, such as UTZ, the Global Coffee Platform, and the Rainforest Alliance, are setting standards for the industry although certified raw coffee is a relatively small percentage of total imports to Italy. For example, in 2014, only about 2300 tons of Lavazza's 150,000 tons of imported coffee was certified by outside bodies. This figure can be compared to the 95% third-party certifications obtained by Starbucks a year earlier.[27] Nevertheless, the education of

---

24   Fulvio Milone, "La tazzulella sfida Torino," *La Stampa Sera*, March 13, 1990, 2.

25   Center for the Promotion of Imports, "Exporting Coffee to Italy," Web site, https://www.cbi.eu/market-information/coffee/italy/. Last accessed April 30, 2018.

26   Sandali, "Italy," 185.

27   Sjoerd Panhuysen and Joost Pierrot, *Coffee Barometer 2014*, Report Produced by Hivos, IUCN, Nederland, Oxfam, Novib, Solidaridad, and the WWF, available

consumers through advertising, such as in Lavazza's recent calendars that feature coffee-growing countries and the stories of what several individuals and groups are doing to improve the planet, represents a change in direction. Earlier calendars tended to use pin-up girls rather than discuss the origins of the product. Today's consumers are interested in knowing more about their espresso and they ask questions about it. Who grows it? Where? How is it transformed into a cup of coffee? This, too, is a departure from the days in which many espresso drinkers perhaps had a favorite brand or a favorite bar but were not necessarily curious about why their tastes led them to buy Kimbo at the supermarket or to get an espresso at the Tazza d'Oro when in the center of Rome.

One of the marked changes among younger espresso drinkers in Italy today is, in fact, learning more about their coffee and making specific choices about what they buy and where they buy it. In some ways, specialty espresso shares elements with craft beer in that a wide menu of options is available to cater to many tastes. Consumers can now choose very specific blends, order organic products, and exchange used capsules for discounts on new purchases in recycling plans. The smaller artisanal roasters are especially attuned to the newer segments of espresso drinkers and to gourmet veterans. As Francesco of Mokadoro explains, "Younger consumers are interested in the artistic aspects of artisanal products since each roaster puts a little of themselves into the process. It's not about speed. Good coffee happens slowly. A lot of Italians are still using the moka to make coffee, too. We're fond of them and we want good tasting coffee from them."[28] Diana Lisci of Vergnano agrees that capturing the youth espresso market is important and says that a "third wave" of espresso drinking has arrived. Vergnano is experimenting with new techniques, such as producing espresso for cold brew coffees, and offering some single origin espressos along with their traditional blends.[29]

for download at hivos.org/sites/default/files/coffee_barometer_2014_report_1.pdf.

28   Interview by Author with Francesco Salomone, Mokadoro, Turin, Italy, March 14, 2018.

29   Interview by Author with Diana Lisci, Caffè Vergnano, Turin, Italy, March 13, 2018.

The biggest impact in the market over the past decade, however, is the realm of pod and capsule espresso. The smaller artisanal roasters have preferred to stick with beans and ground espresso, but the medium and large producers have seen an increasingly important segment of their business in this area. Moreno, Vergnano and Trombetta, for example, now have much larger production areas dedicated to the preparation and packaging of pods and capsules than to the traditional "bricks" of espresso. According to Mara Annarilli of Trombetta, the returns on the single dose machine-based products are much higher than those for arm machines or moka ground coffee for traditional home use.[30] Lavazza and Illy both developed pod machines by the 1980s, but it is really the Swiss company Nespresso that has revolutionized the home and office espresso markets with its capsule machines. Trombetta, Moreno and Vergnano all offer compatible pods and capsules for the machines made by the larger companies and anticipate that this sector will only continue to grow in coming years. Trombetta has purchased new pod and capsule making machines to keep up with demand and is looking to expand into a nearby warehouse shortly. The challenge has been to maintain the same high quality of the espresso in a single-dose product while also focusing on a commitment to environmentally friendly production. The pods tend to be favored in both cases because they contain more espresso, about 7 grams, and use paper casings, versus the Nespresso compatible capsules that use just 5 grams of coffee and are packaged with plastics and aluminum. According to the Specialty Coffee Association of Europe a single shot of espresso, which is 20-30 milliliters, should be made from 6.5 to 7.5 grams of ground espresso to achieve the best flavor. The capsules also generate more waste, but some companies, including Nespresso, offer recycling incentives with discounts on future purchases.

By the time espresso drinkers lift their cups to their mouths and inhale the aroma, the coffee has been through a complex journey that extends across multiple continents and involves numerous individuals.[31]

---

30 Interview by Author with Mara Annarilli, Caffè Trombetta, Rome, Italy, March 20, 2018.

31 See for example on coffee growing and Italian imports, Manuel Terzi, *Dalla parte del caffè: storia, ricette ed emozoni della bevanda più famosa al mondo* (Bologna:

Coffee plants [*coffeeae*] grow only in very specific conditions and so are limited to just a handful of countries in tropical regions. Currently, the Italians buy the most coffee from Brazil (31%), Vietnam (21%) and India (12%). Uganda, Indonesia and Colombia also are significant suppliers, especially for special blends. Particularly expensive raw coffee beans come from Jamaica, Hawaii, and Guatemala. Blue Mountain Jamaican coffee, for example, costs importers about 70 Euros per kilogram and so is ordered in small quantities for the high-end gourmet market, such as for some of the espresso blends Vergnano and Tazza d'Oro produce. The climates in these areas are well-suited to coffee growing because the plants require steady temperatures of about 70 to 80 degrees Fahrenheit (21 to 26 degrees Celsius) and suffer when temperatures dip below 55 degrees F (13 degrees C). Hilly areas with partial sunshine and good drainage tend to offer the best growing conditions and can result in plants that flower up to three times per year. If left undisturbed, the plants can become trees reaching as high as 30 feet but cultivated plants are usually pruned at 5 to 12 feet. Longevous and fertile, coffee plants can yield as many as 8 pounds of beans per year for as many as 50 years, although 2 pounds annually is considered a strong crop. The main enemies of coffee plants are frost, which freezes the tree sap and kills the plant as occurred in Brazil in the 1970s, pests such as coffee bean borers like the broca, and disease, especially fungus, such as the *hemilea vastatrix* that killed all the coffee plants in Ceylon (Sri Lanka) in 1869.

The harvesting of the beans is done by hand using either a wet or dry method. The dry method involves shaking or pulling off the cherries and then raking them out on the ground. In the wet method, machines wash off the hard, outer shell. The wet, or washed method, usually commands higher prices because the beans are fully ripened, and their fermentation closely monitored, versus the dry method in which the beans may ferment for longer than is desirable.[32] Increasingly,

Edizioni Pendragon, 2012); Gabriella Baiguera, *Caffè: varietà e origini, tecniche di preparazione, cocktail e ricette* (Milano: Giunti 2009) and Maria Linardi, Enrico Maltoni, and Manuel Terzi, *Il libro completo del caffè* (Novara: DeAgostini, 2005).

32 David Joel and Karl Shapira, *The Book of Coffee & Tea: A Guide to the Appreciation of Fine Coffees, Teas and Herbal Beverages*, Illustrated by Meri Shardin

Italian roasters are purchasing more raw coffee directly from farmers rather than through brokers who bring green coffee to the large import markets in Genova, Trieste and Savona. However, brokers such as Sandalj in Trieste continue to play a large role in importation, especially for the smaller roasters who count on their expertise for the choicest beans.[33] Larger companies, such as Lavazza and Illy often have a person dedicated to visiting farms and sampling beans as do some mid-sized roasters, such as Moreno, but mid-sized and smaller roasters usually rely on the brokers or have samples sent to them from the growers to roast before committing to a large shipment. Once selected, most of the green coffee arrives in Italy in 60 to 70-kilogram natural fiber sacks made from hessian or jute, although larger quantities of up to a ton are now being shipped in polypropylene bags. All sacks or bags are labeled with the country of origin, weight, grade, certification codes, and a nomenclature code. The beans are traced every step of the way from their arrival through roasting, storage, blending, packaging and shipping.

Before the roasting begins, the beans are sifted to remove any unwanted elements, such as twigs or small pebbles. Moreno, Vergnano and Trombetta use a combination of mechanized and human checks to ensure only the raw beans are ending up in the roasting machines. Humidity levels are also checked, and tasters compile cards to explain how the beans should be roasted. Because the size and shape of the raw beans varies by crop, the different types are roasted separately. It is especially important that the beans be roasted evenly, that is, the surface of each bean must come into contact with the heat. Ideally, the roasting should be done at the lowest temperature possible for the shortest time possible to achieve the desired roast. Traditional drum roasting, in which the beans rotate on a flat surface that is heated from below by an indirect or direct flame, has been the preferred roasting method for artisanal roasters for more than a century. In 1935, Jabez Burns invented the Thermalo process that uses hot air to intensify the quantity of heat while halving the temperature. This

---

(New York: St. Martin's Press, 1975), 42-44.

33   Sandalj Trading Company, Our History of Italian Coffee Passion, Web site: https://www.sandalj.com/about-us/history/. Last accessed April 30, 2018.

avoids burning the beans and allows for a consistent level of heat. The larger companies, such as Lavazza, have introduced a turbo convection system to speed up the roasting but the smaller roasters insist on the traditional methods to guarantee the best flavor. Moreno, Vergnano, and Trombetta's roasting takes about 15-20 minutes per batch at 395 degrees Fahrenheit [200 degrees Celsius]. Each of the Italian companies does what is considered a "dark" roast by international industry standards, but the roasts actually vary quite a bit based on client preferences. Moreno's roasts are the darkest, Vergnano's the lightest, with Trombetta falling in between. The lighter roasts produce more acid that remains in the bean; darker roasting creates and then destroys the acids. Darker roasts contain less caffeine as a result and retain a shinier patina. When the roasting is complete, the beans spill out of the roaster into a large wire basket and are air cooled rapidly to prevent them from continuing to cook. During roasting, about 16-20% of the bean weight evaporates, but the volume increases by 60-70%. Antonio Tota of Vergnano explains that the process is a bit like popping popcorn. He points out that because of the new weight any remaining impurities are easy to remove; there will be a marked difference between the undesirable items and the now roasted beans.[34] Once cooled, the beans are sent to individual silos. The smallest artisanal roasters, such as Tazza d'Oro and Mokadoro then allow the beans to sit for up to a month. Francesco of Mokadoro says the best flavor, especially the pleasant aftertaste espresso leaves in your mouth, results from a short aging process during which more CO2 gasses are let out and more aroma remains. The larger companies working on volume, he notes, cannot devote so much storage space to roasted coffee before it's packaged or ground.

The next stage, and one that especially reveals the talents of the roaster, is the creation of blends, the *miscela*, essentially the recipe the roasters use to achieve the desired aromas and flavors. Most companies offer a variety of miscela options to cater to different tastes and budgets. The creative process begins with the selection of beans. Coffee plants are classified as arabica or robusta. Arabica plants tend to be more

---

34   Interview by Author with Antonio Tota, Caffè Vergnano, Turin, Italy, March 13, 2018.

delicate and produce beans that are lighter, sweeter and more acidic, whereas robusta plants are heartier and result in fuller bodied, earthier coffees that can tend toward bitterness. Robusta beans contain more caffeine as well. Generally speaking, the espresso preference in northern Italy is for a higher percentage of arabica, often 90 to 100%, whereas robusta generally reaches up to 20-25% in southern Italian blends. Of course, quality is a factor in all cases. It is a fallacy that arabica plants always produce better beans; there is a range of quality among arabica and robusta plants. Specific flavors also come from different regions or plants and are sought by the espresso roasters to round out their blends. Francesco of Mokadoro explains that Brazilian arabica is a great base for Italian espresso, which is why it is used by all the companies. However, he notes that it can be a very simple coffee if other beans are not added to the miscela. He compares an espresso made only from Brazilian beans to a red house wine that might satisfy a number of drinkers but not receive accolades for being exceptional. In Turin, he says consumers enjoy chocolatey, nutty and caramel tones, which he finds in arabica and robusta beans from Mexico, Costa Rica, Honduras, and Peru, among other countries. Vergnano and Trombetta tend to favor the sweeter, more acidic blends based mostly on arabica whereas Moreno's blends tend to be fuller bodied, rich and creamy with a higher percentage of robusta. In addition to Italian regional differences, the roasters also cater to the needs of domestic and foreign clients who request specific blends to satisfy their customers and stay within budgetary restrictions. Sometimes this means that a lower quality arabica has to be blended with a greater amount of robusta to achieve a pleasing taste. Some artisanal roasters, such as Tazza d'Oro, create special blends from a variety of arabica coffees. For instance, one of their higher cost blends is a mix of arabica beans from Yemen, called the Queen of Saba, which sells for 53 Euros a kilogram.[35] A current trend in the industry is to create blends from single countries of origin, but they are generally not just from one crop of beans in any case. Illy has featured Brazil, Colombia, Guatemala and Ethiopia in their monoarabica blends that nonetheless rely on some mixing. Andrea Illy describes them as "a unique blend that expressed an ideal

---

35   Interview by Author with Lara of Tazza D'Oro, Rome, Italy, March 7, 2018.

of balance and elegance, in which every variety contributes to the final result, one that pleases the olfactory senses, the palate and the taste of the connoisseur and that offers a richness and an emotion that no single quality of arabica can guarantee on its own."[36] Interestingly, despite great praise for the high quality of all the Illy espressos, some roasters point out that Illy is partially responsible for the myth of the absolute superiority of arabica since the company always uses 100% arabica beans. Illy's higher price point, about twice as much as the other commercial makers, is partially explained by the arabica preference in any case.

Roasters rely on their tasters to discern which beans, blends and preparation methods are the best for their production. Each of the companies features a tasting room where samples can be tried on a variety of machines. Moreno has lever machines, a Neapolitan bar essential, in its tasting room as well as automatic, pod, and capsule machines. Trombetta uses a small home pump machine along with small bar machines and even has a small roaster where tasters can roast very small samples before grinding them. Vergnano keeps cards featuring images of different types of beans on which the individual beans can be placed for comparison of size, shape and color. For the large companies working on maintaining consistency year after year, the tasters are important to determine how much of particular lots need to be used to compensate for annual crop differences that may occur because of environmental factors. As with wine or other agricultural beverages, yields from the same soil may not result in the exact same taste; but whereas wine connoisseurs learn about the particularities of production years, espresso consumers are mainly concerned with knowing that if they purchase the same miscela from Kimbo, Trombetta or Moreno, it will taste the same each time. Tasters are also tasked with suggesting new blends based on interesting samples they receive and keeping up with market trends. Once they have decided on the best recipes, they communicate them to the production staff, which programs the computers to begin the blending process. Beans are released from silos and blended together before entering new silos for packaging. In the case of espresso powder production and the

---

36   Andrea Illy, *Il sogno del caffè* (Torino: Codice Edizioni, 2015), 68.

preparation of pods and capsules, the beans are ground together. The grinding is also key to final flavor. Most of the roasters separate coffee for use with moka stove top makers from espresso for machines for home use. Bars, instead, grind their espresso on the spot. Nando Arenella of Moreno points out that grinding is often an overlooked aspect of espresso preparation. Since humidity levels factor into the density of the granules and powder, the correct size will determine how much liquid passes over the surface and into the cup. If the grinds are too large, the espresso will be too watery. If they are too small, the espresso will be very dense and too intense. A good barista will adjust the size of the grinder accordingly, even perhaps more than once in a given day.[37] In any case, the espresso companies are well aware of all the factors that go into producing a single espresso and work to deliver the best products they can.

Packaging and shipping are part of the delivery system. The mid-sized and larger companies use a combination of robots, machines, and humans to complete the production side. Moreno, which focuses especially on the restaurant and bar industries, prepares large numbers of 5-kilogram bags and large aluminum cans the barista attaches directly to the grinder. Vergnano makes espresso for distribution in Carrefour supermarkets and so prepares the vacuum-sealed briquettes in the chain's labeled bags. Trombetta points to their use of a special valve in packaging that allows CO_2 gasses to escape while preventing oxygen from entering it. Once packaged, the espresso, still carrying labels about origin, is then marked for delivery. Some companies, such as Moreno, include special storage areas in their warehouse where espresso and any related items, such as espresso and cappuccino cups and even machines, are kept organized by client destination. This is especially important to Moreno for the area in and around Naples where the company can offer personalized services. Moreno, in fact, was the only company I visited that provided machines by various makers and serviced them. Because many of their clients are regional bars, they tend to use the lever machines and send them in regularly to be refitted and cleaned. All the companies offer at least some

---

37   Interview by Author with Nando Arenella, Caffè Moreno, Naples, Italy, February 19, 2018.

merchandise to their bar clients as part of their marketing plan. The branding of espresso much resembles the branding of other products; it is also historical and cultural. Lavazza claims to be Italy's favorite coffee. Kimbo writes "espresso italiano" and "espresso napoletano" on its labels while Moreno asserts it is the "real Neapolitan espresso." Vergnano includes 1882 on all its packaging and Trombetta 1890 to remind customers of their company's longevity. Illy's aluminum can, made available for the home market in 2001, is itself a feature of the product and heralded for its simple elegance.

Family tradition is also a key historical component of many of the espresso makers. Vergnano, Lavazza, Trombetta, and Tazza d'Oro span four generations; Illy, Moreno, and Kimbo have been run by family members for three generations. The sons, daughters, and grandchildren of the company's families have been at the forefront of daily operations, sales, design, chemistry, technology, marketing, and development. Family businesses are a mainstay of Italian industry and common in the larger beverage industry as well; beer and liquor companies, for example, are known for family operations. Family members in the Italian espresso companies emphasize the role of informal apprenticeship, namely growing up inside the torrefazione and being exposed to the aromas and sounds of coffee. The sociability of espresso that is woven across family and shared with friends, who are part of an extended family, translates also into business practices. The role of the companies in the regional and national consciousness is noteworthy. For example, employees and bar owners who work with the Percuoco family that heads Moreno all referred to them as exceptional, kind people whose work ethic, commitment to Neapolitan tradition and generosity should be emulated across the trade. The young Francesco who purchased Mokadoro is not a family member, but he, too, underscored the significance of the contributions the original owner, Leonardo Venezia, made to the city of Turin and its environs. His plans for the future of the roaster take into account the family lives and long-term goals of his current employees. The contemporary world of the espresso roasters rests on the heritage of over 100 hundred years of production informed by well-honed traditions and an interest in innovation. The Italian ability to connect past and

present and project it into the future is well-represented in its espresso
industry, which is well-placed to continue to be at the leading edge
of the global marketplace.

CHAPTER THREE

ESPRESSO IN POPULAR CULTURE

In a famous scene from the 1954 film *Questi fantasmi*, beloved Neapolitan actor Eduardo De Filippo (1900-1984) sits on a balcony with a caffè in his hand after waking from his post-lunch nap. He explains to the camera that he could give up everything in his life except for the pleasure of making and drinking that caffè. He prepares the cuccumella, the special Neapolitan coffee maker, with care, grinds the correct amount of his favorite beans and brings the pot to a boil at the right speed. When ready, he carefully closes the spout with paper to keep the flavor from escaping and then carries it out to the balcony overlooking the twisty streets of Naples. His young wife, De Filippo's character explains, does not understand all the fuss and so she is not invited to share in the ritual. It's the perfect caffè, he notes, enjoyed in peace and solitude. Later in the same film De Filippo invokes the spirituality of espresso when he implores, "When I die, bring me a coffee and you will see that I will be revived like Lazarus." Scenes featuring espresso frequently appear in Italian films. It is the national beverage woven into the contemporary Italian consciousness through film, song, advertising, and tradition. Unlike, however, particular brands of food and drink, such as Coca-Cola or Nutella, which are recognizable in specific national or global contexts, espresso is its own category. There are espresso ad campaigns that most Italians recognize, such as Lavazza's Caballero and Carmencita commercials that were featured on the popular Carosello show in the 1960s and 70s, but espresso extends beyond its brands. It is first and foremost the drink of Italy.

It is not merely a casual occurrence that espresso appears in many popular contexts and is integrated into modern life. Coffee is imbued with hospitality, friendship, love, and solitude in ways other drinks are not. And, while it can be asserted that Italian cuisine is at the heart of the national culture and that preparing and eating meals carries historical significance, espresso can be distinguished in several important ways. It involves ritual and tradition but making coffee is relatively easy. There is little toil involved. It is easy to clean up.

It is more casual than food preparation or even opening a bottle of wine. People make and drink coffee throughout the day. It is part of breakfast or the end of a meal, but it is also a key feature of taking breaks and finding a moment to recollect. Espresso is synonymous with contemporary life and, as a result, it appears in numerous ways in all its vicissitudes. Popular sayings, songs, films, and ads about espresso shed light on the contemporary Italian consciousness. They reveal shared experiences such as love and betrayal, and loneliness and joy. They remind us of regional differences but also national unity. They show us the ways in which life has grown more frenetic but open the window on a mythological past and traditions many people believe are worth holding onto. And, they shape identities.

Italian poetry and popular music are rich with references to espresso. Poems and songs, old and new, in regional dialects, and in strict Italian, make use of the beverage's possibilities for forming analogies and recounting moments of both heroism and simple daily life. One of the most famous examples is Cesare Pavese's (1908-1950) 1923 "In un caffè" that begins with the title "In a coffee" and the very simple yet profound statement "I found myself." The poem continues "Reflected in the mirror, infinite, scintillating, I am, curved, enveloped in smoke and I don't even know any more if that is an illusion or if instead I am its empty image."[38] The patina of the coffee is reflective, and it releases smoke for this Italian poet, perhaps much like a foggy pond did for the Romantics or Transcendentalists of the north. Drinking coffee is an activity repeated each day, however, one that might even go nearly unnoticed until that time it comes especially into focus. The 1916 poem "L'eroe ar Caffè" recounts the fantasy of World War I battles in the northeast part of Italy in which a soldier never actually participated; it also modernizes coffee in the popular consciousness. Entering into Trieste and bombing Trento, climbing mountains, shooting and killing are all part of the soldier's life, but so is dipping cookies in a cup of coffee. That simple morning ritual grounds soldiers and keeps them marching on: "Level the mountains, break through,

---

38   In Italian, "Ho trovato me stesso, Riflesso nello specchio, Infinito, scintillante, sto, curvo, ravvolto di fumo e non so neppure più se proprio quella è un'illusione o sono io invece la sua immagine vuota."

shoot, kill. For me, there is only one road ... and there I dip cookies in the mug."[39] Another poem from the same era, the 1918 "'A tazza 'e cafè" explores the tumultuous state of unrequieted love. The young poet, Giuseppe Capaldo (1874-1919), legend has it, wrote the song about the barista, Brigida, with whom he was infatuated, comparing her to an espresso that at first seems a little bitter but sweetens as you stir it/her. The chorus in Neapolitan goes, "Ma i' tanto ch'aggi'a vutá, e tanto ch'aggi'a girá...ca 'o ddoce 'e sott'a tazza, fin'a 'mmocca mm'ha da arrivá!..." [But I have to stir a lot, I have to stir a lot, the sweetness from the bottom of the cup, into my mouth it must arrive.] Apparently, Brigida never sweetened to Capaldo's advances no matter how much he stirred, but his poem was turned into a song popularized in 1974 by Massimo Ranieri (b. 1951).

Neapolitans, going back to at least Capaldo, are proud of their long song tradition and their coffee. In 1958 Domenico Modugno (1928-1994) released "'O Cafè" that distinguishes Neapolitan espresso from all other possible drinks consumed in bars. "Milk is good and chocolate is sweet and chamomile does good. Orzo is refreshing, and wine makes you happy and only water takes away your thirst. But, a million people in Naples, like me, don't want to hear about it and live on coffee. And, good coffee. Only in Naples do they know how to make it. And, nobody knows why. It's a true specialty."[40] According to Modugno and sustained by Neapolitans even today, espresso is the number one drink in Naples and Naples is the number one place to drink espresso. As the song continues we also learn of the social importance of espresso. "To drink a coffee, you find an excuse. I offer one to someone and he offers one to me. No one says "no" because it's an offense. Already had six coffees and it's only 3 o'clock." To turn down a coffee is equivalent to saying, "I don't have time for you" or "I don't really want to talk to you" or even "I don't really like you." In the

---

39   In Italian, "Spiana li monti, sfonna, spara, ammazza...Per me, barbotta, c'è una strada sola... E intigne li biscotti ne la tazza."

40   In Italian, "Il latte è buono e la cioccolata è dolce e anche la camomilla bene ci fa. Rinfresca l'orzo e il vino rende felici e solo l'acqua la sete fa passare. Ma un milione di persone, di Napoli come me, non vogliono sapere niente e vivono di caffè. Ah, che bel caffè. Solo a Napoli lo sanno fare, e nessuno si spiega perchè è una vera specialità."

action comedy film, for example, *No grazie, il caffè mi rende nervoso* (1982) [No thanks, coffee makes me nervous], the protagonist turns down coffee by saying it makes him agitated since the rejection of this form of sociabilty requires explanation. The baristi who spoke to me in Naples confirmed the same. Once you've turned down an invitation for a coffee it can be difficult to regain the offeror's interest or trust. A similar response occurs in Rome but it is possible to recover by later bringing a coffee to the jilted party. Further north, especially in Milan, it is still polite to agree to get a coffee together but not doing so is not generally grounds for a fractured relationship. Regional habits reflect the ways in which people conduct their days and what constitutes friendliness. It is reductive to suggest that all of contemporary life moves forward based on personal connections in Naples and on at least the appearance of being busy in Milan, but the economic development of the country does point to a corresponding culture of habits based on the simple ritual of the espresso break.

Historical and regional espresso lyrics have held on over time and espresso continues to be a part of the national, contemporary Italian music scene as well. At the Sanremo music festival, an annual ongoing music competition held in a seaside resort town and followed by most Italians since 1950, numerous top placing songs have intertwined coffee with love and loss. In 1969, French singer Antoine (b. 1944) came in at fourteenth place with "Ma cosa hai messo nel caffè" ["But what did you put in my coffee"] written by Riccardo del Turco (b. 1939). The song asks what a lover has put in his coffee to make him so desperately lose his head. "What did you put in the coffee I drank at your place? There is something different in me now; if there is poison I will die but it will be sweet by your side, because the love that wasn't there before is there now."[41] Several years later when del Turco and his wife opened an elegant bar in Florence across from the Pitti Palace tourists would come in asking them to sing the famous line when they served espresso. In 2013, classically trained Italo-Moroccan pop singer Malike Ayane (b. 1984) performed her 2012 cover of the song

---

41   In Italian, "Ma cosa hai messo nel caffè che ho bevuto su da te? C'è qualche cosa di diverso adesso in me; se c'è un veleno morirò, ma sarà dolce accanto a te perchè l'amore che non c'era adesso c'è."

at Sanremo to enthusiastic applause. The song now has a more than forty-year history and is well-known throughout Italy; the continued utterance of "what did you put in my coffee?" has become synonymous with suddenly and unexpectedly falling in love. Another espresso song about love and life came in at tenth place at the 1981 Sanremo Festival. "Caffè nero bollente" ["Boiling black coffee"] performed by Fiorella Mannoia (b. 1954) explores slow melancholic moments accompanied by coffee. The young woman ruminates on a lover who has deluded her; she comes to the realization she no longer needs him while she drinks boiling black coffee. "I kill time drinking boiling black coffee in this nest heated by a patient sun that burns inside me that is as strong as coffee. An afternoon like this. I don't want to stay here. But then I stay here to look at myself for a moment. The stretch marks of life are many."[42] Having a coffee alone allows the woman to take a moment to reflect on her failed romance and come to terms with it. It is a rite of passage for moving on. It helps her acknowledge that she is human and complex. Love and espresso climbed even higher in the rankings in 2003 when "7000 Caffè" earned second place for Alex Britti (b. 1968). In the song, Britti has consumed 7000 coffees to be able to reach his lover, whom he "needs like water and coffee," as quickly as possible. The song reflects on the challenges of the modern world that separates lovers and the urgency of reuniting them. There is a frenetic quality to the song that is very much part of the technologically advanced, fast-paced reality of modern life and love. Espresso enables the over-tired driver to stay awake to see the woman he misses. He can't live without her as he can't live without the very espresso that takes him to her. Espresso is much more than a drink. It keeps love on track and fuels life.

Love and espresso songs fill our ears while Italian films bring regional differences and national unity to the big screen. Writers and directors have explored numerous aspects of modern life through the role of espresso. As in the song "O Caffè," the film *Benvenuti al*

---

42   In Italian, "E ammazzo il tempo bevendo caffè nero bollente. In questo nido scaldato ormai da un sole paziente che brucia dentro di me che è forte come il caffé. Un pomeriggio così oh no non voglio star qui e poi mi fermo per guardarmi un istante le smagliature della vita sono tante."

sud [*Welcome to the South*] (2010) underscores the significance of the ritual of having a coffee in southern towns. The movie is based on the 2008 French film *Bienvenue chez les Ch'tis* in which a postal worker (played by Dany Boon (b. 1966)) requests a transfer to the warm, sunny Mediterranean coast but ends up near the cool, rainy Belgian border. In the French version, Boon's character is invited to have a local craft beer in each of the residents' homes while on his route and he ends up quite drunk. In the Italian version, the Lombard worker, played by Claudio Bisio (b. 1957), lands in a small town near Salerno in Campania and is invited in to have an espresso by each of his new neighbors. He comments, in fact, that the locals seem to have nothing else to do but drink coffee all day. In both films, there is at first reticence that is overcome as the postal workers come to appreciate local customs and question aspects of their lives back home. The release of these films, including the 2012 Italian sequel, *Benvenuti al nord* [*Welcome to the North*], which simply reverses north/south and urban/rural stereotypes, is part of a European interest in understanding the role of small town life and traditions in the face of Europeanization and globalization. Of course, the popularity of such films can also be tied to the rise of populism and a desire to reclaim "authenticity" in a world of sameness. While tourism to northern France and sales of its local beer increased after the release of *Bienvenue*, however, the same phenomenon was not replicated in Italy. There is no evidence to suggest that Italians outside the south started drinking more espressos in general or more in its *ristretto* [short] version. While a local *torrefazione* [coffee roaster] is surely important in many Italian towns, it is not directly equivalent to craft beer production. In any case, it is coffee drinking and not any sort of alcohol drinking that marks the integration of an outsider in a new place and becomes a form of social bonding that defines a people.

Espresso similarly unites migrants. Such is the case in the 1959 film *I magliari* in which a southern Italian man migrates to Germany to find work but quickly finds himself in the midst of a shadowy existence. In the film, the restaurant Bella Napoli is a point of reference for the migrant community and many scenes feature espresso drinking there. Espresso serves as a cultural tie that unites the Italian men holding onto their ritual of getting a coffee as they seek to find their way in their new surroundings in Hannover. The climate is harsher, the food is heavier, and there is very little that resembles their lives back in Italy other than drinking espresso. In the 1971 film *Bello, onesto, emigrato Australia sposerebbe compaesana illibata* [*A Girl in Australia*] that tells the story of an Italian mail order bride and the immigrant to Australia who sends for her, espresso, too, is a defining feature of Italian identity, separating the two cultures. Australians prefer beer. Espresso is a comfort of home even in the most distant or disquieting of circumstances. Italian migrants are, of course, linked to pasta and pizza as well but coffee fills more frames and is far less frequently consumed by members of the host country than are Italian food items. Expats and migrants to Italy show they have integrated into their new society by drinking, and enjoying, espresso.

The bar as a site of daily life appears frequently in Italian cinema. *Bar sport* (2011), also starring Claudio Bisio, is based on Stefano Benni's popular comedic 1976 collection of short stories of the same name that recounts the lives of residents in a small town near Bologna. All of the action takes place inside the provincial bar. Although the film did not attain much critical or popular success, it nevertheless offers a glimpse, even if stereotyped, of the day-to-day activities inside a small-town bar where residents play card games and pinball as well as eat and drink a multiplicity of items and have their espresso. Elderly gossipy ladies, a hyperactive bicyclist, a self-proclaimed playboy, and obnoxious teens are among the clients of the bar. It is representative of a sociological cross-section of national popular Italian culture that is at once both diverse, because of the different generations and classes that enter, and unifying, because it is replicated in similar bars throughout the country. *Bar sport* is particularly illustrative of post-1970s bar culture in that sense but the role of the bar as a regular stopping place appears in much earlier films as well. A famous scene in *La banda degli onesti* [*The Band of Honest Men*] (1956) featuring beloved comic actors Totò (Antonio de Curtis 1898-1967) and Peppino (de Filippo 1903-1980) takes place inside a bar. Totò explains the workings of capitalism—the film deals with the ethical question of printing contraband bills—as he continues to pour sugar into his espresso. Finally, seeing the sugar bowl quickly being depleted, the barista asks him to stop with his explanation or pay extra. In other Totò classics, coffee bars are frequent settings. In *Totò terzo uomo* [*Toto the Third Man*], the actor orders a *caffè corretto al cognac* [a coffee "corrected" with cognac], then asks for more cognac than coffee and finally ends by saying "just bring me a glass of cognac and we'll leave it at that." In *I tartassati* [*The Overtaxed*] Totò jokes that he "orders three coffees at once to save two tips," a reference to the Italian custom of leaving a small coin on top of the receipt when placing it on the bar to order coffee and in *I due marescialli* [*The Two Marshals*] Totò complains about the bad taste of his coffee to the server.

Drinking a coffee at home also has special cinematic significance, as the earlier referenced *Questi fantasmi* scene makes clear. The more intimate setting of the personal household means that espresso at home is more closely tied to family, love, and solitude. The actor Peppino was himself captured in domestic images as he instructed his teenage son Luigi how to make coffee with a Neapolitan cuccumella and showed off his vast collection of coffee makers.[43] Photographs of director Federico Fellini (1920-1993) drinking a home prepared espresso while seated next to his 1973 Oscar for *Amarcord* circulated widely in part of because of the more relaxed home library setting in which Fellini posed. Several scenes in which another much lauded Neapolitan actor, Massimo Troisi (1953-1994), appears place coffee at the center of domestic life as well. In *Scusate il ritardo* (1983) [Excuse me for being late], Troisi's character Vincenzo owns a one cup moka, a symbol of his solitude. He lives alone and never has guests and so can manage making just one coffee at a time. The fact that he doesn't even expect anyone to come by for a coffee especially drives home the point that he is a man all alone. As the film unfolds, Vincenzo falls in love at first sight with a woman named Anna but he remains with his moka-for-one throughout the film. Coffee takes a dramatic turn in Troisi's *Pensavo fosse amore ... invece era un calesse* [*I thought it was love*] (1991) when minor character Chiara puts rat poison in Tommaso's espresso after he rejects her advances; the action takes place inside a

---

43 Andrea Albertini, Silvia Pesci and Giuseppe Villirillo, eds., *Caffè & Stars* (Rome: Damiani, 2004), introduction (not numbered), their translation.

larger, darker love story.

Of course, coffee can lead to love and subsequent complications as occurs in the film *Venga a prendere il caffè da noi* [*Come Have a Coffee With Us*] (1970) based on the novel of the same name and starring Ugo Tognazzi (1922-1990). In this story, a simple tax collector marries a rich woman and has affairs with both of her sisters after being invited to have a coffee with them at their home. In one scene, Tognazzi is surrounded by the three adoring sisters as they pour coffee into his ornate porcelain and silver cup. When he tries to make advances on the women's live-in domestic servant, however, the character's philandering comes to light, and the ruse finally ends. Totò once proclaimed "per prendere un caffè e tradire la moglie c'è sempre tempo," [there's always time to get a coffee and cheat on your wife], but it's still better to proceed with caution. In *Venga a prendere*, in any case, the male protagonist certainly makes use of espresso to pursue his sexual desires, but women are not excluded from extramarital activities. In the 1949 melodrama *Catene* an adulterous wife leaves her husband and two sons behind in Italy. The rejected family is seen at the breakfast table with sullen faces having caffè latte. And in the Oscar winning *Divorzio all'italiana* [*Divorce Italian Style*] (1961) actor Marcello Mastroianni's (1924-1996) character stares with contempt and desperation at the wife he wants to eliminate by framing her for adultery as she fills his tazzina. Whether in the absence of love, the presence of unrequited love, or when there is perhaps too much love, coffee and espresso figure prominently in Italian homes.

In addition to the popular arts, the advertising campaigns of the larger espresso producers are rich sources for understanding broad cultural interests throughout Italy. Ads often remain part of the popular imagination for many years after they have been discontinued and they represent characteristics of particular generations. One special source for advertising in postwar Italy was the immensely popular television variety show *Carosello*. The program featured longer commercials that were clearly distinguishable from the regular programming but also ran shorts of about 105 seconds that were integrated into the show and highlighted a product. *Carosello* broadcast more than 7000 episodes from 1957 to 1977; it was watched in nearly every Italian household with a television. Some of the most memorable spots for Italians viewing during those years were produced by Armando Testa for Lavazza. In the best known of them, two conically shaped puppets called Caballero and Carmencita, adorned in Latin American costumes, took Italian viewers on an exotic journey around the world to coffee producing countries, especially Brazil. Caballero tirelessly pursued his beloved Carmencita, with whom he had fallen in love at first sight. The ads ran on Carosello from 1960 to 1969 and in other formats through 1976. There are few Italians even of later generations who do not recognize the pair or know the famous Lavazza tag line, "Più lo mandi giù, più ti tira su" [the more you send down, the more it lifts you up].

Audiences and tastes matured by the late 1970s, which meant that coffee producers, like other advertisers, updated their campaigns to reflect cultural trends of the day. Celebrity ads replaced the exotic animated couple, as Jonathan Morris has noted, "in settings that stressed domestic consumption of the product rather than the distant origins of the bean."[44] More importantly, the new ads directly looked to define "italianità," a special sort of Italianness epitomized by espresso. Actor Nino Manfredi (1921-2004) delivered the first celebrity testimonial for Lavazza, a significant choice because of Manfredi's ability to appeal to the Italian "everyman" by playing the working-class man a little down on his luck but who maintains a sense of purpose and optimism. In the early 1990s, celebrated tenor Luciano Pavarotti (1935-2007), the elegant actress Monica Vitti (b. 1931), political satirist and illustrator Giorgio Forattini (b. 1931), and comic actor Bud Spencer (Carlo Pedersoli 1929-2016) further developed the concept of "Italianity" in their Lavazza spots. Extraordinary talent in the high arts, beauty and glamour, political astuteness and the ability to laugh all exemplified the Italian national character according to Lavazza. Kimbo followed Lavazza's lead and, in the 1980s and 1990s, also produced campaigns with famous Italians. Pippo Baudo (b. 1936), a longtime television personality and frequent host of the Sanremo musical festival appeared in ads in the 1980s and 90s. Well-known voice actors and television

---

44   Jonathan Morris, "Making Italian Espresso, Making Espresso Italian," *Food & History* 8, no. 2 (2010): 177.

personalities Massimo Dapporto (b. 1945) and Gigi Proietti (1940-
2020) spoke on behalf of Kimbo in commercials directed by the
award-winning advertiser Vittorio Sacco.[45] The objective during these
years was to recognize the special talents of Italians who claimed
that espresso helped them achieve their success and to associate the
individuals and their Italianness with their personal choice of miscela.
In other words, if Pavarotti drinks Lavazza Gold then that's the one I
want to drink as well. How the public related to the chosen celebrities
was key to the success of the ads and espresso sales; the biggest stars
had the largest impact.[46]

Miscela options became more integral to advertising campaigns in
the 1990s as the major coffee producers expanded into the European
markets and worked to stay fresh and relevant in the Italian one. Lavazza
launched its still ongoing espresso in heaven commercials. In these ads,
espresso is the only beverage consumed while floating on the fluffy
clouds of paradise. Comic television hosts, such as Paolo Bonolis (b.
1961) and Luca Laurenti (b. 1963) and, more recently, Enrico Brignano
(b. 1966), have played the roles of people knocking at the pearly gates
seeking eternal peace in a resting place where the espresso is always
available and always good. It's even better, of course, if served by the
scantily clad, attractive young women who assist St. Peter. This, too,
is representative of a much-discussed cultural decline connected to the
limited roles of decorative women in Italian television.[47] The coffee
producers, however, generally have not reduced their advertising to
heavily sexualized or objectifying images. Espresso is more often tied
to an idea of love and companionship than to promises of sex, as in
recent ads by Kimbo in which attractive actor Fabio Troiano (b. 1974)
invites friends over and prepares coffee for them in a moka. There is

45   Foreign films in Italy are dubbed. Voice actors often become celebrities in their
own right because of their work dubbing famous Hollywood stars and appear as
actors themselves in Italian films.

46   See the Lavazza website on their advertising campaigns at http://www.lavazza.
it/it/mondo_lavazza/comunicazione/storia-comunicazione/

47   Enrico Franceschini, "L'Italia un paese di veline, le donne sono solo oggetti,"
La Repubblica on-line, July 15, 2007. http://www.repubblica.it/2007/07/sezioni/
persone/paese-veline/paese-veline/paese-veline.html

some sexual intrigue among Troiano's good-looking companions but it is clear that friendship is embodied in the act of serving them coffee and that no fancy, expensive machine is required; Kimbo tastes great even in a simple, old-fashioned moka. Nespresso, in contrast, has taken espresso into the global market in new ways in its ads, many of which feature American actor George Clooney (b. 1961) and the wealth and elegance of his former Lake Como bachelor lifestyle. Clooney's charm and intelligence certainly invite fantasies of a new *dolce vita* but are not sexually suggestive. Despite Nespresso's Swiss base and global reach, its advertising is distinctly grounded in Italian aesthetics to purvey the idea of "Made in Italy" to the public. A 2015 Nespresso commercial for the American market stars Clooney with comic actor Danny DeVito (b. 1944). Saturday Night Live ran a parody skit of the ad in which the unlikely pair visit a tailor, an art gallery and a wine bar, all of which are high style Italian in appearance, to contrast Clooney's worldliness with DeVito's down-to-earth Italian-American tastes. Clooney drinks "Nespresso"; DeVito drinks "cauwfee." Nonetheless, here, too, friendship through espresso unites them.

Fantasy plays into the advertising of espresso in part because espresso is also at the core of many superstitions and ideas, true and false, about health and well-being shared in popular traditions. When coffee consumption first began to spread, some individuals were concerned about its possible ill effects. For example, the treatise "On the Use and Abuse of Coffee" written by Giovanni della Bona and published in Padova in 1760 associated the stimulant with the devil and cautioned against drinking it.[48] The agitated state of those who had had a little too much coffee seemed to suggest that it was a powerful drug that could lead to an altered consciousness and perhaps result in heresy. Most of these older beliefs are no longer taken seriously but several do prevail and continue to influence popular discourse. The fear of the evil eye, for instance, has resulted in several practices that involve the use of espresso. To understand if someone has had the evil eye cast upon him, a psychic puts a drop of oil into a cup of coffee. If it expands, it means the evil eye is present. It can be driven away by

---

48   Maria Linardi, Enrico Maltoni, and Manuel Terzi, *Il libro completo del caffè* (Milan: De Agostini, 2005), 111-112.

chanting a counter-spell while continuing to drop oil into the coffee until it no longer expands. In the case of an evil eye spell that has been cast upon an entire household, the psychic burns an incense made from such items as palm leaves, rosemary, and espresso grounds. Adding a few drops of blood to a cup of espresso is said to make someone fall in love with you; this is especially effective for women who use menstrual blood. According to another superstition, the accidental falling of cake or breadcrumbs into an espresso is an indication of the arrival of an unannounced guest or an important piece of news. Young ladies in some rural parts of Italy might still be stopped from putting milk and then sugar into their coffee; to do so is an indication of spinsterhood ahead. The sugar goes first. And, there is a long-held practice of reading coffee grounds, much like tea leaves, to predict the future.[49] Reading the bottom of the espresso cup is now also possible with an App for the iPhone. After finishing your coffee, you can take a photo and upload it to the App. Some of the most common forms and their corresponding meanings include a mouth, which indicates that there are people talking about you and that they might reveal uncomfortable truths; a heart means reciprocal love or a marriage on the way; a wave points to an upcoming period of ups and downs; a leaf carries positive change; and, a skull and crossbones is a sign that revelations will lead to a dramatic change. Of course, the espresso ground App is intended to be fun rather than taken seriously, but the fact that it exists suggests that superstitions and espresso are not just associated with distant times and small villages. Popular traditions have been modernized and made relevant to today's technologies and forms of socializing.[50]

Italians have long maintained that espresso is good for us for a variety of reasons; today's scientific evidence supports many of those claims. In terms of its curative properties, coffee contains more antioxidants than tea and the amount of caffeine in three espressos per day is mostly beneficial. It limits the action of free radicals, thus slowing the aging process. New studies show that caffeine taken orally

---

49   Edmondo Capecelatro, *L'arte del caffè* (Naples: Rogiosi, 2014), 139-141.

50   Blog on coffee web site http://blog.caffevergnano.com/lifestyle/futuro-fondo-di-caffe-tazzina/.

protects the skin from some of the damage caused by UVB rays.[51] It can be helpful for sufferers of depression, asthma, diabetes, gall bladder stones, liver disease, gout, and Parkinson's and Alzheimer's. The polyphenols in coffee even work against the bacteria that cause tooth cavities and halitosis. Of course, on the negative side, espresso does stain teeth. Some widely believed benefits of espresso drinking are not true, however. It does not help with weight loss, cellulite, migraines (low level headaches, yes, though), or cholesterol. Drinking coffee when inebriated does not make you any less drunk. Anxiety sufferers and insomniacs are better off minimizing their espresso, or any caffeinated beverage consumption. Pregnant women are also advised to go easy on their coffee intake, especially during the last trimester. And, counter to the superstition that coffee increases fertility, evidence suggests that women who consume six or more espressos per day may have more difficulty becoming pregnant than women who consume three or fewer a day. Women taking birth control pills are more likely to feel the effects of caffeine, which tend to last twice as long as in women not using oral contraceptives.[52] As with many other substances, too much coffee has negative effects, including irritability, sleeplessness, heart palpitations, and muscle cramps and can cause withdrawal-like symptoms if intake is suddenly stopped. Coffee does not have any direct nutritional value but does deliver energy with just a few calories per cup, if taken black, of course. All this information about the benefits and possible risks of espresso is spread throughout Italy through popular publications, especially magazines and newspapers and television programming.[53] The popular science magazine *Focus*, for example, delivers health news to more than 450,000 Italian homes each month and regularly runs articles about the myths and realities of coffee consumption. Many women's fashion magazines, such as

---

51   Linardi, *Il libro completo*, 121.

52   Franck Senninger, *Le virtù del caffè* (Vicenza: Edizioni il punto d'incontro, 2014).

53   Some recent examples include Panorama, http://www.panorama.it/scienza/salute/caffe-10-buoni-e-sani-motivi-per-berlo/; La Repubblica http://www.repubblica.it/salute/alimentazione/2013/04/19/news/ricerca_il_caff_fa_bene_ai_sani-56994493/

Vogue Italia, do as well. It is a comfort to many espresso consumers to have their beliefs confirmed by evidence but popular speculation and superstition are unlikely to disappear.

Former mayor of Rome Walter Veltroni (b. 1955) has remarked that espresso is "a ritual characteristic of Italianity...which is not only the relaxing pleasure of drinking a hot beverage, but it is a socialness, aesthetics, worldliness, and art. It is our culture."[54] Since people started drinking coffee centuries ago they have studied and discussed it. The modernization and Italianization of coffee vis-à-vis espresso has transformed a habit shared in many parts of the world into one with a distinct national character. Italian poets, songwriters, actors, directors, and advertising executives, among others, have captured the multiple meanings of espresso through their work and woven it into the cultural fabric of Italy. Espresso is a metaphor for the Italian condition. It is representative of a society in transition from rural life and superstition to urbanization and science. The popular culture of espresso maintains elements of local and regional histories but ties them together in a tradition shared up and down the peninsula and across the borders Italians have traversed. Espresso in each context is paired most often with the stages of love (over sex), lasting beauty (over superficiality), and the complex networks of human bonds (over casual encounters). Espresso-based song lyrics, movie scenes, and commercial jingles underscore the importance of its role and deepen its impact in society. And the dissemination of health news helps perpetuate the justification of its consumption. Although he died just as espresso was born, Italian unification composer Giuseppe Verdi (1813-1901) once stated that "coffee is the solace of the heart and of the spirit." The reach of espresso extends and unites the heart and spirit of Italy. It is indeed Italian culture.

---

54 Albertini, *Caffè & Stars,* last page (not numbered), their translation.

CHAPTER FOUR

ESPRESSO BARS IN TURIN: THE SALOTTO

The *salotto*, whether defined as a living room or a showroom, is a Torinese tradition. From the first chamber of the unified Italian Parliament in the Palazzo Carignano to the displays of Fiat's concept cars in the Lingotto, the history of modern Turin is rooted in sites in which people congregate to share, discuss, debate, and showcase. The city's numerous historic cafés and ultramodern espresso bars are tied to this central element of life in Turin. As Diana Lisci of the Caffè Vergnano espresso producer notes, "The salotto has a strong tradition here as a gathering place. The cafés were the first places where people would meet and talk. They still retain an element of the history of the city."[55] The people of Turin enjoy having an espresso beverage in the same finely decorated places where Italy's founders, such as Count Camillo Benso Cavour, and his successors, such as first president of the Italian Republic Luigi Einaudi, drank their coffee. Unity and continuity are close to the hearts of the residents of Turin. Today, argues Marco Giocoso, a journalist for Turin's *La Stampa*, the bar has perhaps assumed a place of even greater importance as more people have moved away from their ties to other historical structures, such as the local church parish or the neighborhood offices of political parties. He claims, "Bars are where we live a certain reality. They serve as a kind of thermometer of what is going on in society. Not only in Turin, of course. But in Turin, the bars in the center have an important historical place and they have not transformed over time."[56] The historical center has nonetheless modernized. Its new cafés and bars have taken on a European continental, and sometimes even American feel, with elements of high contemporary design and the most recent forms of technology. In these spaces, too, however, coffee drinkers settle into their surroundings. The living room, the showcase:

---

55 Interview by Author with Diana Lisci, Caffè Vergnano, Turin, Italy, March 13, 2018.

56 Interview by Author with Marco Giocosa, Pasticceria Vernier, Turin, Italy, March 15, 2018.

they draw people in and become sites defined by those who inhabit them, even if temporarily.

The Caffè al Bicerin (1763) and the Caffè Gelateria Fiorio (1780) are the two oldest cafés in central Turin that are still bustling with customers. Both are reminiscent of the Enlightenment era in which they were founded and that launched the modern coffee house. The links between the consumption of the newly imported hot beverages of tea, hot chocolate and coffee, and political culture became meaningful and lasting during this time. In these public meeting places, intellectuals and artists contributed to the development of print culture and its permeation into political life. Historians of the French Revolution have highlighted the important role of cafés in sparking the political dissent that overturned the old regime but also in contributing to the development of new drinking habits based on caffeinated rather than alcoholic beverages. The café culture of Turin is a perfect example of how this transformation began and continued into the next centuries. In fact, this historical moment separates what historians define as "early" modern and modern, since many cultural and social behaviors formed in the late eighteenth century continued into following decades while others faded slowly into the past. The geographical proximity of Turin to the French border—Italy and France are separated by the Alps west of the city—is evident in the cultural proximity of the two regions. Turin was built on the grid pattern of a Roman encampment, but its architecture and interiors were clearly influenced by the French. The merging and re-imagining of elements of aristocratic and bourgeois traditions are also shared between the French and the Piedmontese, whose dialect borrows heavily from its western neighbors. Yet the House of Savoy, the royal family of the Kingdom of Piedmont-Sardinia, would become the unifying force behind a nationalist movement to make the state of Italy rather than remain a permanent, passive French ally.

The Caffè al Bicerin combines the atmosphere of the French coffee house with the drinking of caffeinated hot beverages but puts a distinctly Torinese flavor to both, namely the invention of Turin's most famous coffee drink, the bicerin. Viviana, currently one of the three managers of the café, explains that the bicerin, "is a favorite of the Torinesi because it combines our love for chocolate with our love for coffee. The drink is made with equal parts hot chocolate and coffee and then a special creamy milk is added on top."[57] Chocolate in Turin, especially the special hazelnut chocolate variety known as gianduia, was becoming popular at the same time as coffee and many chocolatiers opened throughout the city during the 1700s and into the 1800s. The Bicerin was among them and later expanded from the espresso bar into the storefront next door to sell their own chocolate. Viviana points out that their chocolate recipe has remained unchanged since the café opened but that the bicerin they prepare has seen some modifications. The original bicerin was a variation of the drink known as the *bavareisa*, popular in the 18th century, which combined coffee, chocolate, milk and syrup in a large glass. The creators of the bicerin, eliminated the syrup, reduced the size of the glass, made the milk creamier, and allowed the client to decide on the amounts of coffee, chocolate and milk they put into the mix. She explains, "It used to be that customers added their own proportions of chocolate, coffee, and milk to make the drink but now we do it for convenience." From the nineteenth century on, the bicerin was available in three versions: *pur e fuir* (mostly coffee and milk); *pur e barba* (mostly coffee and chocolate); or *'n poc 'd tut* (a little bit of everything). The bicerin also changed with the invention of espresso, which Viviana says, "made it stronger but better even if the overall recipe is the same." Coffee at the time was prepared using infusion methods and the roasts were greener and less uniform, which produced more acidic flavors. Even if the northern espresso preference continues to be based on sweeter, more acidic tones, the addition of espresso reduced the overall acidity of the bicerin. The Caffè al Bicerin currently uses a blend made for them by the Turin based roaster Costadoro, active since 1890, that Viviana says "works well when mixed with hot chocolate. You don't want a coffee that overpowers the flavors of the chocolate but one that enhances them." The exact recipe of the original bicerin remains closely guarded by its heirs but versions of the bicerin can be enjoyed in many of the historic cafés of the center.

The location of the Caffè al Bicerin across a small piazza from the

---

57   Interview by Author with Viviana, Caffè al Bicerin, Turin, Italy, March 12, 2018.

Church of the Virgin of the Consolation is significant to the history of the café's most important beverage as is its ties to the upper classes. When Giuseppe Dentis first opened the bar in 1763, he served mainly citron based drinks in simple surroundings with wooden tables and benches. The center expanded and became the purview of the growing upper bourgeoisie as well as the aristocrats of the nearby palaces. In 1856, architect Carlo Promis designed the building in which the current Caffè al Bicerin was transformed into a salotto, that is, when it became a quintessential example of the Torinese living room.[58] Finely carved wooden panels adorned the walls and ceiling, large mirrors reflected the light of the elaborate chandeliers, and small round marble tables with velvet covered chairs lined the edges of the small square room. It became a warm, elegant, inviting space, especially for neighborhood residents attending mass. According to café legend, during the Lenten season, church-goers would seek sustenance in the bicerin because beverages were not considered food and so not subject to exclusion during the period of renunciation. The warm, caloric drink was a perfect solution for the cool temperatures of early spring. Even those who did not attend mass enjoyed the bicerin, too. Count Camillo Benso di Cavour is said to have accompanied the royal family to attend services at the Consolata but not to have entered the church himself. Instead, he would sit near the front windows with a bicerin and a plate of cookies and wait for them to exit to go back to the Royal Palace. In its earliest years, the bicerin was available to a limited number of people who could afford it; chocolate and coffee were not accessible to all. Over time, however, the bicerin spread to the lower social classes. Viviana explains that "it was especially important for breakfast because it gives you energy." Today, she says, "because of tourism, the bicerin is consumed at all hours of the day and in all seasons," but the locals tend to drink it mostly in winter and as a treat.

Women are particularly associated with the salotto history of the Caffè al Bicerin and the bicerin itself.[59] Since the café was located close to the church, women felt comfortable about its setting. They,

---

58   Caffè al Bicerin entry, Museo Torino, http://www.museotorino.it/view/s/5e1 57799100d49f79bcc4ff50c79a21e?highlight=bicerin, Last accessed May 3, 2018.

59   Caffè al Bicerin Web site, https://bicerin.it/storia/, Last accessed May 3, 2018.

like Cavour, could look at the sanctuary doors but, unlike Cavour, a noted anti-cleric, the women sat at ease because of clergy passing by the windows. Moreover, the management of the café quickly fell into the hands of women, who limited the alcoholic beverages they served to vermouth, *rosolio*, a rose-petal based liqueur, and *ratafià*, a fruity liqueur. The bicerin, as a non-alcoholic drink, was considered the most suitable option for women, however, and their fondness for chocolate and coffee made it a favorite anyway. The café's lovely décor and intimate ambiance lent themselves to long conversations shared among ladies and free from the distractions of liquor-charged, smoking men generally associated with drinking in public establishments. The female management, living room surroundings, and choice of beverage thus contributed to the creation of a space in which women could meet in public without men and without generating gossip about their activities. The Bicerin has retained true to its line of women owners and managers since the early twentieth century when espresso entered into the bar's habits. Women and espresso modernized the café in the sense of keeping it at the forefront of contemporary life. From 1910 to 1975 the bar was owned by Ida Cavalli. She and her sister and daughter ran the café. The women were known in Turin as "more ladies of the house than coffee bar owners; they lovingly looked after all the penniless intellectuals who took shelter from the bitter cold in the Caffè Al Bicerin."[60] As such, they maintained the female run tradition of the salon. From 1983 to 2015, Maritè Costa took over the Bicerin and contributed to making it famous throughout Italy and around the world. She led the bar to its inclusion as a "best bar in Italy" in the noted Gambero Rosso guide and returned to the original recipes for the chocolate and the bicerin served there. Her heirs have continued to showcase the Bicerin through the internet and social media, linking centuries of history to the latest technologies. The long lines outside the Caffè al Bicerin attest to the bar's continued relevance for the people and visitors of Turin.

On the other side of the Royal Palace in the center of Turin resting under the porticos of the Via Po is the Fiorio, the second

---

60   Ibid.

oldest coffee bar in the city still serving loyal patrons. The bar opened in 1780 and was taken over by the Fiorio brothers just a few years later.[61] The bar has had several nicknames associated with it over its long history that demonstrate its role as a political showroom of the history of Turin, Italy and Europe. In the earliest years of its existence, for example, the Fiorio was known for its conservatism. It earned the name of the Bar "dei codini o dei Machiavelli," or of "the pigtails and Machiavellians" because of the hairstyle aristocratic men wore in the 1700s. By the early twentieth century, the Fiorio was associated with democratic principles. Its nickname changed to the "isola felice," happy island, because it served as a haven for anti-fascists seeking refuge from persecutions during the fascist era. King Carlo Alberto used to ask every morning "what are they saying at the Fiorio?" to have an idea of what public opinion looked like during his reign, but even today the same question could be posed by the mayor of Turin or Prime Minister of Italy to get a read on what educated, well-informed people are saying about recent political developments. Regardless of the political leanings of its clients, the Fiorio has always attracted the most intellectually and politically engaged individuals. German philosopher Friedrich Nietzsche wrote in the Fiorio during his stays in Turin in the late 19th century. As one historian has pointed out, "He loved the fact that the city streets were not crowded, as they were maybe in Rome or elsewhere. He wrote, Turin is the capital of discovery, the first place in which I am possible. So he liked a calm world. And then his excitement was really intellectual excitement."[62] Nietzsche found intellectual stimulation in the Fiorio as did Giuseppe Tomasi di Lampedusa much later. The famed Sicilian author whose depiction of the divide between northern and southern Italy in *The Leopard* continues to characterize regional differences, penned his last short novel *La sirena* at the Fiorio in 1955-56. Set in Turin in the late 1930s, the story recounts an unlikely friendship between two Sicilian

---

61   Riccardo Di Vincenzo, *Il Fiorio Caffè Gelateria: L'isola felice di Torino* (Turin: Landriano, 2011).

62   Interview with Robert Rethy, National Public Radio, February 11, 2006. Available at https://www.npr.org/templates/story/story.php?storyId=5201822, Last accessed May 3, 2018.

men who meet in a coffee bar on the Via Po.

The Fiorio, like the Bicerin, features a dark, but warm and inviting, interior where customers are welcome to sit as though guests in someone's living room. The political and literary history of the bar draws in tourists, but unlike the small Bicerin, where a long wait may deter some locals or prevent a particularly leisurely stay, the Fiorio is quite large and part of the mainstay of nearby residents and workers. The rooms are individually named. Especially popular is the *saletta* Cavour, also known as the wagon room, since it was made to resemble the statesman's train car.[63] As in many other espresso bars throughout Italy, the Fiorio undergoes a daily rhythm based on the consumption of coffee. Riccardo di Vincenzo, the Fiorio's current owner describes it, "Still today, the Fiorio opens its shutters like eyelids waking up, at eight o'clock in the morning. The air is crisp and the first patrons, still sleepy, ask for a coffee to take on the day."[64] The morning regulars share news of the day as they hurry off to work. School kids and university students—the main site of the University of Turin is nearby—stop in next asking for cappuccino and brioche to start their morning as they share photos on their smart phones. Pensioners drift in later to read the paper, drink espresso, and gossip. Moms with young children seek a place to sit and relax over a caffè latte. As is the case for many of the other historic bars along the Via Po, the Fiorio offers a rich lunch buffet in the aptly named *sala da pranzo*, lunch room, complete with espresso and traditional cookies, such as the *bacio di dama*, the lady's kiss, consisting of a chocolate hazelnut cream sandwiched between two butter cookies. The afternoon and evening bring in clients taking breaks from their day or enjoying an espresso before heading home. The conversation in the Fiorio's special salons livens up again after dinner when clients come in with friends as part of their late-night stroll. As Vincenzo puts it, "for a few hours it seems like the splendor of the golden age of cafés has returned, when people went to the café at least two times a day: in the afternoon and after dinner."[65] The lively

---

63   Caffè Fiorio entry, Museo Torino, http://www.museotorino.it/view/s/3ffb3342 51cd48ad96c3922afa143c15?highlight=fiorio, Last accessed May 3, 2018.

64   Vincenzo, *Il Fiorio*, 9.

65   Ibid., 10.

jazz music playing in the background is a reminder of that heyday when, especially in the 1950s and 1960s, the rooms filled with dancers moving along the linoleum floor to the rhythms of a small orchestra.

Several other historic cafés in the center of Turin have retained their rich heritage and the liv(ing)ed room characteristics of their predecessors and contemporaries. Some of the most famous of these are known for their beautiful art nouveau décor and the specialties that accompany their espresso beverages. The Baratti & Milano company, named for its founders Ferdinando Baratti and Edoardo Milano, celebrated 160 years of business in 2018. Candy and liqueurs were the starting point for the two young men who created the business, but a period of living in Paris and the personal influence and financial assistance of a young woman turned Edoardo toward an interest in chocolate and coffee, which he began to study in earnest during agricultural trips to South America and Africa.[66] As the candy and chocolate business grew, the two decided to open a shop in the new Galleria Subalpina in 1875 across from the Piazza Castello and the Royal Palace. The location helped the company become closely tied to the House of Savoy. King Carlo Alberto enjoyed the delicious candies, and soon Baratti & Milano became fashionable among the upper echelons of Torinese society. In 1911, the owners expanded the space and introduced the espresso bar for the Universal Exhibition held in Turin. Bolognese architect Giulio Casanova and Torinese sculptor Edoardo Rubino are responsible for the late art nouveau exterior and interior the bar still boasts today despite having been partially destroyed during World War II; the entire Galleria Subalpina was bombed in July and August of 1943.[67]

The long marble counter and elaborate steam coffee maker are representative of the role espresso has played in this bar and many others nearby. In fact, Baratti and Milano had developed their own special roast to serve upon the bar's re-unveiling in celebration of fifty years of Italian unification. They even began to sell espresso along with the other products they were already famous for; the

---

66   Baratti & Milano Web site, https://www.barattiemilano.it/, Last accessed May 3, 2018.

67   Baratti & Milano entry, Museo Torino, http://www.museotorino.it/view/s/8f0 60bb6d4414b759b2707268c64f5fd, Last accessed May 3, 2018.

fruit candies and chocolate bars sold very well. The current waitstaff manager, Luigi Piranagi, explains that although the cafés of central Turin are known for chocolate or other delicacies and for their elegant settings, espresso is still central to their business. He remarks, "Coffee is already very important to Italians. To have espresso in a historic bar where you can appreciate the surroundings makes it even nicer. The bicerin, cappuccino, latte macchiato, etc. are all based on espresso. It has to be good."[68] Baratti & Milano has received a special three coffee bean, the highest rating, recognition from Illy for being a "best bar" based on the quality of the espresso, the service and the environment. Generations of regular clients seek all three. The same is true of clients of the Caffè Torino, which has been housed under the porticos of the large Piazza San Carlo since 1934. The style is a mix of Baroque and art nouveau, the servers first-rate, and the espresso described by its manager as "the root of the bar." A manager explained to me that the espresso habits of the people of Turin are slightly different than in other Italian cities, but all share certain national characteristics, "the Torinesi have coffee in the morning, just like in Naples. We maybe drink more cappuccino though. The espresso after lunch is also very important here. Perhaps we drink espresso less frequently throughout other times of the day than in other parts of Italy, but morning and lunchtime are nearly universal." The bar has been using a Lavazza blend for about thirty years because, "they are a historic Torinese company and the quality of the espresso is consistent and top-notch."[69] The Lavazza logo features prominently—above the main entrance, under the arches of the portico, and on the awnings outdoors.

Illustrious clients conversing, writing, or dancing the night away have been drawn into the living and show rooms of the historic bars for decades and even for centuries. During the twentieth century, some of the most important bars included the Bicerin, the Fiorio, Baratti & Milano, and the Caffè Torino, but the list of establishments is quite long, as is the list of noted notables who have frequented these spaces.

---

68   Interview by Author with Luigi Piranagi, Baratti & Milano, Turin, Italy, July 8, 2016.

69   Interview by Author with Manager (Anonymous), Caffè Torino, Turin, Italy, July 8, 2016.

The Caffè Torino was a chic spot during the *dolce vita* era, for example, in part because of its numerous tables in the piazza where foreign film stars, such as Ava Gardner, Brigitte Bardot and Jimmy Stewart could see and be seen. Italian literary figures, such as poet Cesare Pavese and publisher Giulio Einaudi, added an element of high culture to the celebrity sightings.[70] The small, at just about 300 square feet, but striking art nouveau Caffè Mulassano (1907), which shares a façade under the arcade with Baratti & Milano, is where nationalist writer Gabriele D'Annunzio is said to have given the name *tramezzino* to the popular sandwich that uses soft bread with the crusts removed. It has long been fashionable among the actors of the nearby Teatro Regio and served as a location for several films, including *Piccolo mondo antico* (1941) by Mario Soldati and *Quattro mosche di velluto grigio* (1970) by Dario Argento.[71] On the corner of the Corso Re Umberto and the Corso Vittorio Emanuele II sits the Caffè Platti (1870), which is a popular spot for fans of the soccer team Juventus who go to see the bench where D'Azeglio high school students founded the team in 1897.[72] The café was popular among the young bourgeoisie of Turin in the same period. The founders of Fiat, including Giovanni Agnelli, met there frequently in the early 1900s. In 2015, the café closed for a period because of financial problems, but it reopened in 2017 with the support of the community that wanted to see its historical legacy preserved. The nobility, politicians, businessmen, writers, actors, musicians, and dreamers are among the clients of the historic bars in the city center who have enjoyed espresso, cappuccino, bicerin and an assortment of other coffee beverages during the entirety of the period of Italian unification, through the devastation of World War II, and into the contemporary age all the while seated in spaces that

---

70   Caffè Torino entry, Museo Torino, http://www.museotorino.it/view/s/6c5cb 76fd38e4f95b4a6514441955183?highlight=caffe%20torino, Last accessed May 3, 2018.

71   Caffè Mulassano entry, Museo Torino, http://www.museotorino.it/view/s/03 d3b4d4055246ecba9248ae7ed756ab?highlight=mulassano, Last accessed May 3, 2018.

72   Caffè Platti entry, Museo Torino, http://www.museotorino.it/view/s/7a74f2df 8dcc4e52a935f9da3a75ce64?highlight=platti, Last accessed May 3, 2018.

have been built and rebuilt to evoke the finery and consistency of a new modern era in the face of transformation.

Agnelli and the founders of Fiat first discussed business at the Platti in central Turin, but they are responsible for the development of the area in the southwest of the city that became known as the Lingotto because of the Fiat factory building and its famous rooftop testing track, the Lingotto, that opened in 1923.[73] The emergence of Turin as a "factory town" is, in fact, after the unification of Italy and Turin's eventual displacement as the capital, perhaps the most important story of the city's growth and role in Italian industrialization during the twentieth century. Fiat emerged in an already evolving automobile sector in Turin—dozens of firms were producing cars and parts by the early 1900s—and came to dominate the industry. The company devoted most of its resources to the war efforts in both world wars but enjoyed enormous commercial success in the post-World War II era with its small, economical vehicles, such as the 124, a family sedan chosen as the European car of the year in 1967, and the again popular 500. By 1970, Fiat employed more than 100,000 people in Italy and was producing over 1.3 million cars annually. The Mirafiori Fiat factory, of course, attracted workers from the time of its inception. The area around the production plant transformed into a thriving neighborhood with residential buildings, retail shops, and restaurants and bars. Many southern Italians migrated north for work at Fiat and related companies and some opened their own businesses to cater to tastes from back home.

Coffee culture was built into the habits of Fiat employees, managers and workers alike. The showroom became the centerpiece of the auto industry much as the café was a gathering place—both *salotti* in which to gather, invent, and admire. As in factories throughout Italy, inside the Mirafiori, employees could eat in the company cafeteria and take espresso breaks at the internal bars. The advent of the espresso vending machine made it possible for workers to take an even quicker pause for

---

73   Lingotto entry, Museo Torino, http://www.museotorino.it/view/s/2da9c2e6c 07446ed89d7480f08820cae, Last accessed May 3, 2018; Museo dell'Automobile, Centro di Documentazione, Website, http://www.museoauto.it/website/it/museo/ centro-di-documentazione, Last accessed May 3, 2018.

an espresso outside regular break times. Fiat and Lavazza became close allies since both companies traced their origins to the turn of the 20th century in central Turin and became leaders in their sectors. Lavazza benefited from the sales and transportation networks established by the auto manufacturer and Fiat benefited from keeping its workers content and caffeinated with good espresso. It is not surprising that the first espresso machine made for a mass-produced vehicle is a Lavazza "Coffee Experience Kit" designed as an option on the Fiat 500L, as of 2012. The pod machine fits into the cup holder and makes a single-dose espresso while you drive.[74] Of course, employees could seek espresso outside the Mirafiori complex and several of the historic bars of the city center, such as the Fiorio, opened locations near the factory. However, espresso was not always the top choice of autoworkers. As Saskia, current co-owner of the Bar Bottiglieria Il Coguaro on the Via Nizza explains, "when the bar opened in the late 1950s it was created as a *piola*, that is, a place where workers would come and sit and order wine by the liter and eat something. It was not a healthy lifestyle. They drank a lot. They ate too much. Many of them died young. The previous owner introduced espresso about thirty years ago but mostly for those of us who work here and a few clients. We use only about 1-2 kilograms a day."[75] Drinking wine or beer at lunchtime is an Italian custom that has slowly faded, except for during special occasions, but the stereotype of heavy-drinking factory workers prevailed for some time. In any case, lunch ended with an espresso and the southern Italian migrant workers generally sought an afternoon espresso as well for the duration of the factory's tenure in the Lingotto. In 1982, the Fiat factory closed. Architect Renzo Piano, known for the New York Times building and London's "vertical city," turned it into a convention center with a hotel, cinema, shops and an art gallery. Nonetheless, the neighborhood and the entire metropolitan area of Turin suffered because of Fiat's decision to open factories elsewhere, primarily in central and south America, and to

---

74 Lavazza Fiat Espresso Machine Product summary at https://www.fiat-accessories.com/fiat-500l-lavazza-espresso-machine, Last accessed May 3, 2018.

75 Interview by Author with Saskia, Bar Bottiglieria Il Coguaro, Turin, Italy, March 15, 2018.

lay off thousands of workers.

The large factory spaces and Piedmontese food and beverage traditions were not forgotten when Fiat changed direction, however. Carlo Petrini from the nearby town of Cuneo launched the Slow Food Organization and movement in 1986 in response to the opening of a McDonald's near the Spanish Steps in Rome. His objective was to promote local and sustainable foods and good nutrition.[76] In 2007, Piedmontese entrepreneur Oscar Farinetti opened Eataly in a former vermouth factory across from the renovated Fiat complex after being convinced of Slow Food's value.[77] The two pioneers steered Turin toward an outward looking business model based on established Italian gastronomical practices. That is, they insisted on the superiority of eating and drinking products that were not made in the industrial sector and they encouraged the use of historical recipes based on simplicity and freshness. They then looked to take those principles of "authentic" Italian eating to other parts of the world. The idea was to replicate the best of how Italians eat in Italy more than to modify Italian food as Italian immigrants had done out of necessity when they were unable to find the exact ingredients they had used in their homelands. By further modernizing and eventually globalizing Italian food culture, Farinetti inserted contemporary design aesthetics into the first Eataly that since been replicated in the more than 35 Eatalys that have opened in Italy, other parts of Europe, Asia, the Middle East, and the United States. Eataly is, in fact, a large store made up of multiple *salotti*, that is, each Eataly is divided into distinctive sections designed to feature special products, such as pasta or fish, and often includes a small restaurant or counter where clients can sample products.

Although Slow Food and Eataly focus especially on food, beverages also feature in their objectives and sales. Along with wine and craft beer, espresso is an important part of the Eataly brand. As is the case for all the locations, the original store in Turin features an espresso

76 Slow Food Organization, "A Delicious Revolution: How Grandma's Pasta Changed the World," Web site, https://www.slowfoodusa.org/history, Last accessed May 3, 2018.

77 See the Eataly Web site, https://www.eataly.net/it_it/negozi/torino-lingotto/, Last accessed May 3, 2018.

bar, the coffee *salotto*, located near shelves full of coffee and tea and related products for sale. During my 2018 visit, the barista was serving a Huehue Guatemalan blend. The Eataly café located inside the Turin landmark the Mole Antonelliana is co-partnered by Caffè Vergnano. The largest Eataly location at Ostiense in Rome is an Illy bar complete with an elaborate hanging mobile made from Illy espresso cups. The downtown New York City location houses a Lavazza bar. Eataly emphasizes its commitment to fair trade and Slow Food in its espresso descriptions, noting for instance, that Illy drinkers can learn about the process of espresso-making from the coffee plant's point of origin in Eritrea to it being served in your cup at the bar through its "storia in un chicco di caffè ("history in a coffee bean") class and related products. And consumers of Vergnano learn that Slow Food representatives oversee their Guatemalan producers to guarantee that biodiversity and the authenticity of farming methods are maintained in the highland regions from which the company selects its beans.[78] Vergnano and Lavazza are, of course, the oldest Torinese producers. Illy, although not based in Piedmont, is highly respected for its business practices and high-quality espresso. The fact that Eataly is not brand exclusive means that there is room for other espresso makers to be distributed by the high-end market and that the current brands must meet certain objectives to continue to be featured in its stores and cafés.

Eataly is now a global phenomenon that has taken quality Italian food and espresso around the world, but Turin is also a city where outside influences are transformed into the local culture. The French influence of the historic cafés is one example, but the global high-tech youth coffee culture typical of Seattle, London, or Tokyo has taken hold in Turin as well. Young people in Turin want places, casual *salotti*, where they can hang out with their friends, use their tablets on free Wi-Fi, and drink coffee. The elegant settings of espresso bars such as Baratti & Milano, Fiorio and the Bicerin tend to attract clients over 30 years of age who are interested in quietly conversing with their companions rather than passing hours on a computer doing homework or goofing around after school. Starbucks has been trying to enter the

---

78   From the Rome Web site, https://www.eataly.net/it_it/negozi/roma/archivio-roma/ristorantini-roma/, Last accessed May 3, 2018.

Italian market to pick up on the youth segment, made up especially of high school and college students, but for now, the closest Starbucks is in Milan. The founders of Busters Coffee have intervened in the meantime and opened American-style coffee houses in Turin, where there are now three locations. In late 2015, they also opened near the University of Rome, the only location outside Piedmont. The resemblance of Busters to Starbucks is striking. The logo, the cases of American pastries, such as muffins, cupcakes, and cheesecakes, and the furnishings and artwork all recall the American multinational as do the droves of students sipping from giant ceramic mugs or large, paper take-away cups as they scroll down their smart phones. Busters offers vegan options on its sandwich menu and highlights its commitment to organic, fair trade, and sustainable products—all factors the younger generations are likely to take into consideration when choosing where to spend their often more limited resources.

The featured coffee at Busters is American, not *americano*, meaning it's made using the drip method through paper filters rather than as espresso to which extra water is added. Busters explains that American coffee requires a high percentage of arabica from central America—they use 85%—and that it should be lightly toasted and coarsely ground. "In Italy," they insist on their web site, "it's not easy to find a true 'filtered coffee' blend commonly called 'American coffee,' that allows you to relive the smells and tastes found on vacation."[79] Presumably, the coffee they are referring to is what Italians drink at Starbucks when on vacation in the United States. Italian reviewers, such as the writers of the Nuok blog created by young Italians living in New York City, have pointed out, however, that the coffee at Busters tastes better than what they have consumed at Starbucks in New York.[80] Espresso, cappuccino, and a version of the bicerin, called a *marocchino*, or Moroccan, in most parts of Italy because of its brown color, which is espresso, chocolate and milk froth, are also available for clients interested in the atmosphere of Busters but who prefer Italian coffee. All versions of its coffee can be

79   Busters Web site, https://www.busterscoffee.it/la-torrefazione, Last accessed May 3, 2018.

80   Nuok Blog, Web site, http://www.nuok.it/turin/busters-a-torino-il-cugino-alla-lontana-di-starbucks, Last accessed May 3, 2018.

taken away in recycled paper or refillable cups, a trend that has spread to other parts of Italy as well. The to-go cups can usually be spotted in the hands of American or English tourists and students. Busters explains the appeal, "Before an exam at the university, during a heavy day at work, or just when you want to walk around and enjoy the city, Busters Coffee offers its clients the possibility to drink its coffee away from the store, as in the great American tradition."[81] The casual living room can be transported in a cup of coffee.

The filtering of coffee traditions, in this case literal, is not only evident in the coffee house that mimics and perhaps even improves upon the American model but also in the neighborhoods in which large migrant populations have settled. A walk through the Porta Palazzo area, known for its flea and antique market called the Balòn, to the Barriera di Milano, an industrial and residential neighborhood with a traditionally large working-class population, reflects the diversity of contemporary Turin beyond they city's bourgeois center. The auto and textile industries employed Piedmontese workers but also southern Italians and later foreign migrants, especially from north Africa, seeking jobs in the manufacturing sector. The indoor and outdoor markets near Porta Palazzo came to include products, food in particular, sought after by new migrant populations seeking to keep their own culinary traditions alive while integrating into Italian society. Many of the permanent eateries in the neighborhoods serve traditional Piedmontese food, such as the *bagna cauda*, a stew prepared for many hours, but also pizza and kebab. There are Moroccan, Turkish, Indian, and Chinese restaurants as well. Many of the bars offer baklava or other foreign pastries and serve Turkish-style coffee in addition to espresso. The Bar Balon is managed by an Egyptian man who has developed a passion for artisanal espresso and uses Caffè Vergnano in the bar. Next door is the Antico Borgo Caffè in which two young Torinese women make local pastries and serve Costadoro coffee, another Turin based espresso maker. Across the Po River in the Via Vercelli, a barista at the Antica Pasticceria, which has been operating since 1904, is the daughter of an Italian and a south American. Caffè Fantino, an espresso maker based in the nearby town of Cuneo, is popular with its clients that

---

81   Busters Web site.

includes natives of Turin and numerous foreigners who have chosen to make it their home. The small Mokadoro bar and roaster further up the Via Vercelli relies on a traditional, older Torinese working class clientele as well as newer generations of immigrants to Italy, many of whom come from coffee growing countries and are interested to try blends based on beans from their country of origin. Despite problems of crime and related anti-establishment sentiment associated with the Barriera di Milano that were exacerbated when the manufacturing sector declined in Turin, the community is integrated, united and moving forward, often because people share circumstances but also because they share their cultures, including those based on espresso and coffee in the *salotto* setting of neighborhood bars.[82]

Turin was Italy's first capital city. Its transformations from the 19th to the 21st centuries tell much of the story of the modernization of the country that was born there in 1861. From a center of politics to a center of industry to a city trying to find a new center for its identity, Turin has been home to some of the biggest names in modern Italian history. Men such as Camillo Benso di Cavour and Giovanni Agnelli contributed to shaping Turin and putting it on display for the rest of the unified state and its observers. The *salotto* of the politician like the *salotto* of the entrepreneur have been essential in the development of urban and national identity. The people of Turin are known for their own variety of *politesse*, perhaps influenced by their European connections and continental climate, versus for the openness and warmth of the people of southern cities such as Naples. Turin is an intellectual city with a strong literary tradition that extends across classes and decades. The coffee bar as a *salotto* has been a continuous presence in modern Torinese life, itself undergoing changes vis-à-vis the arrival of espresso in the early 20th century. The elegance, French style, and sit-down environments of the bars of Turin has held on more than in other Italian cities. Bars are places where the people of Turin congregate as though in a living room. The café culture of earlier centuries lingers in the bars as do the people enjoying the bicerin and fine chocolate. Of course, as the birthplace of Italy's largest espresso

---

82 See for instance the Web site of the neighborhood association, http://www. associazionebarriera.com/, Last accessed May 3, 2018.

producer, Lavazza, and one of its oldest, Caffè Vergnano, as well as being the city of the patent for the first espresso machine, Turin could be said to have united Italy through espresso. Attention to an aesthetic at the leading edge of its creation, whether in the art nouveau of the early 20th century or the post-modernism of contemporary design, is evident in Turin's oldest and newest cafés. And attention to the best possible way to make and drink high quality espresso remains essential to the Torinese coffee tradition.

CHAPTER FIVE

ESPRESSO BARS IN ROME: SOCIAL CHANGE IN THE CAPITAL

In 1870, Rome became the capital of the unified Italian state. It quickly grew to become Italy's largest city, a place it still holds today. Rome is also the most popular tourist destination in Italy and the third most visited city in Europe. One of the first things coffee-loving tourists to Rome take note of is the vast number of espresso bars throughout the city. In the most populous neighborhoods as well as in the city center, it is not unusual to find three or four bars on the same block, none of which is a Starbucks. Office workers step out together for morning and afternoon coffee breaks. Students congregate after their classes. Tourists wander in and out often uncertain as to the process of ordering and consuming espresso and other beverages and food. Guidebooks feature some of the most historic of Rome's caffetterie, such as the Caffè Greco on the fashionable Via Condotti near the Spanish Steps, the Bar Rosati in Piazza del Popolo and, until recently, the Café de Paris on the upscale Via Veneto. Several other bars, however, also represent Rome's position as the capital city, its role in key political and social movements in the modern era, and important modernizing trends of the twentieth century.

This chapter examines the many facets of Rome's espresso gathering spots. Whether they are centuries old or have just been around for a few decades, Rome's bars play a central role in the life of the city and its residents, long and short-term visitors and tourists. Perhaps more than in many other Italian cities, Rome's bars have assumed a position of importance that identifies more than just a *buon caffè* [good coffee] but also says something about social identities. The places in which Italians become regulars indicate multiple points of identity, such as social class and political affiliation, as well as personal preferences, such as the kind of coffee served and the general atmosphere of the bar. Romans usually have a favorite bar near their home, a favorite near their workplace, and a favorite they stroll to with family and friends, and they often have strong opinions about where they do and do not want to have a coffee.

Some of the most popular bars in Rome retain a part of the coffee house culture of earlier centuries, meaning that clients consume seated and slowly, but most residents going about their daily lives participate in the modern pace of espresso culture with a typical bar visit lasting about ten minutes before they rush off to or back to work, school, or home. The notion of long-lasting breaks is largely a fantasy of foreign tourists who often fail to see that the other people sitting and talking for long periods are also mostly tourists or Italians engaged in a business meeting. This is not to say that leisure time has disappeared but that the images of films and photos that populate the imagination outside Italy have not kept up with the realities of contemporary life. Reflecting on the roles of several Roman bars we can see that they are much more than simply a place to relax and drink a cup of coffee. Each location reveals facets of the tensions of contemporary life in Italy.

Like the Venetian Florian, the Antico Caffè Greco belongs to the coffee house tradition established during the eighteenth century in such cities as Paris, London, and Vienna in which artists and intellectuals of sometimes different social strata gathered to discuss the events of the day, new developments in their areas of interest, and even to plot revolutions. The Caffè Greco opened its doors in 1760 at Via Condotti, 86 and has remained open for more than two centuries of uninterrupted service.[83] Although the coffee served there before the invention of espresso was considered good, it was not a principal draw to customers who were more likely to drink hot chocolate and smoke tobacco products since smoking was allowed in only a few public places. In fact, the name Kaffe del Greco refers to the tradition of smoking tobacco, like the Greeks were known to do, in the café's ornately decorated rooms, with walls covered in paintings and small circular marble tables. In its early years, the Greco became known as the Tedesco, or German, café because it was a popular spot among German artists. During the Romantic era, the English poets Byron, Keats and Shelley could be spotted there as it was just a short walk from the Shelley residence at the Spanish Steps. Stendhal, another

---

83   Tamara Felicitas Hufschmidt and Livio Jannattoni, *Antico Caffè Greco: storia, ambienti, collezioni* (Rome: Gruppo dei Romanisti, 1989[?]).

regular, commented that the coffee was excellent. Although few women, especially Italian women, ventured out alone, foreign women artists frequented the Greco on their own in the mid-nineteenth century, among them American sculptor Harriet Hosmer and British poet Elizabeth Barrett Browning.

With the arrival of espresso at the Greco in the early 1900s came also the meetings of university professors who, in the 1920s, were treated to specials on Tuesdays. Publisher Luigi Einaudi and philosopher Benedetto Croce even joined in on the lively debates on occasion. Benito Mussolini's rise to power and the accompanying fear of expressing dissent in a public place kept many anti-fascist intellectuals away from the mid-1920s until the end of World War II. In 1948, once the Greco had been reclaimed as a place for free expression, writer Alberto Moravia commented, "Certificates and newspaper articles remained stuck to the walls and the air was still penetrated by the smoke of so many evenings passed talking and waiting. Waiting for what? For my part, I waited fifteen years at the Caffè Greco for the end of fascism."[84] Orson Welles and Carlo Levi were among other writers who returned the Greco to its place in the literary spotlight in the postwar decades. Today the Greco is primarily a tourist attraction and a site for an espresso break for its residents and retail workers of the high end shops that line the Via Condotti. Most clients are seeking the tea room experience and generally remain seated at the tables served by expert waiters and pay high prices for the privilege. Although brought into the modern era and espresso age, the Antico Caffè Greco is a remnant of the past and characteristic of times when life seemed slower.

Another popular tourist destination in the center of Rome is the Caffè Sant'Eustachio, which has been featured in many guide books and international newspapers and magazines, including the *New York Times*. It is not uncommon to find a line of tourists outside the door of the bar, but the Sant'Eustachio is rooted in a twentieth-century history typical of many Roman establishments that do not draw crowds. It opened in the early 1900s as a *latteria*, or milk shop, and took its

---

84 In Italian, "Restano alle pareti gli attestati e i ritagli dei giornali e per l'aria, l'odore di fumo di tante serate trascorse a discutere e ad aspettare. Aspettare che cosa? Io, per conto mio, ho aspettato quindici anni al Caffè Greco la fine del fascismo."

current form around 1938. In the early years, residents bought their milk and eggs in the bar and sometimes stayed for breakfast. It was also a casual restaurant in which locals stopped for a quick bite to eat. After its re-opening in the late 1930s, the Sant'Eustachio became a neighborhood favorite right away because it was decorated in what was considered the most modern style of the time with a central open area and the marble and copper bar around the periphery. Several round tables were, and still are, placed outside in the piazza.

Its location in a highly pedestrian area near the main site of the University of Rome, the Italian Senate building and a large basilica of the same name made it an important stopping place in a key cultural and political hub of the city, particularly before World War II when Rome was still relatively concentrated and less populated. Theatre and cinema goers went in for an espresso or a drink before heading to their shows. During the Christmas season, families strolled the market of the Befana[85] that was set up in the Piazza Sant'Eustachio in front of the bar; later, the market grew much larger and was relocated to Piazza Navona. The fact that the bar remained open until 2:00 am also made it a draw for people living outside the city center; at the end of a long evening out, young men would exclaim, "Hey, let's go get a coffee at the Bar Sant'Eustachio." It is important to note that although the Sant'Eustachio, like most bars, serves alcohol, drinking excessively is not part of the Italian tradition. In the evening, clients might ask for a caffè corretto, a coffee "corrected" with a small shot of grappa or other liqueur but the purpose is not to drink to inebriation as is the case in many other European countries and the United States where bars and pubs are synonymous with partying. Young people seeking coffee at 2:00 am were really looking for a good espresso and perhaps for the company of others doing the same. More pubs have opened in Rome in the past couple of decades but they are separate spaces from the espresso bar.

Raimondo Ricci took over the Sant'Eustachio in 1999, but it has been in his family for several generations.[86] He has many memories of

85   The Befana is the witch who delivers gifts to children on the Epiphany on January 6, which marks the end of the Italian holiday season.

86   Interview by the Author with Raimondo Ricci, Bar Sant'Eustachio, Rome, June 23, 2015.

hiding under the counters while playing a version of hide-and-seek with other neighborhood kids and the scent of roasting beans filling his nostrils. The Bar Sant'Eustachio is an example of a bar that is also a torrefazione, that is a coffee bar that also prepares its own roast for the bar and sells the prepared roasted beans and ground coffees to customers. The Sant'Eustachio, the Tazza D'Oro discussed in chapter two, and the Caffè Sciascia in Prati are among the oldest and best known of the combined espresso roasters and bars in Rome. Once most neighborhoods had at least one torrefazione, but today many Roman bars buy directly from the multinationals, such as Illy and Lavazza since they offer convenience and incentives. Over the years, the Ricci family has developed its own special miscela, or particular roast, to produce the flavor of coffee their guests seek. Before Raimondo took over, his family bought the highest quality beans commercially available and then wood roasted and ground them on site. Since 2000, instead, Ricci's brother has begun to travel directly to the growers to personally select the best beans available, which are always organic, 100% arabica and produced in an economically fair way, known as fair trade. Most of their coffee today comes from small growers in South America, but north Africa and parts of Asia still factor into their buying to help the expert roasters achieve the flavors they want to offer.

Maintaining traditions is important to the Riccis, and they count on more than eighty years of experience when training their baristi and roasters, many of whom have worked in other espresso bars before coming to the Sant'Eustachio but are then retrained to follow the bar's procedures. Serving large numbers of high-quality espresso beverages very quickly requires that each employee stick to the process, especially since the bar's output is astounding, with between four and six thousand espressos served each day. What may seem like disorder to inexperienced ears as the person taking receipts at the bar calls out numbers to the barista at the machine is actually quite efficient; espresso arrives in front of customers within seconds to a couple of minutes. There is none of the writing of names on cups, and then waiting at length for an order as happens in some U.S. establishments. Instead the choreography in the Sant'Eustachio guarantees clients a tasty version of what they ordered, even if it is not a simple espresso.

Italians, too, order many variations of the basic espresso, specifying even such details as the temperature of the milk they use to make a macchiato or the proportion of coffee to milk in a latte or cappuccino. Ricci notes that very popular bars in New York City serve maybe four to six hundred espressos each day in comparison. Foreigners, Ricci notes, have attempted to capture the Sant'Eustachio experience by buying the bar's roast, but they cannot buy a large stock and Ricci does not have plans to increase production. High-end markets, such as the now defunct Dean & Deluca, never succeeded in convincing him to increase commercial exports.

In a *New York Times* magazine article that mentions Ricci and his bar, journalist William Grimes attempted to determine why it is so hard to find a good espresso in New York.[87] The number served (the higher the better to keep the machines hot and ready), the water (although this is a myth since the water in professional machines is distilled in the boiler), the preparation of the powdered espresso, and numerous other factors have to be taken into consideration. But, what Ricci points out as being key to the experience is, in fact, the location. You cannot expect to have a Roman espresso bar experience in Manhattan or Brooklyn. He explains that "manca l'anima" ["the spirit is lacking"] in most New York City bars. He and his family have always considered the bar a place for family, whether a Roman family or a family from around the world. He has met thousands and thousands of people over the years and especially enjoys receiving updates from former clients. Tourists who stopped in for a few mornings in a row for their cappuccino and cornetto send cards, and neighbors who have moved away stop by with grandchildren and news of graduations and weddings. The bar is at the center of Ricci's identity, one he shares with people near and far from his Piazza.

Although it is quite well-known inside and outside Rome and Italy, the Bar Sant'Eustachio is a part of a tradition of Roman neighborhood bars for local middle and upper-class residents. Many bars share this characteristic, but a few have become famous because of the illustrious

87   William Grimes, "New York's Best Espresso," *New York Times*, May 15, 2002, Available at https://www.nytimes.com/2002/05/15/dining/critic-s-notebook-new-york-s-best-espresso.html. Last Accessed May 16, 2018.

clientele they attracted and because of modern tragedies that are also part of their history. The Bar Rosati in Piazza del Popolo and the Café de Paris of the Via Veneto are two such spots. Both bars reached their heyday during the era of the *dolce vita*, when Italy's economic miracle was at its peak and movie stars at their most glamorous. The Bar Rosati was opened in 1922 by a man of the same name who designed the layout and decor the bar maintains today, a combination of rich woods, red velvets and marble countertops. Rosati occupies a large retail space to the right of the twin churches, Santa Maria dei Miracoli and Santa Maria in Montesanto, that flank Piazza del Popolo and lead to the Via del Corso, a main throughway that leads to Piazza Venezia and is lined by shops, churches and a few museums. As was the case for the Sant'Eustachio, the bar was primarily a latteria but also a pasticceria, pastry shop, until the wider availability of espresso turned it into an espresso bar; Rosati is now a full-service restaurant as well. During the 1950s and 1960s, Rosati attracted a mix of intellectuals, artists, and directors, Pier Paolo Pasolini and Federico Fellini among them, plus families of aristocratic origins and the nouveau riche. In 1956, a few kilometers away, Victor Tombolini opened the Café de Paris on the fashionable Via Veneto, hoping to reproduce the chic French style he had seen in Paris and attract a clientele similar to that of Rosati. The café quickly gained popularity among Italian and foreign film and music stars, such as Sophia Lauren and Frank Sinatra, who were photographed drinking espresso and cocktails by paparazzi and tourists fascinated by the idea of the *dolce vita*; the ambience of the cafe, in fact, inspired Federico Fellini's 1960 film of the same name.

Both the Rosati and the de Paris represented the dreams and realities of contemporary Italian life. Members of different social classes mixed together. Even if many clients could not pay exorbitant amounts of money to sit at a street side table and eat a full lunch while people-watching and being seen, they could afford to drink an espresso at the bar and catch a glimpse of the glamorous life. Money and ideas flowed freely. Beautiful and clever people shaped the literary and film worlds partly through their conversations and encounters at the bars. They wore the latest fashions, read the newest novels, listened to jazz and blues recordings, and socialized in their in-groups. And, largely removed from the unrest of growing social currents, at least for a few years captured in a few moments, life did indeed seem sweet. The *dolce vita* era bars retained some aspects of their tea house predecessors, such as the Antico Caffè Greco, in that they were elegant spaces that encouraged lingering. They evolved from them, however, because they were also contemporary and fashionable. Italian high design replaced old money stuffiness. The espresso machines became more streamlined and moved behind the counter, still a visible marker of the high quality of espresso-making but less of an attraction in themselves as the art nouveau machines of the early years of the twentieth century had been. The *dolce vita* bars created new concoctions, often fancy cocktails, along with the classic espresso and cappuccino drinks customers counted on and served light breakfasts and lunches. The baristi interacted less formally with their customers but still treated them with respect. A clear hierarchy stayed intact, even as a family atmosphere took shape, and the jokes of truly Roman characters were nearly always understood and appreciated, even when a little off color.

The *dolce vita* did not outlast the economic downturn that followed the 1973 oil crisis, however. The Rosati and de Paris both made it through dramatic moments and were the targets of terrorist attacks. In 1980, the Gruppi di Azione Proletaria [Proletarian Action Group] claimed responsibility in a bombing that nearly destroyed the Bar Rosati; luckily, no people were harmed in the attack. The radical political group had intended to target young neo-fascists who had begun meeting at the bar to plan their activities. Since the 1970s, the bar had assumed a politically right-leaning character and became a hangout for attention-seeking upper-bourgeois wannabees and neo-fascists.[88] Far-left groups sometimes directly confronted their opponents in public places, such as the Bar Rosati, and provoked violent outbursts. Whether or not the AP wanted to physically harm anyone was not clear, since they set off the bomb after the bar had closed for the evening. Whatever the intentions of the attackers though, the Rosati nevertheless had to close for many months to undergo thousands of dollars of repairs. Since its reopening, the Rosati has not experienced anything similar. Current

---

88   Liliana Madeo, "E` distrutto a Roma il bar Rosati: bomba," *La Stampa*, March 2, 1980, 1, 5.

manager Mario in fact, fondly recalls several big parties the Rosati has hosted with much "*allegria* [liveliness/happiness]," in particular a big celebration for the horse Varenne that won a championship in 1998. Today many tourists occupy the Rosati's outdoor tables while resting on their treks through Rome. It is still a popular site for members of the entertainment industry, especially Italian television. A former boss of mine, documentary producer-director Brando Quilici, was always happy to entertain visiting writers and editors there.

A few years later, in 1985, the Café de Paris also sustained significant damage when a Palestinian man threw grenades at the bar during regular hours and wounded 38 people, including several Americans on break from the nearby embassy. The precise motives for the attack were never understood, and the attacker, Ahmad Al Hossen Abu Sareja, did not appear to belong to any terrorist organizations. It was Italian organized crime, however, that permanently ended the Café de Paris' tenure on the Via Veneto. During the late 1990s-early 2000s the bar was taken over by the Calabrian based 'Ndrangheta before the state claimed it in 2009 and reopened it in 2011. In 2012, Chinese billionaire businessman Robert Kuok purchased the Café for 116 million Euro to build a hotel, but the 'Ndrangheta retaliated by setting it ablaze in 2014. The site remained in its incinerated state with plates and glasses still sitting on tabletops inside the sidewalk gazebo until the bar was finally torn down at the end of May 2016. For many Romans, the café had come to symbolize the corruption that was inherent in the capital and the ineffectiveness of the Italian state to oversee the flourishing of tourism. Moreover, it would appear that the lavishness of the *dolce vita* the bars represented had been skewed in various ways. Wealth turned into greed, corruption, and resentment.

In addition to the large, elegant historic bars in Rome's central upscale and bourgeois areas, there are several bars that emerged in the midst of specific political movements and cater to Rome's middle-class state and service workers and the working classes more generally. Most of these receive little more than a brief mention in the standard tourist guides, but there are exceptions. In Rome's medieval winding cobblestone neighborhood of Trastevere, I became a regular at the Bar San Calisto while a graduate student. One day I walked by the San

Calisto on my way to a research library. It attracted my attention because it was far less fancy than the bars in the nearby Piazza Santa Maria in Trastevere, the main square of the neighborhood known for its lovely Byzantine basilica. Once I stepped in, I immediately noticed that it was filled with Romans engaged in lively conversation and I appreciated that the coffee was very good. A clipping by an unknown author in a dusty frame on the wall inside the bar's seating area partly captures the charm that kept me coming back, "The San Calisto is democratic: it welcomes everyone – thieves and artists, gypsies and politicians, workers and students. And lately it's even creating a buzz...it seems it's trendy." It's trendiness though has endured for decades. The San Calisto is unpretentious with an outdated decor and old, worn floors that make it look a little squalid despite its actual state of cleanliness. The wooden tables and chairs inside are mismatched and scratched. Photos of the staff, clients and famous regulars share wall space with posters of soccer players and an award from torrefazione Pincicaffè for being a "best bar." Its adorable, now elderly but very energetic manager Marcello Forti has overseen the San Calisto's operations since 1969.[89] He explains that a family atmosphere is what matters most at the San Calisto and points out that the bar has had a major role in the daily life of Trastevere's residents ever since he can remember. During the 1970s and 80s, when Trastevere's artistic community was flourishing, accompanied by drug abuse problems, Forti notes, there were some tough periods that threatened to close the bar. Changes occurred, however, with the appearance of more foreign students and increases in rents. Gentrification, in fact, has largely pushed out newer residents unable to keep up with paying market prices to live in central Rome. At night in the 1990s, it was not uncommon to witness a fist-fight or two break out in the bar's outdoor seating on the piazza that bears the same name. Forti says that today such skirmishes are few and far between. It's a "*posto tranquillo*" now [a quiet place].

A typical day seated at one of the San Calisto's tables is indicative of the bar's role in the neighborhood since it first opened in the 1930s when, like the Sant'Eustachio it, too, was a latteria. Early in the morning—the

---

89   Interview by the Author with Marcello Forti, Bar San Calisto, Rome, June 12, 2015.

bar opens at 5:00 am—long-time elderly residents stop in for their breakfast and to share neighborhood gossip and discuss politics. By mid-morning, shop keepers and office workers take their coffee break. In the early afternoon, students arrive seeking espresso or gelato; the San Calisto is known for high-quality gelato even though it is not displayed in fancy glass cabinets as in many other bars and gelaterie. Evening brings in young people and not-so-young people who are out for a stroll and people-watching. Italians are the most numerous San Calisto customers but Trastevere's large expat population of Americans and Brits and students attending the international college, John Cabot University, contribute to the mix of visitors until the bar finally closes down for the night around 2:00 am. There is nearly constant activity with few long pauses as the ebb and flow of the day moves along. Forti remarks that it is important to have trustworthy baristi who know how to do their job because even if he cannot be present during all of the bar's opening hours, someone has to be. The ideal barista is fast, alert, and able to resolve problems without constant supervision. And, of course, the espresso has to be good. Forti has been using a miscela made by Pinci of Roma for most of the time he has run the bar. In fact, he points out that good espresso is something his clients count on that has contributed to the bar's continuous history. Many nearby bars revert to constant renovations and other novelties to attract and keep customers but the quality of their coffee suffers. You will not find a trendy cocktail list displayed on a board outside while dance music booms from inside a dimly lit stylish locale in the Piazza di San Calisto. There is the just the reliable Bar San Calisto instead. No frills. Great coffee. A smile and story from Marcello and his baristi. That's what keeps people coming back.

As at the San Calisto, the Caffè Vezio was also known for its charismatic owner, Vezio Bagazzini, and its many colorful clients, in this case mostly committed members of the Italian left, especially the Italian Communist Party (PCI). The original bar opened in 1911 on the Via dei Delfini near the Via delle Botteghe Oscure in central Rome. Vezio took over in 1967 and the bar quickly became known simply by his first name. The bar transferred and re-opened on the Lungotevere (Tor di Nona) in 2003 and closed its doors for good in 2010. Ill from Parkinson's disease and diabetes and in debt to two ex-wives, Vezio was no longer able to keep the bar open. When I first visited the Tor di Nona location in 2007 with archivists from the nearby Unione Donne Italiane, I was struck by the posters, photos and other ephemera of the Italian and international communist world – Karl Marx and Vladimir Lenin adorned the walls alongside Che Guevara and Palmiro Togliatti. A heavy-set dark-haired woman in a long skirt served espresso to a group of four small elderly men hovered over a tiny round table in the corner. Vezio, a short, thin nearly bald man with lively, intelligent eyes looked through paperwork and occasionally exchanged a few words with his clients. When I ordered my espresso, the barista joked with my companions that I could not possibly be a communist since I was an American. I just smiled.

Both the bar's relocation and closure made national news since it had for so long been an important gathering point for the Italian left. Many of his clients were surprised to learn Vezio had been unable to claim his pension and was nearly destitute. Several regulars vowed to help him during the period of closure and transfer. After all, Vezio had prepared Enrico Berlinguer's thermos to take to work with him when he was national secretary of the PCI, made sure Walter Veltroni had his ciambella and latte macchiato waiting for him when he was mayor of Rome and, over the years, Vezio served espresso to an array of famous leftists such as director Pier Paolo Pasolini, Prime Minister Massimo D'Alema, and pop star Jovanotti. The Caffè Vezio is testament to the role of the bar and espresso in Italian daily life and to the importance of like-minded individuals frequenting the same spaces because of adherence to a political cause. Leftists could surely consume their espresso elsewhere, but the atmosphere of the bar Vezio brought them back time and time again. The bar allowed for casual conversation and joking around as much as for serious political meetings. The most rigid and closed individuals were more likely to let down their guard and open up in the setting of the bar than in their offices or on the floor of the Italian Senate. Much as the golf course is a bonding place for American businessmen, so is the bar for Italian politicians. Having a coffee together is less time-consuming, however, than playing a round of golf. And while having a Happy Hour cocktail has long played a role in cementing a variety of political and business deals, the absence of alcohol is important to coffee's sociability. It can be consumed at any time without anyone raising an eyebrow.

During his years on the Via dei Delfini, it appeared Vezio was in good standing with his neighbors in the Botteghe Oscure area. Although government offices and research institutes occupy a number of buildings in the neighborhood, there are also long-term private residences and other sorts of commercial activities. Foreigners, including tourists and students but also migrant workers, have grown in numbers since the 1980s and changed the makeup of this and many Roman neighborhoods. Bar managers have responded to the new influx in various ways. In the Botteghe Oscure in the early 1990s, it seemed the nearby Polish church San Stanislao was unable to keep up with the needs of new arrivals and the neighbors grew concerned about public drunkenness, litter, brawls, and the street harassment of women. Although some commentators accused Vezio and the Italian left of being racists, he led a group to try to resolve the problem; Polish migrants often came into his bar asking for wine in a box and plastic cups. Vezio was reluctant to sell it to them because he would then see the men wandering the streets in a drunken stupor.[90] At the same time, he did not want to pass judgment on men looking for a drink at the end of a hard day of work as laborers, a job many new arrivals took. Vezio was also passionate about the Roma soccer team, and it was not uncommon to find a few non-communist friends in the bar during soccer matches. After learning of Vezio's death just a few months after his bar closed for good, Walter Veltroni recalled, "Vezio Bagazzini has gone, too young, too soon. The news of the death pains me. I knew him since forever: a coffee and an exchange of jokes was a daily custom for me as for many other people who worked at the Botteghe Oscure. And with him one thing was always certain: unfailingly we ended up talking politics. It was his passion."[91] For some clients, the closing of the Bar Vezio ran parallel to the larger faltering of the political left.

Another site for coffee and political activism is the bar L'una e

90   Flavia Amabile, "Fuori i polacchi dal bar dei comunisti," *La Stampa*, December 5, 1992, 13.

91   "E' morto Vezio, nel suo bar a Botteghe Oscure la storia del Pci," *La Repubblica*, April 22, 2011.

l'altra at the Casa Internazionale delle Donne in Trastevere. The current establishment has been open for just a few years but there has been a bar at the center of the Roman feminist movement since the first, Zanzibar, opened in 1978 in nearby Piazza Trilussa. Having a woman-only space was of great significance to feminists who wanted to create a place where women could come together to socialize, enjoy a meal, buy and sell crafts and, of course, *prendere un caffè* [get a coffee]. As co-founder Tiziana explained in an article when Zanzibar opened, there was some conflict over the idea for such a gathering spot, even among feminists, which meant that Zanzibar's supporters had to be "careful not to label moments for fun as not intellectual or less political but to consider them an expression of the liberation of our bodies and of our fantasies."[92] In other words, it was not only okay for feminists to socialize and have fun, it was a political statement when they did. After the divorce referendum in 1974, the concept of woman-only spaces flourished, aided by discussions of sexuality and lesbian separatism, and more women joined neighborhood women's collectives and participated in political activities. They usually shared food and drink informally, pot-luck style, until the women established more permanent spaces and did not want to have to interrupt their activities to seek refreshments elsewhere. Unlike commercial businesses, Zanzibar and subsequent versions, such as le Sette Streghe [seven witches] and L'una e l'altra [the one and the other – in feminine gender], stayed open because they were organized as cultural centers. Guests paid a small fee for a *tessera*, the membership card, and the centers were staffed primarily by volunteers. That way they enjoyed tax exempt status. Even the current bar in the Casa Internazionale would not likely be economically viable on its own but is nonetheless considered of utmost importance to the day-to-day activities of the Casa. Women in the more than thirty different women's groups housed in the center, such as the Filipino Women's Council and the Società italiana delle storiche, enjoy access to a low-cost restaurant/bar and it brings in customers, men and women, from some of the nearby offices along the Via della Lungara.[93] It is an

---

92   Clipping from archive at CIDD.

93   The Casa Internazionale delle Donne is in danger of being closed by the City of Rome because of questions about payments of taxes and rent to the city.

inclusive, welcoming space in the Casa's central courtyard adorned by flowers and trees where guests can eat and relax outside or remain inside seated in the large rectangular room with wooden tables and chairs. And, of course, everyone is invited to stand at the bar for an espresso. Giovanna Olivieri, who has been a feminist activist since the late 1960s and currently works with the library and archive in the Casa, notes that espresso has a special significance neither a nice plate of pasta nor a fine glass of wine can match.[94] According to her, espresso is part of Italian identity and Roman life; it is informal, convivial, and economical. She explains that at some of the first evening gatherings at the Casa after it re-opened in 1994, women lamented if there was no coffee served, "No coffee? But that's not possible." They did not say the same about wine.

From intellectuals and movie stars to office workers and students going about their day, the people of Rome have made espresso drinking and the bar central reference points in their lives. The practice of getting a coffee is a moment for sharing while at the same time a moment of distacco, of getting away. A Roman's choices about drinking coffee tell us something about historical identities and sociological belongings. Having the opportunity to congregate in a space with like-minded individuals outside of the usual meeting places of work and home generates meaning, creating affinity and belonging. Roman bars are the heart of their neighborhoods. Espresso is what brings people together but it is rarely just part of an anonymous experience in replicated surroundings. The buildings and their decor, the aromas, the baristi, the clients and the passers-by all affect espresso drinking. Residents of Rome live hectic lives in a major European capital amidst the ruins of a triumphant ancient civilization that tourists flock to in droves. Espresso fuels their days.

---

94   Interview by the Author with Giovanna Olivieri, CIDD, Rome, June 30, 2015.

CHAPTER SIX

ESPRESSO BARS IN NAPLES: THE RITUAL OF COFFEE

"A Napoli, il caffè è un rito" [In Naples, espresso is a ritual] is a phrase I heard from nearly every Neapolitan I encountered who wanted to describe espresso culture in a city known for its food traditions. Pierluigi Barbato of the Chalet Bar in Piazza Nazionale explains, "There are three things that have cult status in Naples—coffee, pizza, sfogliatelle—for bars, espresso; for restaurants, pizza; for pastry shops, sfogliatelle. All are products that were born in Naples and that we do best. We count on coffee; it's our calling card."[95] Giuseppe Madonna of the Intra Moenia publishing house and coffee bar concurs that good espresso is a "calling card" and remarks that, "In Naples, you get together and then say, 'let's get a coffee.' It's a form of conviviality. Neapolitans are very tied to coffee. It's a ritual."[96] Elsa Calise of the Bar Calise on the island of Ischia agrees, "in Naples, coffee is a ritual; it's for getting together with friends. Here, everything revolves around coffee."[97] Neapolitans are fiercely proud of their long and strong espresso tradition and defend their espresso preferences in much the same way as they are proud of their city, an area long lauded and criticized by outsiders for its stunning beauty and internal contradictions. Neapolitan espresso bars are reflections of the city's glorious past, its troubled times, and its ability to keep up with contemporary life and its many demands. Salvatore Riccardi of the Caffè del professore puts it simply, "For us, coffee is culture."[98]

One of the oldest and most beloved espresso centers in Naples is the Gran Caffè Gambrinus. The lovely tea room and pastry shop

---

95   Interview by Author with Pierluigi Barbato, Chalet Barbato, Naples, February 27, 2018.

96   Interview by Author with Giuseppe Madonna of the Intramoenia Publishing House, Naples, February 22, 2018.

97   Interview by Author with Elsa Calise, Bar Calise at Piazza degli Eroi, Ischia, February 16, 2018.

98   Interview by Author with Salvatore Riccardi, Caffè del professore, Naples, June 23, 2016.

still enjoyed by Neapolitans and visitors to Naples dates to 1860, just one year before the pivotal moment in Italian history when Giuseppe Garibaldi handed over the Kingdom of Two Sicilies to the House of Savoy, making Victor Emmanuel the King of Italy and Turin the capital of a newly unified state. Naples at the time was the largest city in Italy with a population of about 484,000 residents and had been the capital of an important European kingdom. Its role in the Bourbon dynasty has been preserved in the Gambrinus, where a lavish décor in white and gold with imposing crystal chandeliers and red velvet upholstery captures the city at the moment of Italian unification. The memories of the aristocrats of the era who frequented the Royal Palace that stands across the large Piazza del Plebiscito from the Gambrinus are reflected in the violet ice cream the café still serves in honor of the Princess "Sissi," Elizabeth of Bavaria, who was much admired by the Neapolitans for her beauty and tall, slender figure. Gambrinus was a gathering spot for intellectuals and artists during the belle époque. The Irish poet and playwright Oscar Wilde and four-time nominee for the Nobel Prize for literature and founder of the Neapolitan newspaper *Il Mattino* Matilde Serao sat at its tables. Writer and Italian nationalist Gabriele D'Annunzio visited the Gambrinus on his trips to the former Bourbon capital. They were all drawn by the atmosphere, the opportunity to discuss the key political events of the day, and by the pastries.

Gambrinus, like many of the espresso establishments in the city, was first and foremost a popular pasticceria, or bakery. Neapolitan specialties, such as sfogliatelle, a ricotta filled pastry, and babá, a rum based treat, could be enjoyed with a beverage. In Gambrinus' first years that beverage was coffee, but it quickly became espresso. As Michele Sergio, the charismatic co-owner of Gambrinus explains, "at first, coffee was made in the old way. It took as much as a half hour to prepare. Italy was an agricultural country. Life moved more slowly. Making coffee was slow."[99] He notes that the arrival of espresso and the new methods for preparing it accompanied revolutionary changes in daily life. After unification, he remarks, "not all southern Italians

---

99 Interview by Author with Michele Sergio, Gran Caffè Gambrinus, Naples, June 21, 2016.

were happy with the new state. Many Neapolitans left Italy for the United States, for New York. And they took pizza, spaghetti and coffee with them." Those who stayed, of course, continued to develop the tradition. Sergio claims, in fact, that "Naples is where coffee became an adult. The love of espresso. The ritual of espresso. Naples is at the center of it." The disruptions of fascism and the war years were felt at Gambrinus, too, however. In 1937, *La Stampa* reported that the historic café was closing, a news item that was reaching even the German and Swiss media because so clamorous a story. Magistrates, professors, and pensioners—artists, writers, and scientists—young men seeking a nice breeze on a hot afternoon, reported *La Stampa*, all of them would have to find a new gathering place. The paper reported that some of the café's clients had been sitting at the same table for forty years, enjoying pastries, coffee, and art to rival the Café Greco in Rome.[100]

Luckily, Gambrinus did not close its doors for good but it did experience, and survive, some of the hardships of twentieth century Neapolitan and Italian life. It continues to thrive in spite of them. As was the case in other historic Italian cities, the fascists re-envisioned the urban architectural landscape in Naples. The central district from the Via Toledo to the Piazza Municipio was demolished and replaced with new buildings, but a large part of the historic center, including Piazza Plebiscito, was left in a state of abandonment or transformed into far less glamorous uses.[101] In fact, after the war and with the spread of the automobile during the economic miracle, the piazza became a large car park and housed a bus terminal; Gambrinus was flanked by traffic and noise. Nonetheless, the café remained a popular spot for special occasions, such as celebrations of baptisms, birthdays and weddings. In the 1960s, the automobile symbolized the growth of the Italian middle-class, and for the Neapolitans, "played a crucial role in ordering the increasingly chaotic traffic of Naples and projecting a modern, *civilized* image of the city."[102] Gambrinus played a part in connecting

---

100   Alberto Consiglio, "Ombre e memorie del vecchio caffè," *La Stampa*, January 21, 1937, 4.

101   Giuseppe Mazzeo, "City Profile: Naples," Cities 26 (2009): 365.

102   Nick Dines, *Tuff City: Urban Change and Contested Space in Central Naples* (New York: Berghahn Books, 2015), 126.

the aristocratic past of the piazza to its new role as a center for families benefiting from the boom. By the late 1980s, however, the Neapolitan love for cars had been replaced by disdain for chaos and pollution, and many environmental and historic revival groups began to call for changes to the ordering of the center of the city. Prime Minister Carlo Azeglio Ciampi's decision to hold the 1994 G7 summit meeting in Naples and the tenure of a new major, Antonio Bassolino, who held the position from 1993 to 2001, brought important changes to Piazza Plebiscito and the entire *centro storico* [historic center]. What began as a temporary closure of the Piazza to traffic became a permanent feature that again re-ordered the place of long-standing businesses, such as Gambrinus. By the middle of the 1990s, the café capped the end of the long shopping district of the Via Toledo, marked the top of the elegant Chiaia district and extended into the pedestrian-only area of the piazza. Essentially, on one side Gambrinus met the high energy and high density of Naples and, on the other, enjoyed the breezes arriving from the sea. It also benefited from the revival of Naples as a tourist destination, attracting Italian and foreign visitors and serving as a port for large cruise ships.

As an espresso bar, the Gambrinus is famous worldwide. Its long history and central position in the Italian south and in Naples' now most important piazza keep locals and visitors returning to enjoy the coffee. Michele Sergio is another reason Gambrinus is one of the most beloved espresso bars today, however. Young, dynamic and passionate about his family's business, Sergio spreads the word about Gambrinus and Naples' espresso tradition through social media platforms, such as Facebook and Instagram. He wants to attract clients, of course, but he also wants to educate the public about espresso. For example, on-line viewers can watch Sergio make *crema alla nocciola*, a hazelnut cream that is the basis of a Neapolitan specialty coffee or see him hop on his scooter to rush to the rescue of someone unable to make good coffee.[103] At the base of the gran café is the espresso. For the past fifty years, the Gambrinus has been using a Moreno espresso blend created especially for them. Sergio explains that the five "Ms" —*macchina* [coffee machine];

---

103   See for instance the videos on the Gambrinus Facebook page https://www.facebook.com/CaffeGambrinusNapoli/.

miscela [blend]; *macinino* [grinder]; *mano dell'operatore* [hand of the barista]; and *manutenzione della macchina* [machine maintenance] – are the essential elements of good Neapolitan coffee. For the locals, an espresso must be strong, potent, and full of flavor. The bar serves upwards of 3500 espressos each day, each "pulled" on the traditional lever machines by expert baristas such as Giovanni Fummo who, at just over 70 years of age, has made more than 15 million espressos since he began working at the bar as a teenager. Sergio compares the lever machines to cars with manual transmissions. He says, "sure, the automatic car like the automated espresso machine will get you there, but it's better to have control. A good barista knows how to grind the espresso and how to work the machine." Moreover, Sergio points out that the Gambrinus is offering great espresso, but also the experience of the location. He notes that while "the Americans tend to propose one product and then send it everywhere, we're interested in maintaining the uniqueness of the product and the tradition. It's reflected even in how we dress, speak, serve our clients. In Naples, we love the sun and we don't sleep much," he jokes, "so we need our espresso." The service is professional and jovial at the same time.

One tradition the Gambrinus has helped to keep alive and that has taken on elsewhere in Italy and worldwide is the *caffè sospeso*, literally, suspended coffee. What it means is that during the earliest years of the Gambrinus, when the aristocratic tradition carried an element of caring for the lower classes, well-to-do customers would pay for two or more coffees when buying one for themselves. The coffees not consumed would be recorded and left for guests who were unable to spend money on what was not considered a life or death need, an espresso. The person desiring coffee could then enter and order a *caffè sospeso*, no questions asked, no judgments offered. Today an espresso consumed at the counter at Gambrinus costs just 1 Euro and 10 cents, slightly above the Neapolitan average of 90 cents yet still quite reasonable, but suspended coffees are purchased and drunk there each day. Many espresso bars in the city use the practice and Neapolitan bars in other Italian cities—I visited one in Turin—have extended the tradition, a version of paying it forward. The Neapolitan twist, however, recognizes the importance of coffee in the city's culture and highlights the warmth and generosity the people are known for, especially in times of hardship. For them, espresso is something no one should have to go without.

The southern Italian sun, the Neapolitan literary and artistic heritage, and the contributions of espresso bars to the changing urban landscape are all prevalent features of another well-known espresso bar in the *centro storico*. The Caffè Intra Moenia in Piazza Bellini is today a lively and centrally located gathering spot for artists, musicians, and writers. When Attilio Wanderlingh, a writer very much interested in the connections between the present and the past in the history of Italian cities, decided to open the café in the late 1980s, it was in part to re-valorize the ancient history of Naples and link it to contemporary life.[104] Like the Piazza Plebiscito, Piazza Bellini had turned into a car park once automobiles took over the city in the 1960s and 1970s. By the 1980s, the Piazza Bellini was controlled by unofficial parking lot attendants, essentially individuals who are not authorized by the city to park cars but collect a fee from the drivers who leave their cars there. Not paying implies a risk of finding a damaged vehicle or missing items upon the driver's return or perhaps not finding the car at all. Growing support for urban renewal and the creation of pedestrian areas allowed Wanderlingh to imagine his plans for the piazza, including a new literary café/espresso bar and a publishing house. He wanted to unite the arts to coffee, using a Parisian model but re-envisioning it in the Neapolitan context, that is, with an emphasis on espresso and the use of the outdoors. The mild climate and ample sunshine of the southern capital were well-suited to seating in the piazza and appreciation for its history. The name Intra Moenia, meaning inside the walls in Greek, in fact, comes from the ruins of Greek walls that are exposed on the edge of the piazza but whose presence had been undervalued because of the piazza's use as a parking lot. Wanderlingh thus mobilized the neighborhood to make the piazza pedestrian only and better demarcate the area surrounding the ruins. When he opened the Intra Moenia in 1989, Wanderlingh became one of the leading figures of the movement to reclaim the city center for pedestrians and

---

104 Intra Moenia, Web site, https://www.intramoenia.it/caffe-letterario/, Last accessed May 1, 2018.

bring the arts and culture back to a place of historical significance.

The addition of a small publishing house that released titles especially on local history deepened the café's role in the neighborhood and in Naples more generally. Giuseppe Madonna, who has been working for the publisher for several years, notes that from the moment it opened, the Intra Moenia became a popular spot for the city's youth.[105] Its location near a branch of the University of Naples, the city's music conservatory, and a classical high school contributed to its draw, but Madonna says, "people come from all over the city, especially in the evening, because it is a reference point. It is known as the first and is maybe still the only major literary café in southern Italy." The café hosts regular events, such as art shows, poetry readings, book presentations, and live music. Madonna acknowledges that the evening events might seem to favor the drinking of alcoholic beverages, but he says espresso is really the café's "reference point. In Naples, you get an espresso for pleasure. You meet up with friends. Then you get a coffee." In the morning, Madonna says you will see many readers and writers enjoying a cappuccino at one of the cozy indoor tables. During the day, friends gather at the outside tables for some sun in the piazza and an espresso. In the evening, clients have espresso, maybe *corretto*, that is, with a shot of alcohol, or a fancy espresso-based cocktail while they listen to a local writer discussing her work. Other beverages are available, of course, but the café managers know their customers expect good coffee. One of their baristas tells me they are currently using Kimbo. The bar had used Illy for several years, which he says is great espresso, but then they decided they wanted to go back to using a Neapolitan brand and chose Kimbo. "Naples is the capital of espresso," he remarks. Intra Moenia could base its business on its location and the arts, but it holds true to the city's coffee heritage as well.

A short walking distance from the Caffè Intra Moenia is the Via San Luigi dei Librai in the neighborhood known as Spaccanapoli because of the street of the same name that cuts through the center of the city with its narrow, cobblestone streets. Famous for its artisans who craft elaborate wooden nativity scenes and produce versions of Naples' beloved Pulcinella, a 17th century stock puppet character, during the

---

105 Madonna interview.

1970s and 1980s, Spaccanapoli gained a less-than-happy notoriety as a center of organized crime controlled by the city's Camorra. Today Spaccanapoli is enjoying a revival brought about by a decline in crime and an upsurge in tourism. There are now twenty-four espresso bars along the Via San Luigi and its side streets, but as Carmine Alcide, owner of the Bar Nilo, notes, "until about twenty years ago, there were just four bars, including ours."[106] His grandfather opened the establishment in 1920 and it became an integral part of the neighborhood. Alcide recalls that it was an especially popular bar among the professors and students of the nearby university who became regular clients. Many politicians stopped in as well. Passion for the Napoli soccer team made the bar a mainstay of the neighborhood when brother and co-owner Bruno created a shrine to Diego Maradona, the Argentine-born Napoli soccer player who led the team to national titles in 1987 and 1990. The year of the second title, Bruno snatched long, curly black hairs belonging to the player from his airplane seat when deplaning from the same flight as his hero. The Bar Nilo then used Maradona's hairs as the centerpiece for an homage to the player known for uniting the city behind him during some of the hardest times Naples faced.[107] Local residents kept the bar going during some of its more challenging moments as well, such as when part of the university, and thus many of its regular clients, relocated and, during the late 1990s, when a series of Camorra-related shootings disrupted daily life in the neighborhood just as it was beginning to improve.

Throughout its history, Carmine says, espresso has been the number one focus and kept the Nilo's customers coming back. "It's our battle call. Coffee for Neapolitans is a ritual, a tradition. When you run into a friend, the first thing you say is 'let's go get a coffee,' and if the friend says no, you get offended. We get offended. Coffee. It's a gesture of getting together. Understand? For me, it's fundamental." He continues, "It's different in Naples. As soon as you get up you

---

106   Interview by Author with Carmine Alcide, Bar Nilo, Naples, June 22, 2016.

107   Emanuela Sorrentino, "Napoli, il vero e il traditore: Maradona e Higuain, i due santi del Bar Nilo," *Il Mattino*, November 4, 2016, https://www.ilmattino.it/napoli/cronaca/napoli_maradona_higuain_santi_bar_nilo-2061635.html.

have a coffee. It gives you energy. Coffee is everything."[108] The bar
uses a special Moreno blend with a fair amount of robusta to enhance
the intensity of the flavor their customers seem to prefer. The Alcide
brothers point out that it's hard work but worth it to be a focal point
of the neighborhood. The bar is open from 7:00 am to 8:00 pm and
constantly busy despite competition from the many newer places
located nearby. The older bars, such as Nilo and the Gran Caffè Ciorfito
located down the street, rely on their heritage and their commitment
to good espresso. Like Nilo, the Ciorfito is run by a second generation
of brothers, Massimiliano and Raffaele Ciorfito, but the bar has been
open for more than a hundred years. The espresso is so good, in fact,
that it has inspired poetry. A framed poem in the bar reads, "Che caffè
com'è squisito! Che scoperto! È di Ciorfito! Io voglio essere servito
il caffè solo da Ciorfito. O sorseggio da Ciorfito o per me il caffè è
esaurito. Rigustato un buon Ciorfito resto triste: è già finito! Finché
torno da Ciorfito: fa il caffè da tutti ambito. Io non so s'è mai esistito
il caffè senza Ciorfito. Tieni in testa ben scolpito tale detto saggio e
antico: Occaffè sta da Ciorfito. O vai lì o si scimunito! [What coffee!
How exquisite! What a discovery! It's from Ciorfito! I want to be served
coffee only at Ciorfito. Or sip it at Ciorfito or for me the coffee is
finished. Re-sipping the good Ciorfito and I am sad: it's already gone!
Until I go back to Ciorfito: they make coffee that's the ambition of all
the others. I don't know if there's ever been coffee without Ciorfito.
Keep in your well-sculpted head the wise and ancient saying: the
coffee is at Ciorfito. You go there or you're an idiot]."[109] The quality
of its traditional espresso is appreciated by Neapolitans and visitors
alike, but the Ciorfito's specialty coffees, made with Kinder candies,
hazelnut cream, or the specialty *caffè del nonno* [grandfather's coffee], a
sort of coffee milkshake, are particularly popular. Following traditions
and creating trends work well for the espresso bars of Spaccanapoli.

The ritual of coffee in Naples is further exemplified at the Chalet
Barbato in Piazza Nazionale where good espresso has been served to
a loyal clientele since 1955. The Chalet sits inside the circular piazza

---

108   Alcide interview.
109   Author photograph from framed poem, February 26, 2018.

and is an open-style bar, closed on the back side toward the center of the piazza but open to the outdoors on the front and sides with the main entrance point resting on the sidewalk near the piazza's parking areas. The location is indicative of the hustle and bustle of the city since the piazza is a main thoroughfare still open to traffic in which clients can pull over quickly in cars or on scooters for an espresso and a sfogliatella on their way to work or to school. The partially outdoor setting also reflects, however, the Neapolitans' love for the sun and being outside whenever possible. Tables placed at the Chalet allow clients to linger in the warmth a bit longer or take a little stroll around the piazza. Pierluigi Barbato, who inherited the business, says that when his parents opened the bar in the 1950s, they had the idea of sun in mind and perhaps already understood the role the automobile would come to play in the city. They did not, however, predict that what was supposed to be a temporary closure, about 18 months, of the piazza for repairs would last for more than a decade. Barbato shrugs off what he calls, "the usual Neapolitan administrative problems" and points to the spot where the bar did business in a shipping container during the period of construction.[110]

Clients kept coming back to the chalet even when it was technically a container because of the Barbato family and the bar's excellent espresso. Barbato continues, "we are not a bar just for passers-by. We know our clients. Everyone who comes in knows my name. They say 'hello.' They have been coming for years, from when my father was here. It's a source of pride and satisfaction." The Chalet is open nearly 24 hours a day, making in a constantly active spot in the piazza with a flow of changing customers who appear throughout the day. The bar opens at 5:00 am and first brings in a number of professionals from the neighborhood, especially doctors and other medical workers because of nearby state clinics, and lawyers who work at the ASLA, the national association of law firms, whose office sits right behind the piazza. Students, other office workers, and retirees also pop in in the morning and lunchtime hours. By the late afternoon, young people start gathering around the chalet after school or work and keep the lively atmosphere going until 2:00 am during the week and 4:00 am

---

110   Barbato interview.

on weekends. They use the bar as a meeting spot for an espresso before heading to discos or cinemas and come back before going home. Some young people stay all evening and chat and joke around with friends into the wee hours. And, here, too, Barbato states, "espresso is our main weapon. If the coffee is good, people come back and you can sell them other things." Barbato's parents committed to Caffè Moreno as their blend about twenty years ago because it was "a guarantee of quality. And they are exceptional people—the owners and the employees. They are a Neapolitan company that puts itself at the disposition of the client. They give us the machines, the product, the full service." A lively atmosphere based on the outdoors, family tradition, client loyalty, and the ritual of espresso. The classic, contemporary Neapolitan bar.

A ten-minute walk from Piazza Nazionale is the Piazza Garibaldi located in front of the main train station, Napoli Centrale. Today, travelers enter and exit the train station that serves as a stop for national and regional trains as well as local commuter transit with relative ease. They can find an espresso inside one the station's bars or in one of the many bars just outside unaware of decades of public debate about the fate of the site. Piazza Garibaldi and the neighborhood surrounding the station has been a contested area since it was first built in the mid-1950s, mainly because it was not well-integrated into an overall urban plan, and again became a site of much discussion in the early 1990s because of its perceived connection to immigration and crime.[111] During the 1970s, when tourism to Naples began to drop, and as occurred around transit hubs in many large urban areas, the train station attracted petty thieves, drug pushers, and prostitutes. What had been grand hotels fell to the lower end of the market and the neighborhood became seamier and less desirable. The influx of migrants to Italy from Eritrea, the Philippines, Cape Verde, and other countries began at roughly the same time. Although many of the first arrivals were women who worked in the domestic sector, migrations of men from north Africa picked up by the second half of the 1980s. Migrants and refugees from war-torn and economically depressed areas, such as Albania and sub-Saharan

---

111 Antonia Dawes, "The Struggle for Via Bologna Street Market: Crisis, Racial Denial and Speaking Back to Power in Naples Italy," *The British Journal of Sociology* (2018): 1-18.

Africa led to new entries by the early 1990s. The area near the station, as well as in other central parts of Naples, such as the Montesanto and Spanish Quarters neighborhoods, became a site for migrant residents and street vendors and most notably the Via Bologna market. Some migrants in more desperate circumstances took up residence inside the station itself, however. When the Bassolino administration called for urban renewal in the early 1990s, they targeted the station and Piazza Garibaldi for an overhaul. Naples had been known for its relatively tolerant approach to immigration, in part because of the idea of "*l'arte d'arrangiarsi*," "the art of getting by" that applies to all residents of Naples, but the desire for an image makeover in the hopes of revitalizing the tourist industry meant projecting an arrival point that was clean, safe and Italian.[112]

The neighborhood bars, especially in the nearby streets named for Italian cities, reflect the interconnectedness and continuity of peoples and decades of change. Near the Via Bologna market, there are bars catering to particular ethnic tastes, such as those that serve Turkish coffee and Arab sweets, but they also feature Neapolitan specialties, such as espresso and sfogliatelle. Young African men can be seen congregating in small groups outside shops to sell knock-off bags and cell phones but also pulling an espresso as baristas inside the bars. Along the edge of Piazza Garibaldi itself heading toward Piazza Mancini that connects with the central Corso Umberto are numerous bars, some decades old and some just a few years old. The Gran Caffè Imperius, which sits in the space linking Piazzas Garibaldi and Mancini, opened in 1999 with the idea of bringing the "grand café" style back to the piazza. A large seating area on the sidewalk outside allows customers to take in the view of a steady flow of pedestrians and drivers passing by while enjoying some sun. Inside is a well-furnished pastry shop with all the Neapolitan favorites, staffed by Neapolitans. The espresso served is a blend made by Caffè del Professore, another famous Neapolitan roaster and bar whose original location is just steps away from the Gambrinus. All signs point to the bar's arrival as a distinctly new and Neapolitan site to greet tourists and serve the nearby businesses and thus very much fits in with the urban renewal plans for the neighborhood. A

---

112 Dines, *Tuff City*, 193.

short distance ahead toward the station is the Luna Rossa, which can be described as simple and unassuming, a standard neighborhood bar. Here though they serve Lavazza and the staff and clients are a mix of Neapolitans and migrants. It's a place for passers-by and residents— the sort of bar one goes to because it's there rather than because it's a destination. The same cannot be said for the best-known bar on the Piazza Garibaldi, the Bar Mexico. Middle-aged, professional baristas serve Passalacqua espresso, which is already sweetened with sugar, in large numbers. The ticket the cashier hands customers, in fact, indicates which of the day's espressos is being consumed, a number that can easily exceed 1000 during a busy period.

The Piazza Garibaldi Bar Mexico, along with two other Bar Mexico locations, one at Piazza Dante and one in the Vomero, opened in the mid-1950s, making them contemporaries of the construction of the train station. The Piazza Garibaldi bar is a reminder of the history of the urban landscape of Naples and an indication of continuity in the face of decades of change. It has endured novelty, decline, and renewal and earned its place among the top bars of the city. Of the original three sites of the Bar Mexico, however, only the Vomero bar on the Via Scarlatti is still part of the original ownership tied to the Passalacqua roasters. There are many Bar Mexico franchises throughout Naples that operate independently but serve Passalacqua. Not all are of the same age or quality, however. In fact, the Via Scarlatti bar won the Mangia e Bevi [Eat and Drink] award in 2017 for the best coffee shop in the region of Campania, not only Naples. Maurizio Capodanno, the current owner who has been working with Passalacqua and the Bar Mexico for more than thirty years, says the sixty of years of the success of the business comes from listening to their clients and the tradition of high quality espresso that is maintained from the origins of the plants to when the *tazzina* [espresso cup] is served at the bar counter. "At the bar we're good at preparing espresso and selling it, but at the base there's the goodness of the coffee. We start from the high quality of the coffee. We have good baristas. We take good care of the machines. All of it is important."[113] The blend is a dark roasted 100% arabica. The baristas are trained, especially on how to grind the

---

113 Capodanno interview.

beans correctly depending on weather conditions. The machine is a five lever San Marco. He notes that repeat customers, the vast majority, have admitted to trying an espresso at a nearby bar when the lines at Bar Mexico become especially long. "They come back and tell me that the coffee was not as good or even that it gave them a stomachache and say next time they'll wait an extra three minutes to be served. It's gratifying to know they can count on us." In addition to the practice of adding sugar to the espresso, unless the client requests it *amaro* [unsweetened], the Bar Mexico initiated the custom of offering a small glass of mineral water, flat or carbonated as the client prefers, with the coffee. It is to be drunk before the espresso to cleanse the palate, not afterwards, as many coffee drinkers think. Most bars in Naples and now even in other parts of Italy provide pre-espresso water. Thought has even gone into the choice of espresso cups, ceramic cups that are the right size and thickness to hold the heat. Glass is available on request as are take away plastic cups, but Capodanno underlines the repeated notion that espresso is not just something to toss back for the caffeine, "it's ritual; it's not just a break that you take super-fast. It's an opportunity to chat with a friend and talk about the family, or soccer, or the government, or anything really, to be together."

Capodanno points out that he has known many of his clients for the entirety of the time he has worked in the Vomero and has watched families grow up, suffered losses, and experienced the numerous changes of the neighborhood. Known for being one of the nicest upper middle-class neighborhoods in Naples, the Vomero sits atop the hill behind the Spanish Quarters and is most easily reachable by cable car. Several spots offer spectacular views of the sea and Mount Vesuvius and, on clear days, the islands and hills beyond. Fans of author Elena Ferrante may recognize the names of streets and piazzas from her first novel, *Troubling Love*, in which a daughter traces her mother's final steps that lead her into the shops of the Vomero. Capodanno explains that there were traditionally two main groups of customers in the bar, office and shop workers who came for their breaks, and residents of the neighborhood who came to purchase freshly ground espresso along with other specialty items such as chocolates, cookies or teas. The second segment has diminished as specialty items have become more available in regular supermarkets and coffee purchases for home use have changed. He notes that more people seem to have abandoned the napoletana and the moka, the traditional stove top methods, in favor of pods and capsules. Fewer customers buy ground espresso. The Bar Mexico sells Passalacqua ground coffee and pods but not capsules. However, some younger clients, especially twenty-somethings, Capodanno points out, seem to have a renewed interest in coffee and its history. "They want good coffee and are passionate about it. They are starting to ask more questions about where the beans come from, what kind of blend they should use. So we do explain to them, for instance, that the arabica coffees are sweeter, more aromatic, less caffeinated, not as strong. They'll ask you for a lighter coffee and so *lungo* [long, with more water] but don't understand that more water isn't the key. They are happy to learn more and to try different kinds of coffee at home. They are going back to the ritual of the napoletana at home, even if it takes longer." Getting younger people interested in espresso and its history, says Capodanno, is important to keeping the Neapolitan coffee traditions going.

Elsa, co-owner of the Bar Calise chain on the island of Ischia, agrees that "young people appreciate the flavor of the local espresso" and are essential to the continued ritual of coffee in Naples and the islands.[114] A woman of youthful vitality in her 80s, Elsa is the granddaughter of the original founders of the first Bar Calise in the village of Casamicciola. When her grandfather opened a small bar near the port in the early 1900s, it mostly served agricultural merchants taking their products to sell in Naples. Today the Calise family owns three bars in different points on the island and runs a special events villa. Elsa's father, Francesco, who took over the family business in 1925, learned the craft of baking in Naples and decided to make pastries and espresso his focus. Elsa explains, "it was never just the coffee alone—it was always espresso or a cappuccino and a brioche for breakfast—but coffee is a ritual. It's like the tea ritual in Japan, only we don't take long breaks. In Italy, it's not just coffee for coffee like in the United States." The bar uses an arabica and robusta blend made by Passalacqua, a company Elsa says, "knows the taste of

114 Calise interview.

Naples." She points out that her family's business has always made espresso the way the locals like it, even if much of their clientele is from other Italian regions or other countries. "Our espresso has always tasted more or less the same since the 1950s." She notes that other regions have flavor preferences, lighter in the north, for example, and that there is a recent trend of offering a choice of multiple blends to clients. But, Elsa remains true to her coffee heritage when she asserts, "Here, you drink the coffee we have. And it's very good." The choice of blend, the lever machines, the choice of cups, as in other historic bars, contribute to the ultimate flavor and experience.

The bars' island settings also attest to the special place of espresso on Ischia. The Casamicciola bar sits just behind the main road that runs along the coast of the island and is connected to the port. The décor inside is typical of bars from the 1970s and 1980s, although the original bar dates to the 1920s. The large outdoor seating area complete with palm trees and umbrellas is where most customers pass their time, however. The bar/pasticceria retains a colonial, old-world feel, as seen in the hanging black and white images of men in suits and women in dresses and hats seated at circular tables with tablecloths taking in the view of the boats and passers-by. The second location at Piazza degli Eroi opened in the late 1960s, an inland setting beneath an expanse of maritime pines, palm trees, orange trees and flowers. Inside, the décor is luxurious with elaborate globe light fixtures, carved wooden display cases for the extensive pastries, and numerous elegant wooden tables. Outside, patrons enjoy the terracotta patio and a terraced garden with private covered seating areas. The last location of the Bar Calise dates to 2002 at the main Port of Ischia that bring boats full of tourists to the island each day. Here, too, clients have the choice of an elegant, if more simple, indoor area or outdoor seating overlooking the port.

In each bar, the natural beauty of the island, the warm climate, and the congregation of people come together to encourage sociability and relaxation. Many clients still consume their espresso at the counter, of course, especially the locals and workers. However, Elsa points out that their clientele and its habits have changed significantly during her lifetime, an indication of Italy's contemporary transformations. From the late 1950s on, she recalls, there were mostly well-to-do families who came to spend a month or more on the island. Steady employees at the time received the entire month of August for vacation plus a month of extra pay, known as the *tredicesima*, or thirteenth paycheck, that allowed families to spend so much time away from home. For most Italian families that meant a month's vacation in a seaside location. Ischia was always known for its high style and elegance and so attracted an upper-middle-class and wealthy set of returning visitors to its villas and hotels for extended stays, but its location across the bay from the city of Naples meant that nearby urban dwellers could escape the city heat for a day or two by catching a ferry. Over the past 25 years or so, however, the August vacation has gradually been reduced and the extra paycheck has disappeared for many workers. Elsa says most people now come for a week to ten days and they have less money to spend, "in part because of economic changes and in part because work life has changed." Despite these changes, customers continue to seek good espresso and pastries on the island of Ischia. The Bar Calise's century of activity will surely continue into the next generation.

The phrase "see Naples and die" was coined during the time of the Bourbons when Naples was a wealthy capital in the Kingdom of Two Sicilies. Contemporaries considered the beauty of Naples to be unparalleled and claimed a visit to the city was a must for anyone seeking new experiences. The city's post-unification struggles have been real and for many years left the Neapolitans a bit ambivalent about outside visitors. Naples has enjoyed a renewal over the past decade that includes a bourgeoning tourist industry, and the city is shedding its unfavorable reputation as a haven for crime and filth. What its residents have known all along, however, is that despite its problems, Naples has never stopped being full of energy, beauty, excitement, spirituality, openness, warmth, and loyalty. It has held onto food and drink traditions that reflect the significance of friends, family and community in good times and bad. The ritual of espresso has taken a fitting place in the city's history over the past more than one hundred years. The slow roasting of beans, the use of the lever machine, the boiling temperature of the espresso and its strong, full-bodied flavor and dense crema have emerged because Neapolitans put thought and time into a simple moment infused with sociability. Whether seated across from the Royal Palace in the splendid Gambrinus or standing at the counter of the Chalet Barbato in the busy Piazza Nazionale, the people of Naples—natives, migrants, or short-term visitors alike— partake in the ritual of espresso that connects them to one another and to modern life in one of Italy and Europe's most fascinating cities.

AFTERWORD

I completed the research and writing of this book before the terrible coronavirus pandemic hit in early 2020. Italy was among the first European countries to be devastated by COVID19. Its espresso industry, like many others, has suffered. Because of the deep-seated cultural history of espresso you have just read about, however, I am confident in its resilience. Espresso roasters and machine manufacturers as well as espresso bar owners, managers and baristi have already demonstrated their creativity and ability to adapt to the changes that have, at least temporarily, altered day-to-day life and patterns of coffee consumption. At the same time, the people of Italy have shown that coffee continues to unite them. An image circulating on social media, which was likely staged but is nonetheless representative of Italian fortitude and solidarity, captured Italians under stay-at-home orders passing a moka pot and espresso cups across their balconies to their neighbors. This moment underscored the Italian desire for the sociability of coffee even, and perhaps especially, during a time of fear and uncertainty. It seems to me the social value of espresso culture will continue to thrive and help carry the country forward as the global community seeks a resolution to this ongoing health crisis.

SELECTED BIBLIOGRAPHY

Albertini, Andrea, Silvia Pesci and Giuseppe Villirillo, eds. *Caffè & Stars.* Rome: Damiani, 2004.

Baiguera, Gabriella. *Caffè: varietà e origini, tecniche di preparazione, cocktail e ricette.* Milano: Giunti 2009.

Baiguera, Gabriella and Rosalba Gioffré. *Il piacere dell'espresso.* Florence: Giunti, 2010.

Baldoli, Claudia. "L'espresso, modernità e tradizione nell'Italia del caffè." *Memoria e ricerca* 23 (September 2006): 13-26.

Capecelatro, Edmondo. *L'arte del caffè.* Naples: Rogiosi, 2014.

Cowan, Brian. *The Social Life of Coffee: The Emergence of the British Coffeehouse.* New Haven: Yale University Press, 2005.

Dawes, Antonia. "The Struggle for Via Bologna Street Market: Crisis, Racial Denial and Speaking Back to Power in Naples Italy," *The British Journal of Sociology* (2018): 1-18.

Di Vincenzo, Riccardo. *Il Fiorio Caffè Gelateria: L'isola felice di Torino.* Turin: Landriano, 2011.

Dines, Nick. *Tuff City: Urban Change and Contested Space in Central Naples.* New York: Berghahn Books, 2015.

Felicitas Hufschmidt, Tamara and Livio Jannattoni. *Antico Caffè Greco: storia, ambienti, collezioni.* Rome: Gruppo dei Romanisti, [1989].

Illy, Andrea. *Il sogno del caffè.* Torino: Codice Edizioni, 2015.

Illy, Francesco and Riccardo. *Dal caffè all'espresso.* Milan: Arnoldo Mondadori, 1989.

Joel, David and Karl Shapira. *The Book of Coffee & Tea: A Guide to the Appreciation of Fine Coffees, Teas and Herbal Beverages.* Illustrated by Meri Shardin. New York: St. Martin's Press, 1975.

Maltoni, Enrico and Giuseppe Fabris. *Espresso: Made in Italy 1901-1962*. Forli: Collezione Enrico Maltoni, 2004.

Morris, Jonathan. "Why espresso? Explaining Changes in European Coffee Preferences from a Production of Culture Perspective." *European Review of History* 20, no. 5 (2013): 881-901.

_____. "Making Italian Espresso, Making Espresso Italian." *Food & History* 8, no. 2 (2010): 155-184.

Pendergrast, Mark. *Uncommon Grounds: The History of Coffee and How it Transformed our World*. New York: Basic Books, 2010.

Rittner, Leona, W. Scott Haine and Jeffrey H. Jackson, eds. *The Thinking Space: The Cafe as a Cultural Institution in Paris, Italy and Vienna*. Burlington, VT: Ashgate Publishing, 2013.

Schnapp, Jeffrey T. "The Romance of Caffeine and Aluminum." *Critical Inquiry* 28, no. 1 (Autumn 2001): 244-69.

Senninger, Franck. *Le virtù del caffè*. Vicenza: Edizioni il punto d'incontro, 2014.

Settimo, Giulia. *Un caffè per favore. L'espresso al bar in Italia. Una straordinaria ricerca su tutto il territorio nazionale* (Milan: Pubblistampa, 1989).

Terzi, Manuel. *Dall parte del caffè: storia, ricette ed emozioni della bevanda più famosa al mondo*. Bologna: Edizioni Pendragon, 2012.

Thurston, Robert W., Jonathan Morris and Shawn Steiman, eds. *Coffee: A Comprehensive Guide to the Bean, the Beverage and the Industry*. New York: Rowman & Littlefield, 2013.

INDEX

ABOUT THE AUTHOR

WENDY POJMANN is Professor of History and Director of the Standish Honors Program at Siena College in Albany, New York. She is the author of two monographs, *Immigrant Women and Feminism in Italy* (2005) and *Italian Women and International Cold War Politics, 1944-1968* (2013), lead author of the textbook *Doing History: An Introduction to the Historian's Craft* (2016), and editor of *Migration and Activism in Europe since 1945* (2008). She has published articles in leading scholarly journals and several edited volumes. She is also a regular contributor to the motorcycle publication *The Vintagent*. Her teaching includes courses in world, European, and women's and gender history. Pojmann earned a Ph.D. in modern European history from Boston College. She is a near-native Italian speaker, holds dual citizenship in the U.S. and Italy, and has lived in Italy and Germany as well as in many parts of the United States. She drinks an average of five espressos per day. Her current project examines motorcycle coffee culture.

SAGGISTICA

Taking its name from the Italian—which means essays, essay writing, or non-fiction—*Saggisitca* is a referred book series dedicated to the study of all topics and cultural productions that fall under what we might consider that larger umbrella of all things Italian and Italian/American.

Vito Zagarrio
The "Un-Happy Ending": Re-viewing The Cinema of Frank Capra. 2011.
ISBN 978-1-59954-005-4. Volume 1.

Paolo A. Giordano, Editor
The Hyphenate Writer and The Legacy of Exile. 2010.
ISBN 978-1-59954-007-8. Volume 2.

Dennis Barone
America / Trattabili. 2011. ISBN 978-1-59954-018-4. Volume 3.

Fred L. Gardaphè
The Art of Reading Italian Americana. 2011.
ISBN 978-1-59954-019-1. Volume 4.

Anthony Julian Tamburri
Re-viewing Italian Americana: Generalities and Specificities on Cinema. 2011.
ISBN 978-1-59954-020-7. Volume 5.

Sheryl Lynn Postman
An Italian Writer's Journey through American Realities: Giose Rimanelli's English Novels. "The most tormented decade of America: the 60s"
ISBN 978-1-59954-034-4. Volume 6.

Luigi Fontanella
Migrating Words: Italian Writers in the United States. 2012.
ISBN 978-1-59954-041-2. Volume 7.

Peter Covino & Dennis Barone, Editors
Essays on Italian American Literature and Culture. 2012.
ISBN 978-1-59954-035-1. Volume 8.

Gianfranco Viesti
Italy at the Crossroads. 2012. ISBN 978-1-59954-071-9. Volume 9.

Peter Carravetta, Editor
Discourse Boundary Creation (LOGOS TOPOS POIESIS): A Festschrift in Honor of Paolo Valesio. ISBN 978-1-59954-036-8. Volume 10.

Antonio Vitti and Anthony Julian Tamburri, Editors
Europe, Italy, and the Mediterranean. ISBN 978-1-59954-073-3. Volume 11.

Vincenzo Scotti
Pax Mafiosa or War: Twenty Years after the Palermo Massacres. 2012.
ISBN 978-1-59954-074-0. Volume 12.

LIFE SKILLS 101:

A Practical Guide to Leaving Home and Living on Your Own

TINA PESTALOZZI

STONEWOOD PUBLICATIONS

Disclaimer: Every effort has been made to make this guide as complete and accurate as possible. It is published for general reference and sold with the understanding that neither the author nor publisher is engaged in rendering any legal, accounting, automotive, medical or psychological advice. The author and Stonewood Publications disclaim any personal liability, either directly or indirectly, for advice or information presented within.

Publisher's Cataloging-in-Publication

Pestalozzi, Tina.
   Life skills 101 : a practical guide to leaving
home and living on your own / Tina Pestalozzi. —
1st ed.
     p. cm.
     Includes bibliographical references and index.
     LCCN: 00-133460
     ISBN: 0-9701334-4-8

     1. Life skills. 2. Finance, Personal.
3. Conduct of life. I. Title.

HQ2037.P48 2000   646.7
                QBI00-500070

Printed in the United States of America

I wrote down a few things to anyone who might need them
and especially for
my dearest Natalya
on the occasion of her eighteenth birthday
and for
Cari
Cris
Ivan Keith
John-Michael
Nicholas
Noelle
Sami
and Sarah Kathryn.
I know you're ready, but in case you forget . . .

Table of Contents

Acknowledgments

This book would still be just an idea waiting to happen had it not been for the support, encouragement and efforts of Cynthia Bischoff. Her program "Leading from the Heart" helped me realize my dream, and I am grateful and indebted.

I also wish to extend my thanks to Theresa Fredericka for her endless support, and Frank Fredericka and David Klamut for their help with the title. Many thanks also to Rollie Welsh, George E. Gessner, Dolores Fredericka, and Genny and George Phillips for their kind assistance.

Thank you, Natalya, for your gentle encouragement, delicate comments, and endless patience.

Most importantly, thank you, to my parents, Nate and Gladys, for everything.

Introduction

On your own. What do you think of when you read these words? Is living on your own a much anticipated time? Are you looking forward to the day when you will have your own "place?"—when you are responsible for yourself and can live as you please in your own style? Or does the idea of living on your own give you a nervous twinge? Do you feel not quite ready? When are we ready to live on our own anyway?

Of course there is no certain time when we are magically ready to venture out of the nest. Some of us live in circumstances where we feel we've been pretty much on our own for years anyway. For some of us, circumstances dictate that once we hit age eighteen we are out the door, ready or not. Living on your own may be going away to college. Sometimes it may be supporting yourself, but living with a roommate.

Whatever your particular age or circumstance, being as prepared as possible makes living on your own an exciting, rather than a difficult, challenge. Having the knowledge and skills required to live successfully alone frees your energy and allows you to grow and fully enjoy the experience. This book is written with the heartfelt intention of both passing along information you may not now know and assembling information you already know into a handy reference to make your new life easier.

There is a tremendous freedom in being a responsible person. Knowing how to easily maneuver through your new world and make it manageable allows you to approach life and receive it at your best. And that is what this book is really all about: acquiring the basic life skills you need to be the best you that you can be—to not only survive, but to thrive.

Chapter 1

Stepping into the Working World

Your Dream—Your Plan and Your Present Reality

I graduated from high school knowing I was going to be successful. Yet I had no idea how it was going to happen. None whatsoever. Not only did I not have a clue as to how I would suddenly have the successful life that I envisioned, I basically had no idea of how I was even going to survive. I was on my own and unprepared. "I guess I'll go to work . . . somewhere," I thought. "I'll find something . . . maybe I'll take a few classes somewhere . . . somehow. . . ." Please don't let this happen to you!

I didn't have a plan of how I was going to go about getting where I wanted to be. No matter what point we are in our lives, having a vision of how we want our lives to be is important. But having the plan, the rough outline, the "road map" of how to get there, is critical.

You must develop a personal plan of how you are actually going to reach your dreams. Outline a plan that will be very easy to follow so that you will stick with it. Just as most of us give up trying to stick to a budget we've made that is too difficult to deal with, you might give up thinking about your plan if you make your road map too complicated. The easiest plan I have seen is the following chart developed by Cynthia Bischoff, a communications trainer. Imagine or visualize your "dream" goal; then divide the steps to reach it into smaller goals. It may help to honestly face facts about your present reality. This will give you an idea of how much you need to do to reach your dream.

Your Dream

Long-Range Goals

Medium-Range Goals

Short-Range Goals

Immediate Action

Your Present Reality

Some people know or think they know at an early age just what they want out of life. Others are not so sure. Once you decide *something* you want to work toward and focus your energy on, you will be giving your life direction. Ideally, you will eventually know and follow the dreams you love.

You can count on adjusting your goals as you move forward. You will find yourself adding, subtracting, and moving around your basic life plan. Life is full of irregularities. The old saying, "Expect the unexpected" certainly applies here. We also change our goals as we grow and mature.

Having a life plan can be quite a comfort. You will worry less about your life's direction because you have an idea of where you are going. For instance, you will probably instinctively know if a certain decision is right for you or not. You will ask yourself, "Is this action going to help me reach my goals or keep me further away from making my dreams a reality?" Your life's path will take twists and turns on the way to your dreams. Your dreams may even change several times. Yet being responsible for your life's direction is part of being a healthy, whole person, and it is where a great deal of fun and fulfillment lies.

Now, let's look at Chart 1. You can use this chart not only for your overall life plan, but also to break down any project you tackle. If one of your personal dreams is to see yourself in better shape, toned up with more energy and stamina, use this chart to create a path to reach your goal. If your present reality is that you are out of shape, not eating the right food, too tired even to exercise, your immediate goal may be something small, like eating more fruit and vegetables every day. It doesn't matter how small the action, just faithfully meeting one small goal after another keeps you heading in the right direction.

If living successfully on your own is a dream of yours, what is your present reality? How far are you from your goal? Are you still living at home with plenty of time to calculate your move? Not everyone has that luxury, but if you do, your plan may look something like this:

Chart 2:
Your Plan

Your Dream

To be out of my parent's house and to be living on my own, with at least three months living expenses in my saving account.

Long-Range Goal

Keep my job, or get a better one, and save all I can, even though I'll also be attending college.

Medium-Range Goal

Open a savings and a checking account. Start acquiring things I know I will need for my own place.

Short-Range Goal

Get a job and work part-time while I finish high school.

Immediate Action

Start organizing for my job search.

Your Present Reality

I'm sick of living here, and I can't wait until I'm on my own.

This is a good plan for someone who has the foresight to start thinking and planning early. Yet it's never too late to come up with some sort of plan of action. Whatever your present reality, a little planning and a little knowledge of basic life skills enables you to start living on your own from a position of strength. Ready or not—Let's go!

Your Social Skills—Don't Leave Home Without Them

A lot of us grew up acquiring our social skills in a hit-or-miss fashion. Now we make do and hope for the best. We manage to introduce people all the time and get by. We shake hands without giving much thought as to whether we are doing it correctly or not. After all, how much difference can it make? Plenty!

Just as the behavior we would expect from a two-year-old is not appropriate for a nine-year-old, somewhere in our young adult years having immature social skills will no longer be considered acceptable. Many people are technically excellent at their work but fail to achieve the kind of career success they would like because they lack good "people skills." Taking the time to acquire solid personal skills is one of the best investments you can ever make. Start from scratch. Develop an awareness of other people and how your actions appear to them. Respect and consideration for others is the foundation on which all social skills and business etiquette is built. How we treat other people is a direct reflection on us. We are judged, favorably or not, by our actions.

One of the most helpful books you can read is *Letitia Baldrige's New Complete Guide to Executive Manners*. Although the book is directed toward people who work in the business arena, the information it contains can be applied to other areas of life and is beneficial to everyone. Learn the basics of interpersonal skills and at a minimum master these few things:

Etiquette Basics

- Shake hands correctly

- Greet people effectively

- Introduce people properly

- Stand for introductions

- Maintain eye contact

- Sound pleasant

- Be aware of others

- Be friendly

Shake Hands Correctly. A good handshake is firm—connecting the space between your thumb and forefinger with the same space of the hand you are shaking. Do not grab just the fingertips. Connect and shake, using a gentle up and down motion, from the elbow. Never squeeze too hard or shake too long. Do not hesitate in extending your hand. Regardless of gender, shaking hands is the acceptable greeting and should be done again when you say good-bye.

Greet People Effectively. Introduce yourself to people you do not know. Offer your hand, say your name slowly and clearly, and give a little information to help get a conversation going. For example, if you are meeting someone at work, you might say something such as, "Hello, I'm Cris Goode. I just started working in the collections department." It is not correct to ever give *yourself* an honorific title such as Mr., Ms., Mrs., or Dr.

Introduce People Properly. Learn the mechanics of both a business introduction and a social introduction. In business, introductions are based on **precedence,** not gender. You must decide who is considered the more important person in the introduction and present the "lesser" person *to* the "more" important person. This means you would introduce a junior person *to* a senior person. Do this by saying the senior person's name first. For instance, "Ms. Senior, I would like to present *(to you)* Mr. Junior, who is our new intern." You would introduce a peer to your boss, where as your boss would be introduced *to* a client or customer. In social introductions, the older or more distinguished person's name is spoken first, and in most circumstances a man is introduced to a woman.

- Try to be consistent in all your introductions. You would introduce Mr. Somebody to Ms. Someone, not David Somebody to Ms. Someone, or Mr. Somebody to Samantha Someone.

- If you introduce someone by saying "I'd like to introduce *my friend...,*" it sounds as if the other person is not also your friend. Avoid using the expression, *my friend,* in an introduction.

Stand up for Introductions. Whether you are male or female, stand when you are introduced to anyone and everyone. Unless there is a compelling reason for not doing so, such as you are squeezed in a tight spot and your standing would interfere with everyone else, you must always stand for all introductions, even when you hear, "Oh, don't get up."

Maintain Eye Contact. Maintain good eye contact with the person you are talking to. This gives the impression that you care and are respectful. Avoid staring by occasionally looking at another feature of the face.

Sound Pleasant. Don't be lazy in your speech. Whether we like it or not, we are all judged by the way we sound, both in person and on the telephone. Listen to how you sound. Constantly using words such as "like," "you know," and "um" will not be to your best advantage. When you greet someone, say something more than "Hi." "Hello" is better, but "Good Morning, Cari" is even better still.

Be Aware of Others. Be aware of how considerate your behavior is in public. Do you hold open doors for someone who may be approaching behind you? Are you quiet and respectful in public areas? Are you a courteous driver? How we treat people matters. The person you cut off at an intersection today may be the person you face at an employment interview tomorrow.

Be Friendly. Smile. Be warm. Learn the social skills you need to be comfortable with all people and practice your new skills until you appear at ease wherever you are.

Work—It's a Good Thing

Do you know that many people continue to work long after they no longer financially need to do so? That even some people who by birth or by circumstance never "had" to be employed, still seek out interesting and meaningful work? Work can be a fulfilling aspect of our lives, and for most of us it is essential to our survival as well.

You must have resources to live on your own, and by now you probably realize this most likely means your getting a job, starting your own business, or developing your career. Even while going to college full-time, countless numbers of students must also work at least part-time. At some point, most of us seek out employment, and the following information will help you reach your goal of being successfully employed.

Job Search Success

Presenting yourself at your best is important in all aspects of your employment, but it is critical to your success in seeking a job. From filling out a neat and complete employment application form to sending a thank you note after an interview, you must present yourself in a manner that gives you an edge over your competition. Like it or not, you will be evaluated by the way you handle the process. Try to make a good impression every step of the way.

Organizing for the Job. Be as organized as possible in your job search. Start by gathering together all the information you will need. Know your Social Security number. If you don't have a number you, can apply for one at your local Social Security office or post office.

If you are under eighteen, you may need to acquire a work permit. Your guidance counselor at school should be able to help you. You may also call your local Labor Department.

You will need three people who are willing to act as references for you. They should not be family members. Make sure you ask permission to include their names, addresses, and phone numbers on your employment application or resumé. Obviously you want to choose someone who you are sure will respond favorably if questioned about you.

Although you may be looking for your first real job, you may already have had some work experience. Have you done volunteer work for a church or community organization? Have you baby-sat for your neighbors or performed yard work? Anyone you have worked for may be a good person to approach for a reference as well as members of the clergy, teachers, or family friends who know you well.

If you are looking for your first job, it is appropriate to prepare a resumé with references. If you have an employment history, it is not necessary to include the references in your resumé; but have them ready and with you at an interview in case they are requested.

Resumé: Even if the job you are applying for does not require you to submit a resumé, it is a good idea to prepare one so you will have all the necessary information with you. Your resumé should look as professional as possible, so be sure it is typed on plain white paper. Do not use notebook paper or creative stationery. Your school or local library will have books on how to write an appropriate resumé.

Here is a guideline for a first-time basic resumé:

Your name
Your street address
Your city, state, and zip code

Your date of birth

Social Security number

Last grade completed and where

Achievements and awards

Any work experience

Areas of interest or classes you have taken that relate to the position you are applying for.

References: Names, addresses, and phone numbers. If you've listed work experience, have the references listed on a separate sheet and present them when asked.

Remember to proofread and check your spelling. Then have someone else double-check your work.

The more positive information you acquire to add to your resumé, the more sophisticated your resumé should become. In addition to being completely accurate, easy to read, and concise, it should also reflect a high standard of presentation.

A common resumé format is reverse-chronological, in which you list your most recent employment experience and work backward through your education and work history. A skills-based resumé emphasizes what you can do and what your qualifications are.

No matter which format you decide will work best for you, make sure the resumé emphasizes your strong points and is written in an active tone, using action verbs such as arranged, organized, tutored, and so forth.

Study samples in resumé-writing guidebooks. Your resumé is the tool you create to market yourself. Work with your resumé until it is as good as it can be and reflects you at your best.

What Job? Chances are good that you will have had some other work experience before you actually find the job that financially allows you to live on your own. Deciding what kind of job or career you want can take time and patience. Thankfully, there are a lot of resources available to you if you need help making your decision. Check with schools and college-career counseling centers in your area.

- If you already have the education and/or experience to apply for your "ideal" job, your job search will be more sophisticated, as will your resumé and your interview techniques. Be prepared to discuss your particular strengths and what you can offer. In addition, you can help yourself out by doing as much research as you can about the company to which you are applying. Review the company's annual report, visit their Web site, and read any articles that have been written about the company.

The Internet is full of sites designed to help you decide what educational and career options are right for you and what jobs are currently available. Check out:

CareerBabe: *www.careerbabe.com.*
Career Builder: *www.careerbuilder.com.*
Career Path: *www.careerpath.com.*
Career Resource Center: *www.careers.org.*
Job Hunt: *www.job-hunt.org.*
Mapping Your Future: *www.mapping-your-future.com.*
Monster: *www.monster.com.*

• If you are starting to look for your first job, have an idea of the type of job you want to apply for. Try to find a job that complements your interests and abilities. For instance, if you enjoy swimming, you might apply for a position as a lifeguard at your local community pool or YMCA. Discuss your plans with your parents or guardians. They may have some ideas about where you should and should not apply for work. Get the word out to relatives and family friends that you are looking for employment. Perhaps you will get a solid lead to follow or a suggestion that you have not thought of. School counselors may provide job leads.

• Check the "help wanted" section of your local paper. An ad may direct you to call or write. If you call regarding an ad, you should identify yourself and state why you are calling. Make sure you answer all questions in complete sentences.

Cover Letter. Your written request for a job interview is typically called a cover letter when you include a copy of your resumé. With or without a resumé, a letter used to initiate communication with a potential em-

Appropriate Responses

Say: Instead of:

    Hello   Hi or hey

    Good-bye   Bye or See ya

    All right   Okay or yeah

    Thank you   Thanks

Avoid:

    Uh . . . cool . . . like . . . um . . . you know . . . awesome . . .

ployer should be neat and demonstrate competence. Your letter should be one page and typed on the same type of paper as your resumé.

- Try to limit your letter to three paragraphs. Introduce yourself and tell how you heard about the job opening in the first paragraph. The second paragraph should highlight specific qualifications and skills you can offer. Close with a third paragraph requesting an interview.

Use these two examples to help you construct your own cover letter:

Your first and last name
Your street address
Your city, state, and zip code

Month, date, and year

Contact person's name (Mr. or Ms.)
Their correct title (example: Director of Personnel)
Name of the company
Street address or P.O. Box
City, state, and zip code

Dear Ms. Doe:

In response to your advertisement in the May 28, 2001 edition of *The San Pedro News Pilot,* I would like to be considered for the position of Counter Person.

I am sixteen years old and a sophomore at San Pedro High School. I am an honor roll student, and I have been recognized by my instructors as being a dependable and hardworking person. I always strive to do my best.

I would like to meet you to discuss my capabilities as they apply to the position with Mama's Pizza. Please call me at 000.000.0000. I appreciate your time and consideration.

Sincerely,

Your signature
Your first and last name
Enclosure: Resumé

Your first and last name
Your street address
Your city, state, and zip code

Month, date, and year

Contact persons name (Mr. or Ms.)
Their correct title (example: Director of Personnel)
Name of the company
Street address or P.O. Box
City, state, and zip code

Dear Mr. Doe:

This letter is in response to your advertisement in the September 9, 2001, edition of *The Daily News*. Please consider me for the position of Assistant Youth Camp Counselor.

I recently graduated from Lakeview High School, and I will be attending Kent State University in the fall. I believe I would enjoy working at Camp Wilderness as I pursue my major in Child Development.

I would be pleased to meet with you to discuss my qualifications. You may contact me at 000.000.0000 or write me at the above address.

Sincerely,

Your signature

Your first and last name

Enclosure: Resumé

The Application. For many positions, such as retail sales or working at large grocery stores, you can walk in any time and request an application which you can complete there; or take home, fill out, and return another time. Even if you are just picking up an application, look presentable.

- Do *not* go anywhere to apply for a job or to an interview, without having a pen with you. Make sure you use black or blue ink.

- Neatness, spelling, grammar, and good penmanship are essential.

- Answer every question on the form completely and correctly. When you are finished, check over the application to make sure you have not left any spaces blank. This shows that you have read the application thoroughly. Write "N/A" for "not applicable" if a question does not apply to you.

- Many applications ask for salary requirements. You may wish to write "open." This leaves room for a later salary discussion and possible negotiation.

Hint: It is a good idea to ask to see a job description for the position you are applying for. You do not want to commit yourself to a job if you are not fully aware of exactly what it entails.

You Have an Interview. Great! Make sure you keep it! Only a true emergency should keep you from showing up at a scheduled interview on time. Excuses like, "I couldn't make it because the friend who was going to give me a ride was waiting for her brother to get back from. . . . etc." will help a potential employer decide you are not the candidate for the job. Sometimes you may be asked to call or return several times before you are told whether or not you have the job. Don't give up, and be sure you follow up, since this may be a test to see how dependable you are and how well you will follow instructions.

An interview is an opportunity for a potential employer to see what you are like and how you handle yourself. It is also your opportunity to make a positive impression.

Your Interview. Attitude is everything. It's why an employer may hire you instead of someone who is just as smart or just as qualified. The proper attitude shows that you are positive and eager to please. It's caring enough not only to be on time, but to arrive several minutes early. It's wanting the job bad enough to make a good impression. Your clothes should be clean, pressed, and appropriate. Mirror, or dress slightly better than, what is worn in the organization at the level you are applying for. Men, now is the time to tuck in your shirt and put on a tie. Women, dress conservatively, wear medium-heel, closed-toe pumps, and be sure to wear hose. For both men and women, hairstyles should not be extreme. Nails need to be neat. Shoes should be shined. Every part of you needs to be clean and look well-groomed and well put together. You are projecting how you feel about yourself by the way you dress and present yourself.

- Watch your posture. Appear energetic and eager. Greet your interviewer properly—which means with a smile, a greeting (such as "thank you for seeing me"), a correct handshake, and direct eye contact.

- Maintain good direct eye contact during your interview. This indicates you are focused and interested. Do not stare; just appear to be listening and friendly.

- Sit when you are instructed to do so. Don't slump, fidget, play with your hands, cross your legs, or tap your feet. Just sit up straight in the chair with your feet flat on the floor.

- Be mindful not to interrupt.

- Answer all questions completely and honestly. Don't say you have experience if you do not. Don't say you know how to do something

Interview Don'ts:

- Slump
- Fidget
- Interrupt
- Stare
- Talk to the floor
- Check your watch
- Chew gum
- Crack your knuckles
- Fiddle with your hair
- Play with your hands, cuticles, ring, necklace, and so on.

if you know you don't. Never lie. Answer all questions in complete sentences which will help to keep you from appearing indifferent.

- Show interest! During the interview you may wish to ask questions such as:
  1. What would my duties be during a typical workday?
  2. Will I be working with others or by myself?
  3. What type of promotions are available from the position?

- Discuss your strengths, skills, and accomplishments, not how much money you want. Let the interviewer bring up salary, even if it's approached in a subsequent interview.

- When the interview is over, make sure you smile, shake hands again, and say thank you. Immediately after the interview, write and mail a short, well-written letter thanking the interviewer for the time given you and restating your interest in the position. This is an additional opportunity to impress the interviewer and to project the positive attitude employers are looking for.

Workplace Savvy

A major part of your life will be spent working. Your job will be important to you on many levels, and hopefully it will give you the financial support you need. Yet, the satisfaction that you can obtain from enjoying your job and performing it well may mean just as much to you as the financial rewards it offers.

You show a great deal about who you are in your approach to your work. Demonstrate that you respect yourself enough to honor your commitment to your job. Be willing to give it your best. Be willing to work. Be happy to be useful. Make sure you are never late. Being late must never be more than a rare occurrence. Show that you are both dependable and responsible.

- Be courteous. Are you pleasant to work with? Are your co-workers happy to spend time with you? Look carefully at your behavior in the workplace. Employers want employees who can get along with everyone and are cheerful to be around. Never put people down in front of others. Do not engage in mean gossip or allow others to gossip to you. Keep your promises and your confidences.

- Make sure you continue to dress appropriately. Sexy clothes are not for the workplace. Dress the way the person responsible for your promotions expects you to dress.

- When you are new to the workplace, you may find that you need to adjust how you manage your time. Develop the habit of planning ahead; for instance, make sure your work clothes are clean and that you have gas in your car.

  You may find you need to change a few old habits, like staying out late on a work night, or that you need to start a few new routines, such as using a daily planner to keep track of things you need to remember. Take the necessary actions to remain organized and to adjust to your new responsibilities.

- Make it a habit to think before you speak. Communicate as clearly as you can and always speak with respect.

- Develop your listening skills. Being a good listener can greatly contribute to your on-the-job success.

- Approach every job and job challenge as an opportunity to increase your skills.

- Whatever your job, remember that there is dignity in work, and great satisfaction can be gained from knowing you do your particular job well and give your best.

The Value of Networking

We are all connected to each other. The way we treat each other matters. There's an old saying, "You never know to whom you're talking." Not only does this apply to being careful of what you say to whom, but it is very true about people and their connections. Making a good impression on someone, projecting competence, and being thought of favorably may be a huge asset to your long-range plans. Perhaps you will someday be in business for yourself and the contacts you make now will be beneficial to you. Perhaps the friend of an acquaintance will some day be just the person with the experience you need to give you expert advice.

We grow as individuals when we keep an expanding circle of acquaintances. Your genuine interest in others and a natural kindness to everyone has its own rewards.

Chapter 2

Taking Care of Business

Your Official Documents

You have probably already found out that there is a bit of official business you have to take care of in order to function smoothly in our society. The few paper documents that you should obtain now are just the beginning of many "paper valuables" you will collect in your lifetime. You will need to decide how you can best protect them, so you won't have to experience the waste of time and the inconvenience of replacing everything unnecessarily.

Safe Spot. Try to keep everything together. If you decide to keep your papers at home, you can create an "Important Papers" file or folder. In the event of an emergency, it is more likely you could locate your file quickly, than all the separate things it should contain. An accordion-type file folder, a plastic document pouch file, or even a manilla envelope, will keep everything contained and organized. Better yet is a strongbox, which is a fire-proof box designed to survive most fires. They are available at office supply and discount stores. You can also put other valuables in your box. Where to put the box becomes another concern, since you want to make it as difficult as possible to be stolen. As you gain more valuables and obtain more important documents, you may wish to consider getting a safe-deposit box at your bank.

    If you are lucky enough to find a bank that offers a free safe-deposit box with a low-fee checking or savings account, sign up! The following is a sample list of what your safe-deposit box or strongbox may eventually include:

Paper Valuables

- Original or certified copy of your birth certificate

- Title to your car, deeds, or other records of ownership

- Legal contracts or documents such as marriage or divorce papers

- Military papers

- Naturalization papers

- Savings bonds

- Passport

- Master list of your financial accounts and credit card numbers

- Home inventory, including receipts for big purchases and appraisals.

Your Will. Whether you want to or not, at some point, you need to prepare your will. There are strict rules concerning wills, and it is best to do a little research before you start. You need to keep your will updated as you acquire more assets. When you have children, you should name in your will who you desire to be their guardians. (Don't let it be a surprise. Be sure to talk it over beforehand with the person(s) you select). Please remember your *original* will is the one thing that does *not* belong in your safe-deposit box. Most states "seal" (limit access to) your safe-deposit box at the time of death. Original wills should ideally be left in the care of a law office. You can keep your original will in a safe spot at home, but you may also wish to give it to a trusted friend or family member, especially one with a safe-deposit box!

Birth Certificate. Obtaining this document first will make acquiring other documents you may need a lot easier. You should have at least one *certified* copy of your birth certificate. This differs from a regular copy in that it has an official stamp or certification. Birth certificates are kept by the county of the state where you were born. Check the phone book or directory assistance for the number of the Office of Vital Statistics. The offices that keep the records are listed under various names nationwide, but generally fall under the jurisdiction of the Health Department. Fees for each copy vary, but are normally only a few dollars.

Photo Identification. This usually takes the form of a driver's license. If for any reason you do not drive, it is still possible to get official photo identification from your local Department or Bureau of Motor Vehicles. Call your local office to find out what the requirements are.

Driver's License. This falls under the jurisdiction of the state where you live, and requirements vary from state to state. Remember to keep the address on your license current. You will also need to get a new driver's license if you change your state of residence.

Vehicle Registration. The Department or Bureau of Motor Vehicles is also where you register your vehicle. There is a fee to pay every year to keep your registration current. Depending on your state's requirements, you may be asked to present verification that your vehicle meets your state's emission standards. You will be told if you need the certification when you register and where you can obtain it.

If you sell or give away your vehicle, it is very important to complete the necessary paperwork with the Department or Bureau of Motor Vehicles *immediately*. The record of the transaction must be on file with your state, so in the event of an accident, parking tickets, or other law infractions by the new owners, you are free from liability.

Vehicle Title. A title to a car is the document that shows ownership. If you buy a car and pay cash for it, you will receive the title, which you must take to your local title office and have recorded. If you get a loan from a bank to buy the car, the title has a **lien** placed on it from the bank. When the loan is paid off, the lien is removed, and you receive a clear title. You may also record a change in title when you change states and register your car in your new state. If you do not know where to record titles in your area, call your local Department or Bureau of Motor Vehicles.

Voter Registration. If you want to vote in any election, generally you must register in advance. Call your local Board of Elections to find out what identification you need to bring with you when you register.

> **Hint:** Visit *www.bp.fed.gov*—The U.S. Government Blue Pages Online Directory—if you need a federal government listing.

Social Security Card. You can't go very long without having your own Social Security number. Hospitals provide applications for numbers to parents of newborns. Chances are your parents obtained your number for you when you were very young in order to declare you as a dependent on their income tax. In the event that you do not have a Social Security number yet, go to your local Social Security office and apply for one. You will need to prove your identity, age, and citizenship or lawful alien status. You should take a certified copy of your birth certificate with you. If you do not have a birth certificate, you can offer at least three other forms of identification and proof of age, such as original school, medical, or religious records. If you are a lawful alien, bring your INS documents.

The Social Security system has been in effect since 1935 to help provide old age benefits to retired workers and their dependents and to help provide for the disabled. The Social Security Administration (SSA) identifies you and tracks your lifetime earnings by the number they issue to you. Your employers need to know your correct number as does the Internal Revenue Service (IRS). It is very important to protect the privacy of your number. Although not common, identity theft and fraud is real and can be a nightmare. One example of identity theft is if someone uses your social security number to obtain a credit card in their name. This can potentially ruin your good credit record.

Protect your number. Find out what the consequences are if you refuse to give out your number when asked. Most of the time you can get by without having to disclose it. Make it your policy not to give out your number automatically, but to consider every request and to be selective as to who receives it. For instance, your bank needs to know your number to report interest earned on your accounts to the IRS, but the local video store can identify you by some other means. You are within your rights to deny giving out your number, but a business is within its rights not to have you as a customer if you do not provide the requested information. Use your best judgment here. Release the number only when absolutely necessary and make sure you never have your number printed on your bank checks.

- To ensure you are credited with your correct earnings, be sure you notify the SSA if you change your name. You will need to show proof both of your old name and your new name. You will get a new card in your new name with your old number.

- The SSA now sends an annual Personal Earnings and Benefit Estimate Statement (PEBES) to workers 25 years of age and older. Be sure to check the statement for accuracy. You can also request a free statement anytime by calling the SSA at *800.772.1213*.

- Memorize your number and keep the card in a safe place. While you normally should not carry it in your wallet where it can easily be lost or stolen, do not rely on your memory for furnishing the number on important documents, such as those involving your employment.

- Don't use the last four digits of your number as your secret PIN (Personal Identification Number) on any of your financial accounts.

- Shred any document that has your Social Security number on it before you throw it away.

• Call the Social Security Administration at *800.772.1213* if you have any questions or if you would like the address of your local Social Security office and its hours of operation. The Web address is *www.ssa.gov.* You can also request factsheets, including "When Someone Misuses Your Number," Publication No. 05–10064.

Passport. A passport is only a necessity if you are planning to travel out of the country. Otherwise it is just an excellent source of identification and a comfort to know you have in case an unexpected opportunity arises; then you're ready to go. You can apply for your passport at many post offices, county/municipal offices, and federal and state courts. Passports come under the jurisdiction of the U.S. State Department. You can check their Web site at *www.state.gov* for complete information and location of a passport acceptance facility near you. Generally you will need:

1. Form DSP-11: Application for Passport. You may pick the form up at the facility and return it later, but you must sign this form *in person* at the passport acceptance facility.

2. Proof of U.S. Citizenship. Proof could be your certified birth certificate or your naturalization certificate.

3. Proof of identity. Such proof could be a current, valid driver's license or current school ID card.

4. The fee, If you are 16 or older, the fee is $60; if you are 15 or younger, it is $40.

5. Two passport photographs. Photos must be 2" × 2". The photos must meet other criteria as well. You can check the yellow pages under passport photos. They are available at fast service printing shops like Kinko's, at some mail center stores, and at many malls.

The State Department accepts other documents if you do not have the ones listed here. If you are in doubt about what you need to bring with you, call your local passport acceptance facility and ask for help. The State Department recommends applying for your passport several months before your departure date. Your passport will be mailed to the address you put on the application, about 25 days after your application is received. It is possible to get your passport issued faster, but you must pay an additional fee to expedite the process.

You can reach the National Passport Information Center at *900.225.5674*. Automated information is 35¢ per minute; it's $1.05 for operator-assisted calls.

Other Licenses and Permits. When I moved from a large city to a small town, I was very surprised to find out I needed a permit to hold a garage sale. Every state, city, and town has different laws and ordinances, and it's a good idea to find out what is required in your area before the event. (Ignorance of the law is no excuse, as I found out!) When in doubt, check with local officials on things such as:

Licenses and Permits

Bikes of any kind

Block parties

Building or remodeling

Burning (leaves, yard waste, construction waste, trash, etc.)

Child care

Conducting a business in your home

Dogs; farm, exotic, or other animals

Fishing

Guns

Hunting

Marriage

Sales of any kind (garage, yard, tag, bake, book, etc.)

Street and/or overnight parking (especially of recreational vehicles)

Your Mail

The U.S. Postal Service delivers over 107 billion pieces of first class mail every year, yet it is still able to provide you with individual service, such as holding your mail upon request. Small towns may only have one post office, but larger cities may have several. "Your" post office is the one that handles your zip code. This is the office where you would pick up anything that the mail carrier was unable to deliver to your address, such as a registered letter or package that required a signature and you were not available when the carrier attempted delivery. It is not necessarily the post office closest to where you live. "Your" post office is also the office that will hold your mail when needed. Just fill out the appropriate form from the post office and your mail will be held on the dates you request. You can indicate on the form if you are going to pick it up or if you want it all delivered to your address on a specific date. Always try to fill out a change of address card as soon as possible every time you move, and your first class mail will be forwarded to your new address. Make sure you notify everyone who sends you mail of your new address. Magazines usually need six to eight weeks notice before the change becomes effective. Most post offices also provide many other services as well, such as selling money orders and handling passport applications.

- The U.S. Postal Service has a 24-hour phone line for general information on post office locations, hours, zip codes, and mailing rates: *800.275.8777*. Their Web site is *www.usps.gov*.

Your Taxes

The following information is an overview to help give you a general idea of your tax responsibilities. The time to start thinking about your taxes is the time you start having income. Income is not only money you make through your efforts, like your salary and/or tips, but may also be money you make from many other sources, such as **interest** or **dividends** on investments. When your **gross income** reaches a specific amount (the exact amount can be different each tax year), you may be required to file a **tax return**. You must keep track of your finances to determine what year you need to start filing a tax return and to know what tax form is right for your circumstances. Call the Internal Revenue Tax Form request number (*800.829.3676*) and ask for Publication number 17—*Your Federal Income Tax*. This free publication will tell you more than you ever want to know about your taxes and what forms are best for your situation. Browsing the IRS publications online can also be very informative.

When you figure your tax form, you will determine if you owe the U.S. Treasury any money or if the Treasury owes you a refund. During the year, your employer typically takes out a set amount from your paycheck every pay period. This amount is determined by the **withholding** information you provided on your **W-4 form** when you were hired. You may find the amount taken out was too much (and you get a refund), or you may need to write a check to the U.S. Treasury for the difference between what was taken out of your check by your employer (or paid) and what you owe.

Record Keeping. You may earn money without having money taken out for taxes. This does not mean you do not have to consider it income. You do! If you have income from a source such as your own small business, your record keeping should be especially detailed. Save receipts for everything, and don't be careless with any documentation.

- Federal personal income tax returns must be filed every year by mid-April, usually the 15th. Filing your own return may not be too difficult or too time-consuming, but it really helps to be prepared for the job. Do yourself a big favor and keep accurate records from the beginning of your earning history. Create an envelope to keep everything together. You need to keep documentation of any income, such as your current cumulative pay stub, and documentation of any **deductions** you may claim, such as cancelled checks *and* receipts. You may receive a **W-2 form** from your employer. This should be provided to you no later than January 31st of the current year. You will also receive Form 1099 from your financial institution if you have interest or dividends that have been reported to the IRS.

- Order IRS Publication number 552—*Recordkeeping for Individuals.* It explains exactly which records you should have and how long to keep them. Hang on to everything for at least three years (Seven years if you want to be absolutely sure). Normally, if you are going to be audited (this is when the IRS takes a closer look at your return), it would be before the time limit **(period or statue of limitations)** for the return expires. Keep in mind there is no time limitation for filing a fraudulent tax return or for not filing when you are required to do so.

- There are plenty of resources available to help you with your taxes, including the IRS who will try to answer any questions you may have. The number for IRS assistance is *800.829.1040.*

- Call *800.TAX.FORM* to request forms and information. Forms can be downloaded onto your computer, faxed, or mailed. Basic forms and **tax schedules** are available at your local tax office, post office, or library. (Schedules are separate forms that may need to be filed along with your return).

- Computer access to the IRS is *www.irs.gov.*

- Software tax programs are available for about $40 to $60. They can help with your year-round tax organization as well as filing your year-end return. This may be an option for you if your tax situation is not too complicated.

- If you decide you cannot figure your taxes yourself and want professional help, ask around for referrals from people you know who have had successful experiences with tax preparers. If you must pay someone to do your taxes, make sure you do as much as possible ahead of time. You do not want to pay an accountant by the hour to categorize receipts and add up totals that you can do yourself.

- Do not forget about your state taxes. It is easiest to figure out your federal return first, then your state return. These forms are also available at your local post office, library, or tax office.

- Make and keep a copy of every tax return (local, state, and federal) you file. They may be useful in helping you prepare future tax returns or if you need to amend (change) a return you have already filed. Tax returns are sometimes requested when applying for loans.

Chapter 3

Gaining Financial Know-How

Starting Smart

You need financial knowledge to take positive financial actions. The little things you do with your money matter. Cumulatively, a fortune will flow your way during the course of your lifetime. How much of it will you keep? How much will you let flow away? Will you be able to support the lifestyle you dream about? Do you have a financial plan? The more knowledge you acquire, the better your money management skills will be.

The following is general information designed to help you start thinking about your personal financial strategy. It is just one way to go about handling your money. As you gain more money management skills you will find what actions serve you best. We all want to be on solid financial ground. You may not earn much with your first job. You may find it's hard to save a dime. That's the way most of us started out. You may be attending college, receiving financial assistance, and find you have a hard time making ends meet. Don't lose your motivation. Remember, it is possible to meet your financial goals, even moving at a snail's pace—Just gain the financial knowledge and trust your instincts.

Know Financial Terms. Familiarize yourself with the following:

Certificate of Deposit (CD)—A savings certificate issued by a bank, credit union, or savings and loan, which allows you to receive interest on the amount of your deposit. The interest rate is determined not only by the amount deposited, but also by the length of time you agree to keep the funds deposited. You will be penalized if you remove funds before this maturity date.

Money Market—A checking account that generally requires a minimum balance, pays a slightly higher rate of interest than a traditional checking account, and allows you to write a limited amount of checks per month. Mutual fund money market accounts usually offer unlimited check writing privileges, but are not insured by the federal government.

Mutual Funds—Investment companies pool the money of small investors into a fund which is managed by a professional fund manager who buys and sells stocks and bonds, and so forth. Every investor owns shares of the fund in proportion to their investment. Make sure you read and understand the funds **prospectus** (facts and terms) before you invest. A mutual fund with a *load* requires a fee to purchase it, a *no-load* mutual fund does not.

Traditional savings account—An account that typically pays a low interest rate, but does not require a high minimum amount to open. It is insured by the U.S. government up to $100,000.

U.S. Savings Bonds—Buying a savings bond is like lending money to the government. Bonds can be purchased at most banks and credit unions. Series EE bonds can be purchased for as little as $25. Series I bonds start at $50. Learn about both kinds.

U.S. Treasury Bills, Notes, and Bonds—These are U.S. government **securities** and are considered the safest of all debt instruments. Treasury bills are issued for periods of one year or less, notes for one to ten years, and bonds for ten years or more. The minimum purchase price is $1,000. You can obtain more information by contacting the Bureau of Public Debt Online—*www.publicdebt.treas.gov.* or by calling *800.943.6864.*

Also understand the difference between the following:

Bank—A business that is designed to offer its customers savings and checking accounts, credit, and loans and negotiable securities issued by the government or by a corporation. There are three kinds of banks: commercial banks, savings banks, and savings and loans.

Credit Union—A group of individuals having something in common (such as a religious organization, labor union, or employees of a company) form a not-for-profit financial institution. A credit union may offer a full range of services, generally paying higher interest rates on deposits to its customers and charging lower interest rates on loans than a commercial bank or savings and loan association.

Brokerage Firm (or brokerage house)—A business that helps you exchange securities, such as stocks and bonds or mutual funds. There are full-service brokers who give advice on picking investments and planning your financial strategy; and discount brokers who charge lower commissions than full-service brokers, but give little, if any, advice.

Creating Your Financial Plan

Did you know just what you were going to do with your first paycheck? Did you buy something or did you save it, or a combination of both? You need to know exactly what to do with your money coming in. You also need to be comfortable with the decisions you make. For instance, you do not want to be so strict with yourself about not spending *any* money, that you break down and make an extravagant purchase because you feel deprived. You need a plan, but it needs to be a plan that takes into consideration who you are, your responsibilities, and what you can reasonably expect from yourself.

You notice I am not saying *budget*. I am not going to tell you to make up a budget because I don't know anyone who successfully follows one in his whole lifetime. I am telling you to be absolutely aware and totally conscious of exactly how you manage your money. Make it a life-long habit to be in control of your money. You choose how to earn it, save it, spend it, and build security for yourself and those you love.

I want you to formulate your own plan according to your own needs. Remember the life goal chart in Chapter 1? After reading through the eight positive actions I'm going to suggest, please use the chart again, this time to organize your financial goals. I recommend that you structure your plan around the following:

Positive Financial Actions

- Live debt free.

- Always pay yourself first.

- Be accountable to yourself for your spending habits.

- Establish an emergency fund.

- Establish a short-term savings account.

- Establish a long-term investment account.

- Always use your credit cards responsibly.

- Establish a retirement account as early as possible.

In addition to being conscious actions, these suggestions are also long-term positive habits. It doesn't matter if you are not able to start all eight at once. What does matter is that you are developing a long-term personal commitment to your positive financial future.

Live Debt Free. I believe your life will never truly be your own as long as you are harnessed to a burden of debt. Owing money is a burden, no matter if you owe an institution, such as a bank or credit card company, or if you owe a friend or relative. Even if you have an interest-free loan (like from Mom or Dad), debt can mentally and emotionally wear you down.

Respect yourself and your financial game plan enough to make decisions that will take you toward meeting your goals, not move you backward. Having debt is going backward. When you take out a loan, you are charged interest for the use of the money you borrow. When you pay interest, you are not only losing that amount, you are also losing the amount your money would earn if it were working for you, as in an investment. It is not uncommon to still be paying on a loan for a purchase when the item you bought has long since broke or is no longer important in your life.

Before you take on any debt, I suggest you ask yourself, "Is what I want to purchase truly worth the obligation?" For example, is that particular SUV you can't stop thinking about really worth five years of monthly payments? *Every* month? No exceptions?

You will take on debt in your life. We all do. A home mortgage is generally considered an acceptable form of debt. We all know it is going to cost us something every month for shelter whether we rent or buy. Student loans may be considered tolerable obligations because hopefully the education we receive will help get us get a better job and salary. Few people are fortunate enough to be in the position to pay cash for their car, and so take on an auto loan out of necessity for transportation. There are logical reasons for taking on debt, but maintain the mindset to obligate yourself to debt *only* if it is in your overall best interest; assume the least amount possible and pay it back as quickly as you can. I suggest you seriously think about and research the *true* cost of any debt you want to take on. Know exactly how much interest you will end up paying. Is the payment so high it will interfere with your savings plan? Would you be better off financing a less expensive vehicle that is just as reliable? Would you be better off investing what you would save by having a lower payment?

Staying debt-free requires determination. You will be tempted. You will make tough choices. Yet the rewards of a debt-free lifestyle more than compensate for the challenge.

Always Pay Yourself First. If you are like most people, you tell yourself, "If there is anything left over at the end of the month, I'll try to put it in my savings account." In much the same unexplainable way as how our earthly possessions take on a life of their own and expand to fill every empty space we have to store them, money also seems to have a life of its own and tries to keep flowing out, in spite of what our intentions for it may be.

One way to deal with our outflowing money is to grab it at its source. Take your savings first! There will never be enough left over. No matter how much money you make, if you are like the rest of us, you will be inclined to spend more. Develop the lifelong habit of taking a certain amount right off the top of any money that comes in. Once you have a regular paycheck, you may want to consider setting up an automatic deposit from your checking account straight into your savings. The old rule of thumb is to save at least ten percent of every paycheck. If you are working, but do not yet have the financial responsibilities of living on your own, perhaps you can save a much larger percent. You can adjust that amount, taking into consideration what your personal goals are and how fast you intend to reach them. It is the habit of consistently adding to your savings that is important here. Don't put it off. Do you know people who pass up a gourmet cup of coffee because they want to save the money, then drive to the bank to deposit the two dollars they saved? Of course not. Don't give *all* your money the chance to flow out. Paying yourself first assures that you save *something,* and a little something over time helps build your financial independence.

Be Accountable to Yourself for Your Spending Habits. Have you ever thought you had more money in your wallet or purse than you did? Did you have a hard time trying to remember what in the world you spent the missing money on? Inattention to our spending is another area that trips us up.

While it would drive you crazy to account for every single cent you spend, you do need to have an accurate idea of where your money is going. Is the amount you are spending every month on target with your financial game plan? Do you recognize your spending habits? If you feel bad, do you regularly buy yourself something to cheer yourself up? Are you an impulse shopper? Do you give yourself convincing little lectures on why it's okay to buy something now when you know darn well you really should wait?

Some people are better at watching their pennies than others, but most people spend more money every month than they realize. This is where the danger starts. Benjamin Franklin had it right when he said, "Beware of little expenses; a small leak will sink a great ship." It's hard to visualize how saving on little things can make a significant difference to your long-range financial goals. It's also hard to remain committed and motivated to stick to being accountable for how you spend your money. Make up your mind to remain motivated to stick to your financial game plan. Even a small thing like eating lunch out every day can affect your long-term financial picture. Maybe you've heard you can save hundreds of dollars every year by brown bagging your lunch. It's true. This may be an area where you can save money. Yet the decision to pack your lunch is just one example of the attention, the mindset, and the conviction it is going to take for you to live within your means and to be true to your financial plan. It also requires a daily consciousness about your goals and what you do with your cash. How important to you is your financial independence? Will you take your financial game plan seriously? Every day you will be required to commit yourself again to your financial future. Every expenditure requires thought.

The need to be aware of how you are spending your money doesn't go away when you start making more. Your financial portfolio will change, but the necessity of spending your money wisely does not. No matter how much money you have, you will still be accountable, at least to yourself, for your spending. I'm not suggesting you turn yourself into a real cheapskate. Just keep in mind you will need to act responsibly, not only for the rent and the car payment, but also for the extras like magazines, compact discs, and those huge buckets of popcorn at the movies. The little totals do add up.

Another danger, of course, is in thinking you've been so good at saving on the little things that you make a huge purchase you are not ready for. Be careful of those big ticket items! The wrong one at the wrong time may throw you financially off balance. Meeting your financial goals is too important not to give every purchase the consideration it deserves. You are accountable to you. Just pay attention to both the small and the large expenditures, and you won't have to answer to yourself for messing up.

Bringing versus Buying Your Lunch

Spending **$5** on your lunch

    <u>× **4**</u> days a week

    $20 (Treating yourself
            out to lunch
            once a week)

    <u>× **50**</u> weeks a year
            (allowing 2 weeks
            vacation)

  $1000

If packing your lunch costs even half of that—($500) (and it would be much less) you save: **$500**

Establish an Emergency Fund. You know you need a savings account. You should also have money set aside in an emergency account. This means, of course, for emergencies *only.* It is not the money you use when your friend wants you to go along on a spur of the moment vacation to Aruba. It is the money you have set aside for *when,* not *if,* unexpected expenses come up. And they will. Cars break down. You may get sick and miss a lot of work. You may even lose your job. Having this safety net in place may mean the difference between being able to meet your rent or having to move.

Ideally, if you have not yet set out on your own, you should try to make sure your emergency fund is in place before you move. Estimates vary, but it is generally recommended you have from two to six months living expenses saved. This means you figure out how much you will need every month just to get by (include everything: rent, utilities, food, gas, etc.) and multiply it by the number of months you want to have in reserve. Sounds like a lot, doesn't it? Make sure you have at least *two* months worth of expenses saved. After that, guess what? *Then* you can actually start saving to move out. Yes, only after you have enough put away for emergencies can you even begin to think about saving to move out.

You notice I said ideally. Perhaps you are already on your own, struggling just to pay the rent. Whatever your circumstances, make funding an emergency account a priority—even if you have to take on a second job temporarily to come up with the money. It's that important. I'll tell you why. In addition to wanting to be prepared for an emergency, you are also going to need to build a solid financial future. Part of that process involves saving and investing. You will not be able to invest effectively if you have to take money away from your investments to cover life's surprise expenses. It is very hard to build a solid financial future without benefiting from solid investing. Investing just a few dollars regularly helps you tremendously over time. Having to interrupt your investment strategy may end up costing you more than you realize.

If you have several years to save and invest before you will need to have your emergency fund in place, you may wish to consider using a mutual fund to build this account. The **return** on an average mutual fund will most likely be more than those offered by a bank or credit union, and it may be possible for your balance to grow much faster. Always remember, with a mutual fund, there is a chance that your account value will go down as well as up. Understand there is risk involved. Mutual funds serve you best when you have a time frame of several years to work with, not just a couple of months.

Once you are on your own, an important thing to remember about an emergency account is to make sure you can get to the money without delay and/or penalties. With some savings vehicles, such as certificates of deposits (CDs), you will be penalized if you make a withdrawal before the agreed-upon time has passed. If this is all the money you have, don't tie up the entire amount.

Another consideration is that you may not want to keep such a large amount of money in your checking account or regular savings account that pays you a very low interest rate. One reasonable option may be to have your emergency fund in a money market account. Money market accounts generally pay more than a regular savings account, and you can get to your money whenever you need it. You are allowed to write a limited amount of checks per month, which you hopefully will not need anyway. Generally, a minimum amount is required to open a money market account, so you may need to plan accordingly. Money market accounts that are insured by the government are available at many traditional financial institutions such as banks, savings and loan associations, and credit unions. There is a similar fund called a money market mutual fund. This is a type of mutual fund, and it is *not* insured by the government. There is a difference. If you open a mutual fund money market, I suggest you use a large and well-known fund. Make sure you read and understand all of the available information on the fund.

When you are living on your own and you have more than two months' living expenses set aside, you may want to spread the money over a couple of different accounts. Perhaps use both a money market fund and a short-term CD. Wherever you decide to put your emergency fund, knowing you have a safety net to fall back on will give you peace of mind. It will also play an important part in your saving and investment strategy. As you prepare to step out on your own, an emergency fund should be one of your top priorities.

Establish a Short-Term Savings Account. A short-term savings account is for saving up for the near and sort-of-near future. It is better than having a stash around the house because you cannot get to it on a second's impulse and because you can put the money somewhere that pays you interest, or a return, on what you deposit. I believe saving up and paying cash for a purchase is always best. (Using a credit card to make the purchase is fine, but don't buy the item unless you already have the money set aside and can pay the credit card balance when it arrives.) This is the account you use to save to meet those not-too-distant goals. This is where you park the money that you are hiding from yourself. Remember that ten percent rule from "Pay Yourself First?" You may want to divide part of the amount you decided to save into a short-term and part into a long-term account.

Make it easy on yourself to save. Use whatever method of saving that works best for you. It's the development of the habit of systematic saving that is so important here. Time and compound interest is a powerful combination. Saving even a small amount of money regularly is the secret to successful savings.

Establish a Long-Term Investment Account: Did you notice I used the term "investment" here and not "savings"? Investing is taking your capital (money) and using it in a way in which you expect to gain more capital or income in the future. There are many ways to invest your money. Start as soon as possible. Using both your youth and your dedication to your financial game plan to your advantage, you can certainly obtain financial independence and enjoy security for yourself and those you love.

Being ready to start investing means not only do you need to have some dollars available for investing, but that you have also educated yourself as to what types of investment opportunities are right for you. Investing may involve risk. You could lose all or part of your money, depending on where you put it. A savings account at a bank involves almost no risks, but buying the hottest stock of the day certainly has risk involved. Yet, typically it is the investments that have the highest risk that also have the potential for the greatest return.

Everyone has a different comfort level when it comes to risk. Putting your money in securities issued by the U.S. government may not give you much of a return, but you may be someone who requires the peace of mind of knowing your money is insured by the **full faith and credit** of the government. Someone else may be very comfortable with the higher level of risk that investing in the stock market brings. Educate yourself as thoroughly as possible to decide what are the best investments for your risk level and never commit yourself to an investment you do not completely understand.

Always Use Your Credit Cards Responsibly. A credit card company is not your friend. Issuing you a large credit limit is giving you enough rope to hang yourself with. Don't get caught in the credit card trap! It is so easy to get in the habit of using your credit card and end up spending more than you can afford. It takes less time than writing a check and credit cards are accepted almost everywhere. The convenience, however, is not worth the price you pay if you lose touch with your money. If you use cash for every purchase, aren't you just a little more careful of how you spend your money? Do not become desensitized to the fact that charging is spending *real* money. The green stuff. Treat your credit card like you treat your cash.

If you do use a credit card for convenience, make sure you pay off the balance every month. If you find you spent more than you should have and think you'll carry a balance "just this once," you will be best served by putting the card away until the balance is paid in full. You can easily start carrying a small balance and end up over your head. If you cannot get by without charging, you are living beyond your means and need to fix the situation immediately. Does this sound a bit harsh? Well, few things can ruin your financial life as quickly and as painfully as credit card debt. Clearing your credit card debt can be one of the best investments you can ever make. It is true that you need to establish a credit history. It is also true that a credit card can be invaluable in an emergency. Yet, promise yourself that you will not succumb to the temptation of using credit to purchase the things you really should save up for. Credit cards are best left for emergency use *only*.

Establish a Retirement Account as Early as Possible. I bet you can't believe I'm writing this. Just two chapters ago I was telling you how to get your first job and now I want you to worry about your retirement? Am I kidding? No way! Funding your retirement account now will pay you colossal returns later. Just about any book you pick up on investing for your future will have charts, graphs, and tables explaining how much more you can earn for your retirement by starting sooner rather than later. There's a mega difference.

The best part of saving for your retirement is that the U.S. government wants to help you and has created some incentives for you to save. The Roth IRA (Individual Retirement Account) is one such incentive. It allows you to put up to $2,000 worth of earned income away every year, with the benefit of being able to take the money out tax-free in the future. Money accumulating tax-free returns is about as good as it gets. The other great thing about the Roth IRA is that you can take your money out and use it for other things besides retirement, like paying for your education or buying your first home.

You decide where you want to set up your IRA, whether it's at a bank, credit union, or brokerage firm. Insurance companies also offer IRAs. Make sure you are aware of any fees or loads that may be involved with the purchase of fund shares. Setting up a Roth IRA is as easy as opening any other account, and the benefit of starting now is tremendous. Make funding your IRA, as fully as you can, a habit you start as soon as possible and continue all your working years.

Chart Your Financial Game Plan. Now, I encourage you to take the time to make your financial game plan. Keep in mind the information from the eight positive actions. Here's an example:

Your Financial Game Plan

Your Dream
I want to be financially independent and have all the money I need.

Long-Range Goals
I want to purchase a home of my own and do some traveling. I'll continue to save and watch my spending.

Medium-Range Goals
I'll finish acquiring the skills I need to have a job that supports the lifestyle I want. Even though I'll have the expense of living on my own, I will still try to put 10 percent of every paycheck straight into my IRA, and when I meet the maximum contribution allowed for the year, I'll put the 10 percent into a long-term investment.

Short-Range Goals
I want to have two months of living expenses saved just in case I ever need the money. I will have a savings account in place and save enough so I can eventually move out on my own. I will find a better job.

Immediate Action
Since I'm not yet on my own, I'll try faithfully to put at least 50 percent of every paycheck in a savings account. I'll manage my spending so I don't spend more than 50 percent of what I bring home.

Your Present Reality
I'm broke, and I can only work part-time because I'm still in school.

Make your plan as detailed or as sketchy as you wish. The details of your plan will change, but your overall commitment to become and remain financially independent should not. The main thing is to have an idea of what you want your financial life to be like and to know some of the steps involved in turning your financial goals into your reality.

There is a great deal involved in maintaining a healthy financial life, but with financial know-how you can and will make the right choices. Make up your mind that you will respectfully manage your money. Trust in your knowledge and in your intuition that you can and will do the right things. Remain motivated for as long as it takes to reach your financial goals and you will give yourself the best chance at having a solid financial future.

Your Checking Account

You've seen checks. They are pieces of paper that stand for money. You deposit money into your checking account. You write a check to someone, that person cashes it, and the money is taken out of your checking account. Checks are especially good for all the bills that you need to pay by mail. (Never send cash to pay a bill by mail.)

Once you have a regular paycheck and are paying your own bills, you are probably going to want to open a checking account. Until you consistently have several bills to pay each month, it may be more cost effective to purchase money orders to pay those occasional bills that need to be mailed. You can purchase money orders for a very small fee at banks and at many post offices and convenience stores. Money order costs could add up to be less than the service charge or cost of having a checking account.

When you find that the fees are exceeding what it would cost you to have a checking account, it's time to head for the bank. Or the savings and loan, credit union, or brokerage firm. There have never been so many choices available for handling your money. In today's world, you can bank all over the country without leaving your computer screen. You may end up doing most of your banking online. You may want to do all your banking at one location close to where you live. Check out every available option and go with what feels right. Make sure you are happy with the services you get. Unlike the old days when many towns only had one bank, today you have many different options from which to choose.

Once again you are going to have to do some research and leg work. Here are some things to consider when trying to find the checking account that is right for you:

- The best checking account is the one that is totally free. This means there is no fee or service charge to pay every month to maintain the account, no per-check fee, no per-deposit or per-withdrawal fee, no minimum balance required, and no regular charges whatsoever. As you can imagine, those accounts are few and far between, and you will be really lucky if you can find one.

- Keeping in mind that absolutely free is best, the next best checking account is the one with the overall lowest fees and the best services. Find out:
  - What is the monthly service charge? (Don't forget a $10 a month service charge equals $120 every year!)
  - Do you have to maintain a minimum balance?
  - Are you charged to use the banks automated teller machine (ATM)?
  - Does the account have **overdraft protection** in the event you bounce a check? Does the overdraft protection involve an additional fee?
  - Are there any other fees you need to be aware of?

- Generally, the accounts that charge the lowest fees do not pay interest. This may work out just fine for you because you might not earn much interest on your checking account funds anyway. Some checking accounts pay a low interest, but it is offset by higher monthly service fees. Some checking accounts are free if you maintain a minimum balance. Calculate how much that balance would earn in a higher-yielding account before you commit that amount to being tied up in your checking account. So much to consider, but you can do it!

- If you think the time is right for you to open a checking account, you must also consider your age. Some banks allow minors to open checking accounts, but their parents' names must be on the check. When you are writing a check in person at a business, will the check be accepted without your parent being present? Do you have an acceptable photo ID? Don't get caught paying fees to maintain a checking account that is of little use to you.

- Don't be shy about asking for the services you want if they are not offered to you. Can you have your monthly service fee waived if you direct deposit your paycheck? Want a higher rate of interest on your savings account? Ask the bank manager. A lot of financial institutions are trying to attract students and young people because they are interested in establishing long-term relationships. You may want a checking account right now, but you may need a home loan in the future, and your bank will love the additional business.

- The small bank in your neighborhood may have fewer and smaller fees than the larger one. Be sure to check it out.

- One of the decisions involved with opening a checking account is what cute little checks you are going to pick out. Unless you really do find that totally free checking account, you are going to have to pay for your checks. Keep in mind that those custom designer checks cost more and may just be an expense you can live without. Consider purchasing your subsequent checks from a discount check company. You may want to check out:

  Checks In The Mail: *877.397.1541* or *www.checksinthemail.com.*

  Checks Unlimited: *800.204.2244* or *www.currentchecks.com.*

How To Write a Check. Write clearly and use a black or blue fine line waterproof *permanent* marker or pen.

- Today's date goes on the "Date" line. Putting a future date on a check is called postdating, and very few places will accept a postdated check.

- The correct name of the person or business goes on the "Pay To The Order Of" line. Draw a line over to the dollar sign.

- Write out the payment amount on the blank line that leads to the word "Dollars." Use xx/100 for the cents. Draw a line over to the printed word "Dollars." *Example:* Twelve 34/100. Noting the cents and adding a line over to the dollar prevents any additions, such as:
  Twelve hundred————————————————DOLLARS.

How to Write a Check

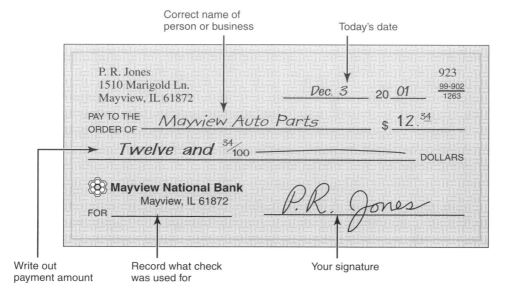

Correct name of person or business

Today's date

P. R. Jones
1510 Marigold Ln.
Mayview, IL 61872

923

Dec. 3 20 *01* 99-902/1263

PAY TO THE ORDER OF *Mayview Auto Parts* $ *12.³⁴*

Twelve and ³⁴/100 DOLLARS

Mayview National Bank
Mayview, IL 61872

FOR

P.R. Jones

Write out payment amount

Record what check was used for

Your signature

- Put the amount of the payment, written in digits, by the dollarsign. *Example:* $12.34.

- Your signature goes on the blank line at the bottom right. Make sure you always use the same signature, matching your printed name on the check.

- Never sign your name to a blank check.

- The "Memo" line is for recording for your own purposes what the check is purchasing. For example, "concert tickets" may help refresh your memory of exactly how much your friend owes you for his ticket that you paid for by check.

Watch Out for Bouncing Checks. Bouncing a check can be expensive. This means you wrote a check and your checking account had insufficient funds to pay the amount. A single **returned check** can easily end up costing you over $50 in fees: a charge from your bank for bouncing the check and a charge from the business to which you wrote the check. Being familiar with your financial institution's policy on *"funds available"* will help you avoid this particular mistake.

When you deposit a check (like a personal check from someone else) into your checking account, a portion or the whole amount of the check may not be available for you to use right away. If you do not have other money in the account and you write a check from your account, you may bounce the check you wrote if that check is presented to your bank before the funds you have in the account become available. Trying to guess when a check will get back to your account can be tricky. Some checks are held by whomever you write them to; some checks may clear the same day you write them. It is, of course, best to always have the money available in the account before you write a check. Some funds you deposit into your checking account will be available immediately; some may be available in five days.

Find out if a **hold** is placed on your payroll check. If this happens, introduce yourself to the manager and explain that you will be making regular deposits of your payroll check. Chances are very good that you will not have a hold placed on your paycheck. Be sure you understand your financial institution's policy. Knowing the policy is a good way to avoid those high returned check fees.

ATM/Debit Card. When you open your checking account, you will probably receive an ATM (automatic teller machine) or **debit** card. An ATM is a terminal that provides you with 24–hour electronic access to your accounts. You can withdraw cash or make a deposit. To use an ATM, you need a personal identification number (PIN) and an ATM or debit card. The same card can be used at many other places as well, such as grocery stores and gas stations.

Using a debit card can be convenient. Keep these things in mind if you are a debit card user:

- When you make a purchase or withdraw, the money comes out of your account immediately—that instant. The money has to be there. You must keep track of every transaction you make. Write down any account activity right away. This is the trickiest thing about a debit card. Forgetting to write down just one withdrawal from your account could lead to being overdrawn. As with a credit card, don't forget that you are spending real money. If you spend cash, you can tell if it's gone. When you use a debit card, it is not that easy to realize you have spent real money unless you write it down and deduct the amount from your balance.

- ATM charges can add up. If your banks' ATM is free, make it the ATM you use. Using an ATM other than your own bank's can end up costing you plenty in **surcharges.** Want to check your balance before you make a withdrawal? Well then, you may get charged for two transactions! Don't forget that when using your debit card in the grocery store, you can request extra cash. This might save you an ATM fee. Be sure you're using your debit card and not a credit card!

Online Banking. Online banking is a fast-growing, fast-evolving banking option. For those who have computer access, this may be an effective way to pay your bills, add to your savings, and maintain an investment portfolio.

Online banking can be done through the Internet, encrypting your personal information; or by using special software with a direct link to your bank that bypasses the Internet altogether. The industry claims that both ways are secure.

Many banks offer free or low account service charges and a minimal fee for automatic bill paying. When checking out your online options, make sure you understand every feature of the service, exactly what the charges are for, and if there are any hidden costs. Will you have to pay an additional charge if you need to pay a bill by phone or mail?

Knowing when a fund transfer takes place is critical to preventing yourself from becoming overdrawn. If you pay your bills online, you need to make sure you know when the bank debits (or takes the money from) your account. Are your bills mailed to the recipient or electronically transferred? This may make a difference in deciding when you want a bill to be paid.

Whether you do your banking online or at the local bank, make sure you are comfortable with your banking decision. If you really don't like the choice you made, shop around until you find what you do like. Being uncomfortable with your decision may make handling your finances an unpleasant chore, and may keep you from paying close attention to your money. Try to create a system you enjoy and you will be inclined to stay on top of your finances.

Keeping It Straight. No matter what banking option you choose, you will need to spend a little time keeping things straight and on track. Reconciling or balancing your checkbook will help eliminate your chances of bouncing a check and it is your opportunity to catch a mistake made by your financial institution. If you do not take the time to balance your checking account down to the penny, at least be sure you faithfully check the following things as soon as your statement arrives.

- Check that the written amount of every canceled check is the same amount debited from your account.

- Be sure the check amount is exactly the same amount you entered in your register. For instance, a check may be made out for $13, but you wrote $18 in your register.

- Check your receipts of deposits made during the statement dates to be sure every deposit has been credited to your account. Make sure you entered every deposit into your register.

- Deduct from your register any service charges that you incurred during the statement period.

- Add any interest payments to your register that were paid during the statement period.

- Notice if you have correctly entered all ATM transactions and fees into your register.

Checking these things every month will head off most serious errors. In addition, you can work with your account until the amount of money you think you have and the amount of money the bank says you have agree exactly. Do this only after you have made the necessary adjustments mentioned above.

Keep in mind that your statement only reflects transactions that have taken place during specific dates. If you made a deposit into your account after the statement closing date, it will be noted on next month's statement, so you'll need to *add* the additional deposit to the ending balance noted by your bank. This is your new total. (The flip side of the statement should have a spot for figuring this out—don't use your register.)

Since the checks reflected as debits on your statement are only the checks that have cleared the bank, not necessarily all the checks that you wrote out, you need to add up the outstanding checks and *subtract* the amount from your new total. This new amount should be the same as what is in your checkbook register. If it's not, look specifically for the amount that you are off. For example, if you are off by eight dollars and that is the amount of your monthly service charge, you may have forgotten to deduct that charge from your total. Staying on top of your bank statements and not letting them go for too long makes the job a whole lot easier.

Establishing Your Credit Record

Credit card companies will find you. Some credit card companies offer cards to students still in high school. Credit card offers multiply mysteriously fast, and before you know it just about every credit card company will be trying to entice you into their web. Well, don't be flattered. They are only after your money.

It is to your advantage to build a good, solid credit history. Employers sometimes look at a potential employee's **credit report** to determine how responsible they are. Your credit history will be examined when you rent an apartment or apply for an auto or home loan. You need a positive credit history to prove you are a financially responsible person. If you ever mess up—for example, are late with a payment or miss one altogether—it will be reported to one or all three of the major credit bureaus. It could take years to get a negative item off your credit report. So it is important not only to establish a credit history, but to keep it unblemished.

- Start small. You may want to start with a credit card from your favorite clothing store. This could be the easiest card for you to get, but it is also the worst type of card to have if you carry a balance. The interest rate could be over twice that of a major credit card company. Yet, if you do not spend more money than you have, paying the total balance due in full and on time, this may be the card you need to get you started.

- With every credit card application you consider, you not only need to read and understand the terms of the account, but you should compare the terms to that of another credit card company. Shop around and get the best card you can qualify for.

- You want the lowest interest rate.

- You want a rate that is calculated on a one-month balance, not a two-month balance.

- You do not want to pay an annual fee.

- Know every category of interest charges. For instance, you are charged a higher interest rate on cash advances.

- Make absolutely sure you are credit card savvy. Be happy if you receive a low credit limit and do not be fooled into thinking you "have" the amount of your credit limit. You do not, or you would not be charging. That is just one way credit card debt can sneak up on you and get a stronghold over you. (Again, please remember; if you don't have the real money, don't use the plastic.)

- Be extra careful of "special low introductory rates." These rates can be wonderful if you do not carry a balance or even if you know for sure your balance will be paid off by the time the rate expires. Don't be suckered into "payment holidays," especially when you have a low introductory rate. They are designed to keep your balance as large as possible when your introductory or promotional rate expires. Having a large balance on your card when the low rate expires is not a good thing! Your next rate is going to be *significantly* higher. Then you may be tempted to open another credit card account and transfer the old balance. There may be balance transfer fees involved. It can turn into a vicious circle. If you haven't been responsible with one credit card, please do not open another. Not only does having more credit increase your chances of getting in over your head, but having too much credit can sometimes work against you. Often banks are reluctant to give loans to people who have large lines of open credit.

- You may be offered a secured credit card. A secured credit card is one in which you have funds on deposit with the issuer of the card in the amount of your credit limit. This money acts as security in the event you are late with or miss a payment. Before you open a secured credit card account, make sure the issuing company will let you switch to a regular account after a reasonable period of time, usually six months. If you decide on a secured card, try to find a secured card that does not charge a fee to open the account.

- Be careful not only with your real credit card, but also with the virtual use of your credit card. Do not include the card number in any e-mail message and do not shop from an Internet merchant that does not claim to be on a secure server.

Don't be in too much of a rush to get all the credit you can qualify for. Build your credit record slowly. Obtain only one or two credit cards. Find low fixed rates. Stay with a low credit limit, and forget you have the cards.

Paying Your Bills

Most of your bills will be on a monthly cycle. This means your rent, phone, credit card payments, and so forth will all need to be paid every single month. Some billings are every two or three months (such as gas, water, trash, etc.), depending on your situation and location. Then there are the bills that may be due quarterly or semiannually, like insurance premiums. They arrive just about the time you forget all about them. Bills arriving at different times may not be a problem if you always have more than enough money in your accounts to pay them. For those who cut it close every month, balancing the bills can require skill and attention.

- Anticipate not only your monthly bills, but all the bills that will be due in the near future. Don't spend extra money one month because there is no utility bill, only to find you are short when the utility bill does arrive. Plan ahead. Mentally take something out of your checking account every month to cover a bimonthly or quarterly bill. You may even want to subtract the amount from your check register to fool yourself, so you won't spend the money you will be needing.

- Try to pay the bills that are accruing interest as soon as they arrive. Credit card interest is calculated on your average daily balance, so don't let money sit in your checking account while you wait for the statement due date. Pay them as quickly as you can. If you are carrying a credit card balance and have extra money, make an additional payment any time during the month.

- If you pay rent, this will probably be your number one concern. You do not want to be charged a late fee, and you do not want any negatives on your renting history or credit report.

- If you have an interest-bearing checking account, you may be tempted to leave your money in the account until the last possible moment before paying your bills. That may be fine if you are good at it, but misjudging once and incurring a late charge can eat up more than an entire year's worth of interest earnings. Be smart about it and mail all payments at least a week before they are due.

- Don't forget—be good to yourself and pay yourself first!

Loaning Your Money

There's an old saying that goes something like this: "Don't ever loan anyone more money than you can afford to lose." Chances are good that you won't get your money back. Only you can decide if loaning money to someone you know is the right thing to do. You'll need to consider what the loan will do to your own personal financial situation. What will the loan do to the relationship you have with the person who wants the loan? Is it possible the loan could put a strain on the relationship? Do you feel pressured into making the loan? Put on the spot? If you decide that you want to loan someone money (and it's more than just a couple of bucks), it is reasonable to ask the person to sign a promissory note. You can get one at most office supply stores. Include the amount borrowed, the amount of the monthly repayment, and the amount of interest the person will pay for the loan. If your friend refuses to sign the note and says something like, "You know I'll pay you back," etc. reconsider loaning the money. Trust your instincts.

There should be a *really* good reason before you ever make a large purchase with your credit card for a friend. Your friend is not being respectful of you if he or she asks you to charge the purchase and tells you, "Don't worry, I'll make the payments." Chances are you *will* end up having to worry about it, every month as you have to track down the payment. Forget it.

It is natural to want to help your family and friends when they need your help. Yet, do it within reason. Like every other decision you make with your money, consider loaning money to anyone very carefully.

Reminder: I wrote in the section called "Live Debt Free," that owing money to anyone is carrying a burden. Although it may sound like a great idea at a time when you need extra money, borrowing money from relatives and friends can be even more of a burden than having institutional debt, like credit card debt or a bank loan.

Getting a loan from someone you know may change the relationship. A friend may begin to resent you for owing her money, even if it was her idea to loan you the money in the first place!

If you must borrow money from family or friends, make sure you treat the loan the same way you would an institutional loan. Be responsible. Sign a promissory note. Meet or exceed the agreed-upon repayment schedule and get rid of the obligation as soon as possible.

Using Your Financial Know-How

Because it is so easy to crash and burn on the personal financial obstacle course, many people do. Plenty of adults would love the opportunity to start their financial life over again. While it's not quite possible to go back and have a financial "do over," many people do spend years trying to straighten out the financial mess they've made.

This chapter was designed to prevent you from having a financial blowout and will help start you on the right course—mainly, not to make a mess of your finances before you really even get going. Cleverer, funnier, and cooler marketing campaigns entice us to spend, spend, and spend some more. Credit card companies try to seduce us with more and easier credit, and our economy-driven culture tries to sell us on the erroneous idea that our personal net-worth equates to our personal self-worth. You know better!

Wearing the designer label of the moment may be great if you can afford it, but you are not less of a person if you shop at *Kmart*. As a matter of fact, I know several millionaires who faithfully shop at discount stores and clip coupons, too!

Spending money on yourself and those you love is a wonderful thing, but only if you can afford to do so. Spending more than you should and trying to support a lifestyle you really can't afford are the quickest ways to fall into financial trouble.

How do you know how to make the right moves with your money? Gain financial knowledge and practice putting that knowledge to work in your everyday life. Read everything you can about money management and the energy of money. Go to the library and read the monthly money magazines. Ask for advice from the people in your life who appear to be managing their money successfully. You may be surprised at what you hear. You will benefit by hearing the mistakes others have made and from learning the strategies that others have found helpful.

Many interesting Internet sites offer useful information on how to manage your money. You may want to start with these:

Check Free: *www.checkfree.com*.
    Online banking services.

FinanCenter: *www.financenter.com.*
   Helpful financial information, including calculators.

Investorama: *www.investorama.com.*
   This site offers a comprehensive directory of financial tools.

Mutual Fund Investor's Center: *www.mfea.com.*
   Information from the Mutual Fund Education Alliance.

Roth IRA information: *www.rothira.com.*
   Current information on the Roth IRA.

Savvy Student: *www.savvystudent.com.*
   Helpful information for students about saving money.

There are several popular software programs available to help you handle your money, including *Microsoft Money 2001* and *Quicken 2001,* basic and deluxe versions.

Chapter 4

Setting Up Your Home

What You Need

You can eventually live a very sucessful life even if you start out with nothing more than the clothes on your back.It's been done. Yet, I hope you start out living on your own by being as prepared as possible. As you plan ahead, take into consideration all the wordly goods that are involved with setting up a home. Fortunately, if we have to, we can get along just fine without most of the stuff. There are things that you need and things that would be nice to have. You don't have to come up with everything at once.

The Basics:

- Mattress
- Set of sheets
- Blanket
- Pillow
- Towels
- Table and chairs
- Frying pan

- Sauce pan
- Can opener
- Large mixing spoon
- Plate, bowl, glass, and mug
- Knife, fork, and spoon
- Lamp

Looking at the previous short list, you can see that if survival depended on it, we really could get by without most of the items. The same goes for the following expanded list of the things that would be great to have when you move into your own place. Don't worry if you don't have everything. You will eventually.

Try to Acquire:

- Mattress
- Box springs
- Bed frame
- Table and chairs
- Sofa
- Bed pillows
- Mattress cover
- Blanket
- Set of sheets
- Washcloths
- Hand towels
- Bath towels
- Beach towel
- Tablecloth or place mats
- Kitchen towels
- Pot holders
- Clock
- Vacuum
- Bucket
- Set of dishes
- Flatware
- Drinking glasses
- Salt and pepper shakers
- Set of pots and pans
- Can opener
- Spatula
- Kitchen knives
- Vegetable peeler
- Mixing spoon
- Baking dish (9 × 11)

- Mixing bowls

- Set of measuring cups

- Set of measuring spoons

- Cookie sheet

- Muffin pan

- Mixer

- Coffeemaker

- Toaster

When your family and friends ask, "What do you want for your birthday?", you know what the answer is. Letting the word out that you will soon be living on your own may bring household donations that you could really use. You can also find items that have plenty of use still in them at garage sales and thrift stores. Consider bartering as well as shopping at clearance and close-out sales.

Tools. In addition to household items, I recommend you start collecting the basic tools you will need for your tool kit:

Minimum Tool List

- Hammer and assorted nails

- Pliers

- Scissors

- Screwdrivers—Phillips and flat-head, and assorted screws

- Utility knife—with reversable, retractable blade

Expanded Tool List

- Duct tape

- Hammer and assorted nails

- Industrial-strength glue

- Pliers

- Plunger

- Scissors

- Screwdrivers—cordless power screwdrivers are great!

- Staple gun

- Tape measure

- Utility knife—with reversable, retractable blade

- Wrench—adjustable

Where Will You Live?

The highlight of moving out on your own is the actual moving into your own place. You've planned, worked, and thought about it for such a long time, and the day finally arrives when you are ready to start hunting for your new home.

The city you choose to live in will most likely be dictated by your job, school, or family connections. The actual address you decide to call home will most likely be chosen on the basis of what you can afford. We all want to live in as safe and as comfortable a place as our finances will allow. The first experience most of us have living on our own is not with home ownership, but with renting. So how do you know how much rent you can reasonably pay each month?

When you set about renting a unit, you must supply the owner or manager with some of your personal information. The rental application will ask your income. Your verifiable income (that which can be proven, such as from your employer) should be at least three or four times the rent you are considering. This means you probably won't be able to qualify for the unit if more than 25 percent to 33 percent of your monthly income is to be used for your rent. For example, if you bring home $1,500 a month, you shouldn't consider spending more than $500 a month for housing.

Your verifiable income (that which can be proven, such as from your employer) should be at least three or four times the rent you are considering.

This rule is not etched in stone. You may find a landlord who doesn't care how much you make as long as you pay the rent in full and on time. Perhaps you know you can easily go without spending money in one area, such as on entertainment, if it means you can afford to live where you really want. Take your personal spending habits into consideration and arrange your priorities, keeping the 33 percent rule in mind. Once you figure out how much you can afford, don't be tempted to spend "just a little bit more." The amount of $530 sounds pretty close to $500, but reaching for that extra $30 every month might turn into too much of a stretch. Remember, starting and keeping your monthly rent payment as low as possible will be to your advantage.

It's not uncommon for a young person to have some help with the first rental experience. Perhaps if you cannot qualify for a rental unit due to lack of a credit history, for instance—a parent or other family member may be willing to co-sign or be responsible with you. That person includes his or her financial and credit information in the application and enters into the agreement, even though he or she will not be living with you. If you get a cosigner, make sure you treat the agreement responsibly. Take extra pains to pay the rent on time and in full. Someone has stepped out on a limb for you and you need to show that person that his or her trust and efforts were not misplaced.

Before Your Search Begins. After you have decided the maximum monthly payment you can afford, it's time to prepare for the search. Before you begin looking at rental units, take the following steps to ensure your search goes smoothly:

1. If you have a credit history, get a copy of your credit report. This ensures that you are aware of its contents. You do not want to be caught off-guard if there's a negative item in the report. If the report contains a mistake, do what you can to correct it. You can order your credit report from one of the three main **credit bureaus:**

Equifax :   800.685.1111

Experian: 800.301.7195

Trans Union: 800.888.4213

2. Obtain permission from two or three people to use their names and telephone numbers as possible references.

3. In addition to references, have other information ready that will be requested, such as:

The name, address and phone number of your employer

Current pay stub

Previous employment information

Social Security and driver's license numbers

4. Decide what you are looking for. What factors are the most important? How much room do you need? Do you need a place that allows pets? Do you want the responsibility of a yard? Having an idea of what your requirements are will help you focus your search.

5. Get a street map of your town. Are some neighborhoods more convenient for your situation than others? Do you have favorite areas where you would like to live? For instance, finding a place that is close to your job or university may be important to you.

6. Make a list of the available rentals which meet your needs. Today, even with online searches, the best resource is still your local newspaper, especially the weekend real estate section. You can also obtain rental guides. They can be found at grocery stores, gas stations, colleges, real estate offices, and so on.

You may want to look into professionally run properties, such as those offered by a property management company or real estate office. Real estate agents are paid their fee by the property owner, so you do not directly pay for the assistance. Professional property managers are typically very much aware not only of owners' rights and responsibilities, but of the rights of tenants as well. Not all real estate offices handle rentals, but you may want to try to find one in your area that does.

What to Look For. In choosing the place that is right for you, knowing what to look out for is as important as knowing what to look for. Try to give yourself as much time as possible to make the decision that is right for you. Don't be in such a hurry to move in that you overlook something important, such as realizing after it's too late that you've moved into a building in which neighbors start to party just about the time you need to get to sleep. You cannot be passive in your search. You have to take the lead and ask the right questions. Here are a few suggestions:

- Pay close attention to the neighborhood. Is it well tended? Do you feel safe? How far is it from your work, university, place of worship, and so forth?

- Try to visit the unit in the daytime. This allows you to notice how much natural light the unit gets and helps in identifying what kind of shape it's in. You can see dirt, marks, and stains, better in daylight.

- If a unit becomes a real possibility, try to revisit it at night. Look at the neighborhood again. Look at the exterior lighting. Notice the lighting in pathways, alleys, hallways, and stairwells. Does the surrounding environment appear to be a safe one?

- Once you think you have found the place that is right for you, don't be shy about meeting your prospective neighbors. Ask them about their experiences with the building's management and if they would recommend a move into the building. Ask about their experiences getting repairs taken care of. Ask about noise. Ask about bugs. Are the neighbors being friendly? You may find out more than you expected.

- Take notes while you are searching. After looking at many different units for several days or weeks, it is easy to get confused. When you find the unit that is the one for you, and you think you are ready to commit, take detailed notes about the entire condition of the unit and what has been discussed with the owner or manager. For instance, if the carpet is stained, write a detailed description of the condition and have the landlord or manager sign the documentation. This acknowledgement may help prevent any disputes over responsibility when you move out. You can also take photos or make a video before you bring in your belongings. This will show the exact condition of the unit when you moved in.

- Always look at the exact unit that you will be living in, not one similar to it, such as a model. Never sign a lease for a unit sight unseen. Never.

- Find out if any utilities are included with the rent. For instance, the water bill is often paid by the owner and not the separate

If your first impression of the unit is positive, look a little deeper. Make sure everything works as it should. Don't be shy. Ask questions and run some tests:

- Does the shower have enough water pressure?
- Run the water in all the faucets; check the pressure and determine if the water is hot.
- Flush the toilet.
- Open and close the windows; do they stick? Lock securely?
- Do all the doors close as they should?
- Try the locks. Find out if they have been changed or rekeyed since the last tenant. Ask if you can have this done.
- Look for leaks and water damage on the ceilings and floors. Look under the sinks.
- Do you smell mold or mildew?
- Does the thermostat work properly? Heater? Air-conditioner?
- Do the walls have holes, dents, marks, or cracks?
- Do all the kitchen appliances work?
- Are there smoke detectors in working order in the unit?
- Where will you park your car?
- What do the common areas look like? Are they clean and maintained? What kind of shape is the laundry room in?
- If there are shared facilities, such as a pool, what are the hours of operation?
- Is the prospective landlord or property manager friendly and responsive to your questions?
- Does he or she appear to be someone whom you will be comfortable entering into a contract with?

tenants. You may want to ask what the average utility bills cost for heating or cooling to determine if your budget allows for this expense.

- Make sure your questions and concerns are stated directly and to the point. It is considered misrepresentation if an owner or manager lies to you, but it is your responsibility to ask the questions that may be of importance. For instance, you should ask, "Has the carpeting been professionally cleaned since the last tenant moved out?" instead of asking, "Is the carpet clean?"

- Find out the policy regarding your pet before you get too involved. Pets are forbidden from some units entirely. Some rentals allow pets only if an additional security deposit is paid. Check first.

- Is the asking rent in line with comparable units?

Your Rental Agreement

Great! You have finally found the place you want to call home. It suits both your needs and your wants. You have checked absolutely everything for potential problems. You are ready to pay the rent and pick up the key. Right? Well, almost.

The last big consideration here is your rental agreement or lease. You need to read, agree, and honor it completely. It's a contract. It spells out what the obligations are for both you and your landlord. It is in your best interest to make sure you thoroughly understand the document.

The time to request changes to a rental document is before you sign it and assume responsibility for its terms. As you read the lease or rental agreement, take note of any modifications you wish to make. If the landlord agrees to your requests, make sure the necessary changes are made on the document and that the landlord initials each change and signs and dates the modified version in ink. Make sure you get a copy.

If you accept the terms of the document, but only if certain conditions are met by the landlord, such as the unit must be painted first, make sure you get the exact conditions in writing, with a date and the signature of the landlord or manager.

Make sure you are clear about what will occur if you breach or break the document. For instance, if you sign a 12-month lease, but your employer transfers you to another state after 7-months, what will be your financial obligation to your landlord? Can you **sublease** the unit?

Take your time and read the document carefully. All rental documents are not the same. Ask questions and refuse to be rushed into signing. Make sure you understand the terms regarding the following:

The Monthly Rent. You are obligating yourself to pay the agreed-upon amount of rent for the agreed-upon amount of time. Find out exactly how your payments are to be made. For instance, where is the payment to be mailed? What day is it due? Are there additional fees involved if you are late? By how many days?

Term of the Tenancy. The length of time you and the landlord agree to be obligated to the rental document is called "the term of tenancy." A rental document is either a fixed-term lease or a rental agreement. Rental agreements may run for several months or run month-to-month and self-renew unless terminated by either party. Leases are usually for one year. When the lease expires, either party can decline to renew it, or it continues on a month-to-month basis.

Security Deposit and Other Fees. In addition to the rent, you will almost always need to make a **security deposit.** This is money that will be held by the landlord to offset any damages made to the property while you are living there. Make sure you understand the conditions for getting your deposit back when you eventually move out. This is why documenting the condition of the unit before you move in is important. Is any portion of your security deposit nonrefundable? Will a cleaning charge be deducted from your deposit when you vacate the unit? How and *when* will your deposit be returned? There may be other fees involved with your lease. Are you required to make an additional deposit for your pet?

Repairs and Maintenance. You will be required to keep your unit clean and sanitary and will be held responsibile if you damage the property by abuse or neglect. It is your responsibility to inform the landlord of any defective and dangerous conditions to the property. It is the landlord's responsibility to keep the premises in livable condition. As you can imagine, this can be subject to interpretation. The landlord is not legally responsible for strictly cosmetic-type repairs. Of course you can request the yellowing wallpaper be replaced and of course the request may be denied. Find out what kind of repairs or alterations you are allowed to do yourself. Most property owners understand the importance of keeping their property in good shape and appreciate being alerted to a potentially serious problem. Make sure your rental document outlines how repairs will be addressed.

Special Rules or Restrictions. Being well-informed on the rules and restrictions relating to your unit can save a lot of misunderstandings. If you are renting a condo, the rules are called the CCRs. These codes, covenants, and restrictions spell out very clearly what is acceptable and what is not. The same may apply to the terms of your rental document. There may be a clause relating to disruptive behavior. There may be a restriction on the lengh of time a houseguest can stay with you. Understand the restrictions before you agree to adhere to them.

Vacating the Property. What does the rental document require of you when it's time to move on? How much notice do you need to give? Will you be required to allow the unit to be shown to prospective tenants when you are not present? When you move out, you may want to do a "walk through" with the landlord and also document the condition of the unit by photographs or video tape to make sure no misunderstandings arise regarding the condition of the property.

When you sign a lease or rental agreement, you are entering into a legal contract, but the agreement itself must be legal. This means that it must comply with all relevant laws. Laws and ordinances exist to protect both the property owner's and the tenant's rights. Learn what your rights are with regard to your landlord entering your unit. This can be a flashpoint if both parties are not aware of the law. A good rental document is thorough and clearly outlines the responsiblities of all persons involved.

A good rental document is fair to all parties. For instance, you should probably avoid signing a rental contract that states you "agree to pay all costs for court proceedings." Use your common sense and get everything spelled out as clearly as possible, right down to the use of nails for hanging pictures.

Do not hesitate to try to negotiate the terms of your rental document. It is better than trying to live with conditions you find objectionable.

Roommates

Often, the only way it's financially possible to move away from home and live on your own is to live with a roommate. This does not necessarily mean that you are not making it on your own. You still must be responsible and meet all your obligations, but sharing expenses may make the dream of being independent financially possible.

Of course, you must choose your roommate carefully. Often it helps if you and your roommate both like the same lifestyle. Yet, even the oddest couple can survive together if they thoughtfully make and honor a mutual agreement. Yes, this does mean another *written* agreement.

There will be differences. Differences between people who live together are a way of life. Yet the differences do not have to be a problem. Having an agreement worked out ahead of time will help head off issues before they become big problems. Work on the agreement together, keeping equality in mind.

Are both of your names on the lease? One person being responsible for the terms of the lease and the other being able to walk away at any time may not be the best arrangement. How are you going to split utilities? Consider a policy on all aspects of living together, such as the cleaning, mutual expenses, guests, food, and even quiet time.

Make sure you are both of the same mindset right from the start. Sign and honor the agreement. Knowing how you will deal with the issues of living together will prevent them from developing into sticky situations.

Utilities

You've signed your lease, paid your rent and security deposit, and just picked up the key to your new place. The next step is getting the utilities turned on and in your name.

Your new landlord, manager, or agent probably has the names and numbers of the utility companies that service your area. You may even be able to transfer services from the previous tenants and avoid full set-up charges. Be sure to ask. The utility companies are listed in your local phone book, or of course you can ask your new neighbors for the names of the companies.

When you call to set up your new accounts, make sure you have your personal information handy, including:

- Your driver's license number or other identification information

- Your Social Security number

- The exact address of your new place

- The day you want the services to start

- Your employment information, including the company's name, address, phone number, and the date you started working there

- Your bank information, including a credit card number if you have one

Depending on your credit history or the utility company's policy, you may be required to submit a deposit for the services. This will be returned to you after a certain amount of time, usually one year.

Since some utilities require more time than others to get setup, make the necessary arangements as soon as possible after your rental agreement is finalized.

Water and Sewer. If your rental unit does not include the water and sewer, you will need to contact the Water Department.

Gas and Electric. These utilities are often combined or may require separate accounts. Generally your account can be set up in a day.

Phone and Cable. Depending on your area, these services may take several days or over a week to get in place.

Garbage. Depending on where you live, you may need to set up an account with the Sanitation Department.

Reminder: If you are sharing expenses with a roommate, consider very carefully the arrangement regarding the responsibility of the utilities. Will the bill be in both your names? If so, your roomate will also need to provide the necessary application information to the service providers.

Moving

The day I moved away from home, everything I owned fit into the back of a pickup truck. The whole maneuver took less than an afternoon from start to finish. Each subsequent move got more complicated, and my last move took months of planning and several days of hard work, even with the help of a moving company.

No matter how simple or involved your move may be, keep the following in mind:

Be prepared. Do whatever you can do ahead of time. If your new place requires any attention, such as a cleaning or some shelf paper, now is the time to get it done. It will be much easier facing it now than waiting until after you've moved in.

- Fill out a mail forwarding card from the post office. Be sure to include the date you want the forwarding to begin.

- Notify everyone of your new address and phone number.

- If you are moving out of town, wrap up any unfinished business. For example, did you get your dirty clothes out of your locker at the gym? Return your library books? Return everything you've borrowed from friends? Pick up your dry cleaning? Visit or call your family and friends?

- If your pet is going with you and will need a new license or tag, make sure you have it's imunization certificate.

- If you are not using a moving company, make sure you have plenty of help. You may want to line up more help than you need just in case someone doesn't show.

- If you are renting or borrowing a truck, make sure it is one you can drive. Don't get stuck with a stick shift U-haul if you can only drive an automatic.

- Do you need to rent or borrow a dolly? This can make a huge difference if you are moving large, heavy items.

- Think about where you are going to place your furniture. Even good friends run out of patience picking up and putting down a couch a dozen times.

- If you are planning to use a professional moving company, obtain at least three estimates before you decide which company to use. The estimates will either be binding (you will not be charged more than the estimated amount) or nonbinding (there is no guarantee that the final cost will be as low or as high as the estimate.) Here again, you will be entering into a written agreement so make sure you are aware and understand all the details. It is important not only to finalize the pick-up date and time, but to make sure you will have your things delivered exactly when you need them. Get it in writing.

• Gather some things together to have available on moving day:

Moving Supplies

• Tools: utility knife, hammer, screwdrivers, and pliers

• Carton sealing tape

• Paper towels and toilet paper

• Hand soap and dish soap

• Towels for the bathroom and kitchen

• First aid kit that includes a pain reliever

• Cleaning product and cleaning cloths

• Paper cups for water or drinks

• Snacks

• Can opener

• Light bulbs

• Trash bags

Moving Out. If you use any boxes that are not new, such as from the grocery store or a friend's garage, check each one for insects and insect eggs.

You don't want to inadvertently *bring* cockroaches, or other insects into your new place.

Even if you are only moving down the street, you'll need to pack carefully.

- Keep in mind the heavier the item is, the smaller its box should be.

- Heavy items go in the bottom of the box with smaller, lighter items on top.

- Try to use unprinted newsprint instead of old newspapers to wrap items. Newspaper ink will rub off.

- Prevent items from shifting in their box by crumpling up the wrapping paper to fill all empty spaces. You can also use towels or clothes for this, but it makes unpacking more complicated.

- Think about unpacking when you pack. Items that go together should be in the same box. Packing by room will make unpacking easier.

- Clearly label your boxes—bedroom, kitchen, and so on.

- When loading the trailer or truck, be sure to put the heaveist things in first and keep them the lowest.

- Carefully keep track of your valuables, important papers, and medications. Keep them with you.

Moving In

- Turn on the refrigerator.

- If you have not already done so, take time out on moving day to familiarize yourself with the electric circuit breaker or fuse box.

Find the location of your gas and water main valves. Learn how to shut them off in an emergency situation.

- Put the boxes in the room they are labeled to go in. Keeping all the boxes together in the dining room, for example, and unpacking them one at a time may be neater, but may also involve more time and effort.

- Prioritize your unpacking and setting up. For instance, set up and make your bed before you get too tired. If you have to go to work the next day, make sure you can find your clothes.

- Once everything is moved in, take your time unpacking. If any item is dirty, now is the time to clean it. Consider very carefully the best way to set up your new home.

Reminder: If you have permanently changed states, you will need to get a new driver's license and change your vehicle registration. Also contact the Board of Elections if you wish to register to vote.

Organization

Chances are you will organize your own place similarly to the home you grew up and were comfortable in. The point here, though, is to actually do some thoughtful organization. Being well-organized will not only save you valuable time, but will save you unnecessary stress as well. Who wants to run around hunting for car keys when late for a movie? Yet, the forces of natural law are working against you here. Are you familar with entropy (the measure of the disorder of a system)? If you don't work to keep your place clean, it's going to turn into a mess. Order goes to chaos. It's a fact of life. The quip we are all familiar with—"a place for everything and everything in its place"—has been around forever with good reason. It's the key to maintaining order. Here are a few tips you may want to consider:

- Remember your cubby from day care or kindergarten? It was your personal little area to put your own stuff and you knew right where everything went. Having such an area in your own place can be a great time-saver. Choose a convenient, *private* place by the door to throw your keys, purse, wallet, and so forth. Faithfully put your outgoing mail here, and you will automatically grab it on your way out. The same goes for library books that need to be returned, outgoing dry cleaning, the gift you need to deliver, and anything else you need to have with you when you run errands.

- Organize to fit your lifestyle. Are you more inclined to come in the door and toss your jacket somewhere than to walk to the closet and hang it up? If you are, you may want to install a wall coatrack. Do you need to set up a special area to do paperwork or will anywhere do just fine? Think about what will work the best for your needs.

- Whether it's clothes, bedding, or kitchenware, items that are used together should be kept together.

- Items should be kept closest to where they are used the most.

- The most frequently used items belong in the most accessible spots.

- Think ahead and organize to make getting out of the house in the morning as easy as possible.

- Put cleaning supplies in the area where you use them, not together in a closet somewhere, unless they are in a plastic caddy with a handle that you can carry with you from room to room.

- Arrange the area by the phone to include:
  - List of emergency numbers, including those of a neighbor, your doctor, poison control center, and your landlord.

  - List of frequently called numbers, like your favorite take-out restaurant.
  - Pens and paper
  - Calendar (Fill in all the birthdays you need to remember for the year when you put the calendar up.)

- Invest in a good quality flashlight and keep it close to your bed.

- Establish and maintain a simple, logical filing system:

    Basic File Headings
    - Automobile
    - Bills That Need To Be Paid*
    - Checking Account Statements
    - Credit Card Information (account numbers and customer service numbers)
    - Insurance
    - Medical
    - Paid Bills (statement stubs and receipts)
    - Tax Documents
    - Warranties and Manuals

- Process your mail every day. You may want to do this standing by the trash can.

- If you are going to recycle, set up a system that makes it easy for you to faithfully keep at it. Even if you think it is too much for you to think about now, perhaps you can at least commit to recycling glass and cans.

- Most importantly, deal with things as you go along. If you bring home dry cleaning, take the time to walk it to the closet. Clean the kitchen after you eat, not three days later.

---

*If you create a "Bills That Need To Be Paid" file, make sure you check it regularly. Otherwise, use a container to keep the bills organized and in sight so you will not forget about them.

Experiment until you find the organizational solutions that work for you. But remember, even the best organization ends up being useless if you don't work at maintaining the order.

Supplies

Shopping List—Nonfood Items

- Aluminum foil

- Cellophane tape

- Coffee filters (if you make coffee)

- Dishwasher detergent (if you have a dishwasher)

- Dishwashing detergent

- Facial tissue

- Garbage bags

- Light bulbs

- Matches

- Muffin pan liners

- Paper napkins

- Paper towels

- Plastic food storage bags

- Plastic wrap

- Soap

- Steel wool soap pads or sponges

- Toilet paper

- Waxed paper

Additional Items You May Need

- All purpose stain remover

- Batteries

- Chlorine bleach

- Cleanser

- Color safe bleach

- Fabric softener

- Glass cleaner

- Laundry detergent

- Leather cleaner (for shoes)

- Leather conditioner (for shoes)

- Liquid detergent for fine fabrics

- Multipurpose cleaner

- Shoe polish

Medications and Emergency Supplies. Having basic medications and emergency supplies around the house is part of setting up your new place. Use the following lists to help you prepare the essentials that you should always have on hand. Decide whether you want to combine your medications with your first aid supplies. Either way, store all the supplies in an easily acessible, easily transportable container. In the event of an emergency, you will want to have them with you.

Medications

- Antacid (such as Mylanta)

- Antidiarrhea medication (such as Imodium A-D)

- Antihistamine (such as Benadryl, for allergic reactions)

- Cough syrup

- Decongestant

- Pain reliever (aspirin or nonaspirin)

- Throat lozenges

- Good thermometer

Note these important tips:

- Read all labels carefully and take medication only as directed.

- Keep all medications in their original containers, and toss them after the expiration date. (Be sure to take the full dosage of prescribed antibiotics.)

- Store your medications in a cool, dark, and dry place.

- Keep up-to-date with your prescription medications. Plan ahead to get your refill *before* you run out.

First Aid Supplies. Keep your first aid supplies in an easily accessible place (preferably the kitchen where accidents are likely to occur.) Store the supplies in a container with a handle to make it easy to grab on the go. Be sure to return or replace items after use.

Household First Aid Supplies

- Adhesive bandages (assorted sizes)

- Adhesive tape

- Antibiotic ointment

- Antiseptic (such as rubbing alcohol)

- Calamine lotion

- Elastic bandage

- Hydrogen peroxide

- Latex gloves

- Safety pins (large and small)

- Scissors

- 2 small bath towels

- Sterile cotton

- Sterile dressings (assorted sizes)

- Sterile roll of gauze

- Tweezers (to remove splinters and glass)

- Wooden tongue blades (for finger splints)

Emergency Supplies. While natural disasters may be more likely in some geographic areas than others, you should be prepared for an emergency situation no matter where you live. Many emergencies, such as a hazardous material evacuation, can happen anywhere. We may never know when a disaster will strike, but we can take comfort in knowing we are prepared. The following information is a short excerpt from "Disaster Supplies Kit" developed by the Federal Emergency Management Agency (FEMA) and the American Red Cross. Visit the Red Cross online at *www.redcross.org.* and print out the entire text. Call your local Red Cross chapter for geographically specific, natural disaster preparedness information. For instance, if you live in southern California you should keep a survival kit in your car as well as in your home. Keep your supplies in a lightweight container that is easy to carry if you have to evacuate.

- Store at least a three-day supply of nonperishable food. Include ready-to-eat canned meats, fruits, vegetables, and juices.

- You need at least one gallon of water per person per day. Have at least three gallons.

- One complete change of clothes, including good sturdy shoes.

- Blanket or sleeping bag

- Flashlight (with extra batteries)

- Battery-operated radio (with extra batteries)

- Can opener (nonelectric)

- Cash and change

- Paper cups and plates, plastic utensils

- Matches in a waterproof container

- Toilet paper and towelettes

- Soap

Safety and Security

Fire Safety. Few people realize how fast a fire can take hold and how quickly it can become uncontrollable. Please take the danger of fire seriously.

- Make sure you have at least one smoke alarm and that it has good batteries. Many people use New Year's Day as a reminder to change the batteries in their smoke detectors.

- Buy one or several ABC multipurpose fire extinguishers. At a minimum, keep one handy in the kitchen and know how to use it.

- Keep baking soda or flour by the stove. Have it at arm's reach, and if something on the stove starts to burn, you can quickly douse the flames.

- Be careful not to set your pot holders on fire.

Burning candles is once again very popular. Use extra caution here. I know a woman who burned down the apartment complex where she and many other tenants lived by burning a candle close to a window. The wind blew her curtains over the candle's flame and within minutes the entire complex was engulfed in flames. Yes, she was held responsible.

The National Fire Protection Association offers tips regarding candles. The following is taken from their recommendations:

- Make sure the candle is in a sturdy holder that will not tip over.

- Place the candle on a sturdy piece of furniture in the center of a one-foot "circle of safety." This means you have checked and there is absolutely nothing within at least a one-foot radius that can possibly ignite, such as wallpaper, curtains or draperies, towels, shelves, plants, and silk flowers.

- Absolutely *never* leave the room or fall asleep with a candle burning.

- Stop burning your candle when it gets down to half an inch from the base. Throw it away.

- Blow out candles or use a snuffer, but never use water to extinguish the flame. Water can cause wax to splatter and can spread the flames.

Personal Precautions. Take a class in self-defense. Please don't put it off. You will feel more confident and secure knowing you know the basics of protecting yourself. Check for classes at your local YMCA, community, or adult education center.

- Do not label your keys with your name or address. Give an extra set of keys to a relative if you wish, but do not label them correctly. Doing so may allow someone to enter your home if the keys are lost or stolen. Carry a spare car key or key card in your wallet.

- Always have your door key ready before you approach your home.

- Always pay close attention to what is happening around you.

- Buy a small flashlight that hooks onto your key ring. This is a big help in locating a keyhole in the dark.

- Set an interior light or radio on a timer when you are away at night.

- Make sure you look in the rearview mirror and close your automatic garage door (if you have one) as soon as your car clears the door.

- Make sure your garage door opener is always in the same place, such as fastened to the sun visor. You should not be sitting in your car scrounging around for the opener.

- Take your parking ticket with you when you park in a pay lot.

- If you leave your car somewhere overnight, remove all identifying information. You don't want to return to find your car stolen *and* your home broken into.

- When driving, never let yourself get caught between two cars. Car-jackers often work in pairs.

- Don't ever pull off the road when driving by yourself at night, except in a true emergency.

- If you believe you have been intentionally rammed from the rear, proceed to a populated, well-lit area or a police station for help.

- When driving, be alert to the signs of a drunk driver:
  - Swerving
  - Weaving
  - Wide turns
  - Driving to the left of center
  - Driving in the dark with the headlights off
  - Driving on the shoulder
  - Unusual stopping

$ Watching Your Pennies—Around Your Home $

✔ Lowering the thermostat even one degree saves money. Turn down the heat when you go to bed.

✔ Turn off the air conditioner when you are going to be gone for more than four hours.

✔ If you do not have an economy cycle on the dishwasher, skip the dry cycle. Let the dishes air dry.

✔ Get your deposit back from your utility company if you've had the service for over a year.

✔ Set your water heater to 120 degrees.

✔ Consider carefully what cable and satellite services you sign up for. Will you really use all those premium channels?

Chapter 5

Maintaining the Basics

Staying on Top of It All

Successfully living on your own requires that you take good care of yourself, your home, your possessions, and your time. Order goes to chaos unless we expend the energy to maintain the order; and maintaining order and balance in life makes thriving, not just surviving, possible. It's hard to grow and really get the most out of life when you are continually bogged down in unnecessary situations that need attention. If you don't change the oil in your car, you will ultimately end up dealing with the inconvenience and the expense of repairs. If you don't maintain your health, you may suffer the inconvenience of an illness and the expense of medical bills. While you cannot control every aspect of your life, working at maintaining the basics will help you avoid living your life moving from one mini-crisis to another and will give you the freedom you need to enjoy the life you are building.

Your Home

Most people I know seem to have definite feelings regarding housework, ranging from fanatical obsession to absolute loathing, with almost everyone having very strong opinions about the best way to go about the chore. You, too, will find the way to maintain your place that works best for you. I recommend you just get the job done to your own satisfaction and do not even think about the "dusting before or after vacuuming" debate. No matter what your particular style of housecleaning may be, have a few cleaning supplies on hand:

Cleaning Supplies

- Vacuum cleaner

- Bucket

- Toilet brush

- Dust cloth

- Clean rags

- Glass cleaner

- Liquid detergent

- Cleanser

- Multipurpose cleaner

If you use several different chemical household cleaners, make sure to read the labels carefully. Never mix different cleaning products together. Sometimes combining products makes each individual product ineffective, but depending on the chemicals, mixing or using the wrong products together could create an extremely dangerous chemical reaction. Follow the instructions exactly.

It may be hard to believe, but there are some people who actually love to clean. They can't get enough of it. In case that does not sound like you, here's a reminder of the things that you should attend to regularly. Your lifestyle, dirt tolerance, and your definition of clean will dictate how often *regularly* is for you. If your home is a high traffic zone, you may need to clean more frequently than someone who spends most of their at-home time alone. (Clean once a week, and you will make both your mom and me proud.)

Regular Housecleaning

- Put away clutter

- Thoroughly clean kitchen

- Clean bathroom, including toilet and shower

- Vacuum floors

- Wash kitchen and bathroom floors

- Dust

- Change your sheets

Cranking up the music volume and cleaning your whole place at a break-neck pace may work great for you, or slowly, meditatively cleaning one room at a time may be more your style. Just get it done. Put off cleaning and you will just have a bigger mess to eventually take care of. Stay on top of your housework and you won't have to take large chunks of time out of your schedule to get the jobs finished.

Clutter. Your place can be clean but still look like a mess if you create mounds of clutter. Even the thought of picking the stuff up and putting it away will seem overwhelming. If you have things lying around in every room, you may want to take time the day before you do your housecleaning to deal with straightening up. Start with the things you have thrown on the floor and work your way up. Go room by room, putting things where they belong or find a better place to keep items if the place you had for them isn't working out.

Keep in mind that even though you may still be acquiring things you need for your place, there may be items you own that are no longer useful to you. Pass things along to your friends. Keep a bag or box handy in which to put items you no longer need. When it is full, give it to charity. Throw things away that are beyond use to anyone. Don't fall into the clutches of clutter.

Cleaning the Kitchen. This is the one room that really should be kept clean. It's so tempting to just leave the dishes, the sticky pots and pans, and the yucky stuff spilled on the bottom of the oven. Yet, if you do, you will find yourself spending your precious nonworking hours working hard—cleaning up a horrendous mess!

- Wipe up spills and put ingredients away as you cook.

- Wash down countertops with liquid detergent, hot water, and a clean dishcloth.

- Stay on top of the dirty dishes. If you only have a few dirty dishes to wash, you may want to wash them by hand instead of running the dish washer. If you have a dishwasher, always run full loads.

- Soak sticky pots and pans and wash them with the next round of dirty dishes. If the food is burned or baked on, try boiling water and a squirt of dishwasher detergent in the pan for several minutes to loosen the stain, then scrub the pan with cleanser. Repeat if necessary.

- Wipe appliances after you use them.

- Wipe up drips and dirt in the refrigerator before it starts to smell. Throw away anything that looks like a biology experiment.

- Wash the floor and empty the trash at least once a week.

Cleaning the Bathroom. Ick!

- Start with the countertop. Remove everything from the surface and wipe down with all purpose cleaner and hot water.

- Get the goop out of the soap dish.

- Scrub the tub/shower with cleanser or soap scum remover. Clean the glass shower doors. If you have a shower curtain, run it through the washer every month or two. Adding a quarter cup of Clorox liquid bleach helps remove any mildew.

- Scrub the inside of the toilet bowl with a toilet brush; scrub the outside, the seat, and surrounding areas with multipurpose cleaner and hot water.

- Scrub the sink.

- Clean the mirror.

- Vacuum and wash the floor.

Vacuuming the Floors. Some vacuum cleaners have one attachment for cleaning noncarpeted surfaces and one attachment for vacuuming carpet. There are some vacuums that are for carpet only. Make sure you are aware of what you are buying. If you can vacuum the kitchen and bathroom floors before you wash them, you will find it's much, much easier. Use a broom if you do not have a floor attachment.

- Vacuum as often as needed, but don't think you need to make a big deal out of it every time. Yet, several times a year, move all the furniture and vacuum every square inch of your place. You may want to purchase an allergen product to sprinkle on your carpet before you vacuum to help kill and remove dust mites.

- Keep extra vacuum bags on hand. Stopping in the middle of cleaning to run around town looking for the correct bag may get you totally out of the mood to continue with your efforts. Write the bag refill information in your organizer or planner.

Washing the Floors. Here's another area where people seem to have strong preferences—either toward using the mop or getting down on your hands and knees. Whatever you decide, use a cleaning product that is appropriate for the surface. Walk all the way into the room and work as you move backward, using hot water and a clean mop or cleaning rag. Scuff marks or stains may need to be scrubbed with cleanser and then washed. You may need to go over the floor again with hot rinse water.

Hint: When you get sick and tired of keeping your floors clean and you want to cut down on the amount of vacuuming and washing you are doing, there is a painless solution. Kick your shoes off every time you walk in the door.

Shoes track in all the worst little bits of our world—not only dirt, but also germs, pesticides, and other toxins. People spit in parking lots and drip in public rest rooms. Businesses spray to control insects, and we all know what dogs do. We bring it all into our home every day on the bottom of our shoes.

Initiate a "no-shoes in the house" policy, and you will dramatically reduce the amount of pollutants in your home and the amount of time spent cleaning them up.

Dusting. There are those who swear it's best to dust before you vacuum because all the dust gets on the floor, and those who think it's best to dust after you vacuum because vacuuming creates more dust. Whatever side you join, you'll find dusting can make your place look better, and it's much healthier for you, too.

- If you use treated dustcloths, make sure they are appropriate for the type of furniture you have. Otherwise, use a cloth that does not leave behind lint. Old cloth diapers work great.

- Generally you won't need more than a dustcloth to get the job done. You can easily ruin the finish on a piece of furniture by applying the wrong furniture cleaner. Be careful of spray furniture polish, as it can actually dull some shiny finishes. Furniture oil, although sometimes necessary to prevent wood from drying out, attracts dust. Furniture wax repels dust.

- Dust top to bottom—high shelf to low shelf.

- Pick up an item, dust it, dust where it was, and replace the item. When you do your more thorough cleaning, remove everything from the shelf or piece of furniture, dust each item, and clean and wax your furniture.

- Shake out the dustcloth often (outside).

Change Your Sheets. Please. If you have two sets of sheets, you can alternate. If you have a washer and dryer nearby, putting the same sheets back on your bed after you wash them will save you the trouble of folding them up. Always wash new sheets before use.

Less Frequent Chores. As I already mentioned, there are a few things that you will need to do *occasionally* in addition to your regular housecleaning. That's another subjective term that means different things to different people. You'll come up with your own definition of exactly how often *occasionally* is to you.

Occasional Chores

- Vacuum under the couch, bed, and behind the refrigerator

- Remove cobwebs from the ceiling and room corners

- Wash the windows and sills

- Wash your mattress cover

- Wash your shower curtain

- Wash any throw rugs

- Clean the refrigerator

- Clean the inside of the oven

Reminder: If you have a home computer, you will need to clean that, too. Use cleaning products that are designed specifically for computers. For instance, use compressed air to remove the dust from the keyboard, disk drive, and mouse.

Your Laundry

Even though I enjoy doing the laundry, I often tend to try to cut corners. When I'm too lazy to take the time to be more careful, I'm guilty of haphazard sorting, frenzily overstuffing the washer, and forgetful overdrying. And my clothes have paid the price of my carelessness. Ruin a couple of your favorite outfits and you'll agree that taking proper care of clothes helps them last longer and look better.

If you are fortunate enough not to use a coin washer and dryer, you can really dig into the world of correct clothes keeping. If you use a coin-operated washer and dryer, doing your laundry can get pretty expensive. You may want to limit the variations in your wardrobe to save on the number of different loads you have to wash. If you wear only t-shirts and jeans, you are not going to have a problem, but branch out into finicky fabrics and bold colors and you'll have to spend a little more time and money on the upkeep. Consider at least keeping all your towels in the same color group (light, bright, or dark) to prevent having to pay to wash several small loads.

Laundry Supplies

- Laundry detergent

Extras

- Fabric softener

- All purpose stain remover (such as Spray 'N Wash, Shout, etc.)

- Chlorine bleach

- Color safe bleach

- Iron

- Ironing board

Sorting. The idea behind careful sorting is not to discolor, stretch, shrink, wrinkle, wear out, or wreck what you wash. You already know to separate the whites from the colors. Taking it further, you can sort not only by color, but also by weight, water temperature, and how much lint the item makes. For example:

- Delicates

- Whites and light colors

- Dark colors

- Bright colors (reds, etc.)

- Heavyweights (like jeans and sweat shirts)

- Towels (terry cloth robes, etc.)

That may be taking it a little far, but you get the idea. Sure, you can throw white towels in with a load of white clothes. Towels are listed separately because they tend to create lint and because they can be very heavy. If you are washing lightweight cotton blouses with heavy bath towels, you may end up doing a wee bit of ironing. The more experience you acquire, the more you'll learn just where you can and can't cut corners.

- Give wadded-up socks and clothes a shake before you throw them into the washer.

- Turn pockets inside out.

- Tie drawstrings and sashes to avoid wet tangles.

Hand Washing. If you have a hand wash cycle on your washer, you're set. Otherwise, it really is best to hand wash an item labeled "Hand Wash Only." Also, washing out a few things by hand may tide you over until you can get around to all of your laundry.

There are special detergents and soaps available for washing by hand, but you can also use just a little bit of your regular detergent. Read the product's label. Add the garment to the sudsy water. Be careful not to add the detergent directly to the item or it may spot. Swish and soak for a few minutes, then let the soapy water out, and fill the sink with rinse water. Swish some more, let the water out, and rinse the item thoroughly under running water. Be careful about not wringing and stretching delicate fabrics. Press the water out instead. When you are sure all the soap is out, fold the item in a dry towel and blot out the excess water.

Follow the garment's instructions about drying. "Line dry" means to hang it on a line or hanger to dry (a plastic hanger if you have one.) "Block" or "flat" means to lay it on a dry towel and try to arrange it back to what it looked like before it was washed.

Dry Cleaning. You may have clothes with care labels that read "Dry Clean Only." Generally, garments labeled "Dry Clean Only" really mean dry clean only. This is usually because at least part of the garment is not washable. You may have more leeway with care labels recommending "Dry Clean." If you are tempted to wash any of your dry clean garments— for instance something silk, cotton, or linen—make sure the item does not have interfacing, lining, or complicated construction. Dab a small hidden area with a wet cloth to make sure the color is not going to run. Hand wash in cold water. When money is tight, stay away from "Dry Clean *Only*" garments.

Laundry Detergent. This is the one essential laundry supply you need. You may want to use the same brand you are used to or experiment with the ones you find on sale.

- Liquid detergents are usually better on greasy stains; powder detergents work best on the muddy ones.

- While it's best to follow the recommended instructions for the detergent you are using, you will soon figure out the correct amount of detergent that works best for your water type. If you add too much, it won't all rinse out, and you'll find that your laundry is stiff with detergent buildup. If you don't add enough, the lint and dirt will not lift out and your laundry will not get clean.

- Buy a detergent designed to work best in the water temperature you use most often.

- First, let the washer begin to fill, then add the detergent. Next, add the clothes. Some detergents will spot fabrics if they are not dissolved first.

Stains. Most spills and spots need some type of immediate attention or they will never come completely out.

- There are several products available to treat stains before they are washed. If you buy one that does not require you to wash the garment right away, you can treat the article and let it sit until it's washed. These prewash products work especially well on greasy stains like butter, oil, and lipstick.

- Enzyme detergents, such as Wisk or Biz, are good for soaking protein stains, such as grass, blood, and egg.

- Muddy clothes may need to be treated with a stain remover and soaked in detergent before being washed.

- Lemon juice and vinegar are both mild bleaches. Mix one part juice or vinegar with one part water. This should remove the color left behind by most stains.

Bleach. Chlorine bleach is used to keep whites bright—yet, not *all* whites. Be sure to read labels carefully before you bleach anything. If you do not have a bleach dispenser, add the bleach after the wash cycle has started. Never pour bleach onto dry clothes. It must be diluted before it hits the fabric. Only bleach your whites occasionally, since the bleach will weaken the fabric.

- Use only color safe or all fabric bleach on colored fabrics.

Machine Settings.

Permanent Press: Use this cycle for normal loads. It adds cool water to the load before it spins to reduce wrinkles.

Regular Cycle: This cycle is best for heavy, sturdy, and very dirty loads.

Delicate Cycle: This cycle is for lightweight and loosely woven fabrics.

Clothes need room to move around in the washer. A load of laundry should fill the washer three-quarters of the way full. Overstuffing the washer will also set in wrinkles.

Water Temperature.

Hot—best for keeping whites bright

Warm—average loads

Cold—bright colors and delicate fabrics

Fabric Softener. Liquid softener is added during the rinse cycle and fabric softener sheets are put into the dryer.

• If your washer does not have an automatic dispenser, dilute the fabric softener with warm water and add to the rinse water. Do not pour it directly onto any fabric since it can cause spots.

• Fabric softener can also build up in your laundry. If your laundry begins to feel slippery and look dingy, cut down on fabric softener. Use it only every few washes.

• Don't use fabric softener on your kitchen towels and dishcloths.

• If you have asthma or allergies, check with your doctor before using dryer fabric softener sheets. An unscented brand is available if your allergy is to fragrance.

Drying. Clean the lint filter after every load. This will cut down on the drying time and allow the dryer to be more energy efficient.

• Shake out each item as you take it from the washer.

• Heat from the dryer will really set a stain, so make sure treated spots and stains have washed out. Re-treat and re-wash any stain that's still noticeable.

• Hang up delicate items and those with elastic.

- Do not overload the dryer; it will cause your clothes to wrinkle.

- Shake out sheets and pillowcases during the drying cycle to avoid them drying in a ball, with some parts remaining damp.

- Follow the care label's drying instructions. The dryer will shrink fabrics, so be very careful not to get clothes too hot.

- Overdrying will cause your clothes to fade. Remove clothes when they are just dry.

The Laundromat. If you have a shared laundry room where you live, or if you go to the local laundromat, here are a few extra things to keep in mind:

- Find out if there is a time when the laundry room is normally not crowded. I have a cousin who does her laundry on the same day each week—at four o'clock in the morning—but she never has to wait for a machine!

- Sort all your loads before you get there. Put each load in a plastic bag and use your laundry baskets for transferring clean clothes from the washer to the dryer, and for bringing the clean laundry home.

- Check the washer for anything left over from previous use before you add your clothes. You may need to wipe a machine out before using.

- Make sure you don't leave any leftovers in the washer or dryer.

- Do not leave your laundry sitting in a machine. Be courteous to others who also use the facilities.

Ironing. This task is definitely not as popular as it used to be. If you have items that must be ironed, remove them from the dryer while they are still a little damp.

- Familiarize yourself with your iron. Use the correct setting for the material you are ironing. When in doubt, start with a low setting and move up to a higher or hotter one if necessary.

- Cotton and permanent press fabrics can tolerate quite a bit of moisture and steam. This makes removing wrinkles much easier. Use a spray bottle filled with warm water if you need more moisture than your iron's steam setting provides. Use distilled water in your iron to prevent mineral deposits.

- Iron with the grain of the fabric, back and forth, not in a circular motion.

- Allow the fabric of the area you are ironing to cool a few seconds, to set the press, before you move on to another area.

- On hard to press items, try using spray sizing or a light spray starch.

- If you really hate to iron, press only the parts of the garment that are going to show.

Sewing Kit. Buttons fall off, seams rip, and pockets mysteriously develop holes. Yet, you'll be able to fix the problem in just a couple of minutes if you have the basic sewing tools available.

Sewing Supplies

- All purpose thread: Buy a few of the basic colors that are in your wardrobe.

- Dual-duty thread: Heavy-duty thread used to sew on buttons. You may want a couple of small spools.

- Needles: Buy a package of assorted sizes.

- Pin cushion

- Sewing scissors: Use this pair for cutting fabric and thread only. Label them "Fabric Only" with a permanent marker. They will never be the same if you use them to cut paper.

- Seam ripper: Use to remove stitches easily, like when a button falls off and leaves a clump of thread behind.

- Safety pins

- Straight pins

- Tape measure: The soft fabric or paper kind. You may be surprised at how often you'll use this.

Hint: If you have thread leftover in the needle, save the needle in your pin cushion. You'll be that much more prepared for your next sewing emergency.

Your Shoes. Shoes? Yes! Don't underestimate the importance of the appearance of your shoes. People notice, especially if you are working in the business arena. To keep your shoes well-maintained you'll need:

Shoe Care Supplies

- Leather cleaner

- Soft cotton cloths

- Flannel cloth for buffing

- Leather conditioner

- Polish

- Shoe cleaning brush

If you are not really into taking the time to clean your shoes the traditional way, there are one-step shoe care products available. Kiwi makes disposable shoe shine wipes and *Kmart* distributes Wipe 'N Shine—a polishing pad that does it all.

Don't forget about your athletic shoes. Clean them before the stains are set for life.

Your Car

Getting your first car is exciting! No matter what it looks like, there's a certain thrill involved; a certain independence. I started with an old, old car and bought a newer old car when I could. The day I bought my first brand-new car, I put a blanket down on the seat *and* the floor before I let anyone sit down! I fussed over that car. I washed it by hand. I kept it away from other cars in the parking lot. It was a whole new world for me. I loaded it with all the recommended safety paraphernalia, earthquake readiness supplies, travel necessities—even beauty supplies and a pillow. I made my little traveling world as comfortable as I could. I made sure the car ran safely and looked good.

Practice preventative maintenance with your car, whether it's old or new, even if you are not as crazy about it as I was about mine. Here are a few things to keep in check. Cars require all of the following fluids which need to be checked for levels and leaks:

Car Fluids

- Battery

- Brake

- Coolant (antifreeze)

- Engine oil

- Power steering

- Transmission

- Windshield washer

With the convenience of fast, economical servicing facilities, or quick lubes, you may not want to actually do the labor yourself; but you do need to make sure to take the car in to have the regular servicing done. Your owner's manual outlines a maintenance schedule you should follow. If you do not have an owner's manual, call the manufacturer of the car for the information. Some quick lubes "top off" fluids between visits free of charge. Or, you can always pull into a full-service gas station and ask the attendant to check under the hood. Or, of course you can learn to do it yourself!

Hint: If you change your own oil, or add to it when the level is low, use a good quality synthetic oil. Synthetic oil will help your car obtain its best gas mileage and will also reduce engine wear. This is one area where you don't want to buy the natural product.

Also Check:

- Battery

- Belts and hoses

- Brakes

- Filters

- Tires

- Windshield wiper blades

Battery. Not only does the battery require a fluid check, but also a check to ensure it has the proper charge and that the terminals are free from corrosion.

Belts and Hoses. Belts need to be checked for wear and proper tightness. Hoses need to be free from bulges and cracks.

Brakes. The Car Care Council recommends brakes be checked every 20,000 miles.

Hint: Anticipate stop signs and signals. Slow down gradually. Zooming from one red light to the next shortens the life of your brakes as well as wastes gas.

Filters. Your car has both fuel and air filters. If you are told you need a new filter, look at your filter to determine whether you really do or not.

Tires.

- Check your owner's manual for the proper amount of air pressure.

- Tires need to be rotated and aligned on a regular basis. Your car pulling to one side or starting to jiggle at certain speeds could be an indication that the tires are out of balance.

- Tires are legally bald when there is less than one-sixteenth of an inch of tread remaining.

Windshield Wiper Blades. Replace blades twice a year or sooner if you notice streaking or signs of splitting or cracking.

Car Trouble. The more you learn about maintaining your car, the less dependent you will be on others. You will also be more in touch with your car and better able to detect and avoid car trouble. Cars often give early warning signs of upcoming problems. The Car Care Council offers a list of common signs. Here are a few:

- More often than before, you're finding it necessary to add oil between changes.

- There is a squealing or scraping sound when you apply the brakes.

- You hear knocks and pings from the engine when you accelerate or climb a hill.

- There is a rumbling or hissing sound coming from your muffler.

- Your engine keeps chugging after you've turned off the ignition. Contact the Car Care Council for the complete list of signs and for additional valuable information about caring for your car. The Web site is *www.carcarecouncil.org.*

Repairs. When your car needs more help than you know how to give, you'll need to find an automotive repair shop. This is another time when it's good to ask around for recommendations from family and friends. Someone may know a shop that does excellent work at reasonable prices, which is exactly what you are looking for.

- Look for professional certifications, such as from: the National Institute for Automotive Service Excellence, the American Automobile Association, or the Automotive Service Council.

- The shop you choose should give you a free estimate of the repair costs and obtain your approval before starting to work on the car.

- The shop should be willing to work with you. This means they should be courteous, listen to your explanation of why you think the car needs attention, and understand when you need to have the repairs completed.

- If the shop discovers additional work that needs to be performed which was not included in the original estimate, the shop should provide you with an estimate of the extra work and obtain your approval before starting the additional repairs.

- The shop should give you written invoices for the repairs, labor, and parts.

- Just as with getting a diagnosis from your doctor, it is reasonable for you to seek a second opinion concerning the diagnosis of your car. If your gut instinct tells you to go somewhere else, then do so.

- Your local Better Business Bureau and Consumer Affairs agency will be able to tell you if there is a significant history of complaints and disciplinary actions against a shop.

Hint: Keep a file about your car. Include a dated service record and the receipts for all service and repairs.

Keeping Your Car Clean. Dirt, grime, bugs, bird droppings, sap, and air pollution can all have damaging effects on your car's paint, which can lead to body rot. You may want to take your car to an automated car wash or save some money and wash it yourself. Here are some suggestions for washing your car by hand:

- Buy a liquid detergent specifically designed for washing cars. Dishwashing liquid can strip car wax.

- Wash the wheels first.

- Hose the entire car, top to bottom, with medium stream pressure.

- Gently clean the roof, trunk, and hood. Use a car wash mitt, sponge, or *soft* cotton cloths. Wring and rinse out frequently.

- Rinse each area when finished.

- Clean the sides, bumper, and grill.

- Rinse.

- Use clean, dry, lint-free cloths or a synthetic chamois to *blot* the car dry.

- Open the doors, hood, and trunk to wipe up any water that leaked in.

- Vacuum the interior.

- Clean the inside windows and rearview mirror.

- Wipe down the inside surfaces with a clean damp cloth.

Car Keeping Hints:

- If you notice bird droppings or sap on your paint, wash the spot off right away; don't wait until the next car wash.

- Keep your headlights clean between washings. Dirt diminishes their effectiveness.

- Wax your car by hand at least a couple of times a year. Buy a good quality wax and follow the directions on the label.

Car Supplies. Here are two lists of supplies you should have in your car. The first list of items should be kept in your trunk. Use a plastic storage container, a duffel bag, or tote to keep everything together. The second list is for supplies you may want to have on hand inside the passenger compartment. Items inside the passenger compartment should always be kept secured, for example, in the glove compartment.

Car Safety Supplies—Trunk

- Blanket

- Can of instant puncture seal

- Flashing, battery-operated emergency light

- Jumper cables

- Reflector triangle

- Spray window cleaner and paper towels

- Tire jack

- Water (in a plastic bottle or jug)

Seasonal

- Small bag of sand, cat box filler, or rock salt.

Car Supplies—Inside

- Car's owner manual

- Change for parking and tolls

- First aid kit (including motion sickness medication—for a passenger, *not* for the driver)

- Flashlight

- Map

- Paper and note pad

- Proof of insurance and registration

- Trash bags

- Umbrella

Seasonal

- Snow brush/ice scraper

- Spray de-icer (can)

- Sun screen

- Sun shield

Important: A loose item rolling under the accelerator or brake can be a potentially dangerous situation. Loose items can also be extremely damaging in an accident. Put small items in the glove or other compartment. Buy a behind-the-front-seat organizer if your car does not provide storage space.

- If you do not already know how to jump-start a car or change a tire, please take the time now to learn.

Your Well-Being

I've been telling you what to do—and what not to do—for over five chapters now. Of all the information in this book, the single thing I hope you will most incorporate into your life is: *Take care of yourself—physically, emotionally, mentally, and spiritually.*

It's easy not to give our health much attention when we are well. Yet, in my opinion, we need to be attentive to our health or we will not stay well. Without meaning to, we can do ourselves a disservice. Have you ever been tired beyond belief only to realize that you either haven't been eating much, or eating all the wrong things? Or have you ever been surprised at how irritable you feel, only later to realize how much stress and strain you were living under? Paying close attention to all aspects of your health, or wellness, will help keep your life in balance. It's much harder to live life to its fullest when you are not caring for your wellness.

Life requires a certain amount of energy from you each day. You have to find that energy somewhere or you will be operating from a deficit position—which means, clearly not at your best.

Since we are all wonderfully different, we all seem to have different ways to keep going and remain energized. I happen to be someone who feels at my best when I've had about *ten* hours of sleep, but I know people who can function perfectly fine with half that amount. Even though the specifics of what it takes to keep us well and running at our best are different, we all share common ways to become energized and to care for our wellness:

Wellness Watch

- Nourishment

- Sleep

- Exercise

- Lifestyle

- Indulgences

Nourishment. The next chapter will be entirely devoted to food because it's so important in your life, or should be. Do you remember the analogy we learned in grade school about how the body needs food just like a car needs gas? Well, I guess it has been around for generations because it's so true. We have to have nourishment to keep our bodies energized.

You've seen the charts of the food pyramid and what you are supposed to eat. Do you know anyone who actually eats the recommendations *every single day?* It's a goal we all need to shoot for. If you had trouble eating right before, use living on your own as an opportunity to take charge of your nutritional intake. Please don't fall into the routine of not feeding yourself well. It is tempting not to take the time and the trouble to prepare yourself wholesome meals. You may even feel a little silly about fixing a full meal, with a nice table setting, to enjoy all by yourself. Yet, your well-being is certainly worth the effort.

You may want to take vitamin and mineral supplements to ensure you at least receive the basic nutrients your body needs. If you do, please be mindful that vitamins and minerals should be supplements to, and not substitutes for, whole food. Whole food contains additional nutrients, such as phytochemicals, that our bodies need. Phytochemicals are naturally occurring, health- enhancing compounds that are proving to be beneficial to our bodies at a cellular level—which makes it truer than ever that we need those veggies, fruits, grains, and legumes.

- Eat a variety of different foods and food combinations. Eating the same things over and over is not only boring, but is also not as healthy as enjoying all the wonderful foods that are available to us.

- Everyone has time to eat. If you are spending your life with no time for meals, you need to do whatever you have to do to fix the situation. Eat!

- If you use the excuse that you don't like cooking for just one person, cook several servings and freeze the excess in individual containers that you can heat up another time.

- Invite people over for meals. Friends will enjoy and appreciate even the simplest meal.

- Cooking actually is part art and part science. Give it a try. You may find cooking to be a way to relax or possibly to be your creative outlet. You may discover you have a gift!

Sleep. While the effects of poor eating habits may not be apparent immediately, the effects of poor sleep habits become apparent right away. We can feel terrible, can act terrible, and can even get in terrible accidents when we are suffering from sleep deprivation. Living on your own may mean you can sleep whenever you choose, but your body clock is going to have its say.

The benefits of sleep are not cumulative: Get a good night's sleep and you may feel strong enough to push yourself and cut back on several hours the next night. Well, that's where the trouble starts. You are going to feel tired if you do not maintain an overall reasonable amount of rest for your body.

Your lifestyle should accommodate your sleep requirements and sleep patterns. You know how many hours of sleep work best for you, and rarely is it a good idea to skip or scrimp on getting the amount you need. Uninterrupted sleep is the best. Turn off the ringer on the phone if you have to. Say no to a social invitation if what you really want is a solid night's sleep. Put extra covering over your bedroom window if you sleep best in an absolutely dark room. Fix your environment and your timetable to get every bit of sleep you crave.

There are those among us who live to sleep. I am one. Whatever your unique sleep patterns are, if you notice a prolonged increase or decrease in your sleep time, you may want to talk to your doctor.

Exercise. Isn't it odd that an antidote to fatigue can be exercise? If you've ever been the kind of tired that has nothing to do with how much sleep you get, you understand why I think it's odd. Pushing yourself to exercise when you feel fatigued can take a tremendous amount of energy—even just talking yourself into it can take energy!

The American Cancer Society recommends at least 30 minutes of moderate activity most days of the week. The American Heart Association wants us to exercise also. We know they're right, don't we? I, at least, am convinced I'll turn into just another sad statistic if I don't get my recommended daily requirement of physical exertion.

You may need to do some searching to find the activities that are right for you. Sticking with exercise is much harder if you're not enjoying what you are doing. The good thing here, though, is that activities that didn't used to be counted as "exercise" now are! Yes, that dancing you did on Friday night and the housecleaning you accomplished on Saturday can be applied to your exercise tally. How great is that?

You may need to enlist the support of a friend or coworker to help you keep up with your exercise routine. Knowing you have a standing appointment to work out with a friend may be all you need to keep on track.

Lifestyle. Well, this word is certainly thrown around a lot, isn't it? Your lifestyle, or your typical approach to living, affects all aspects of your happiness and well-being. Living a life that goes strongly against your heartfelt and soulful desires can be a painful existence. We all make lifestyle choices. Sometimes our choices enhance our lives, sometimes the choices hinder our well-being. Stay in touch with how the choices you make affect you.

When your lifestyle replenishes your inner vitality, you will be at your best. Not only will you feel better, but you will also have the energy to grow into an interesting and productive individual. We all experience times when we feel out of balance, when parts of our lives just aren't working. It can sap our strength straight out of us. Those are the times when we need to examine our lifestyle and see what areas need attention. Are we trying to accommodate the desires of too many other people? Are negative personal habits draining our energy? Pinpointing areas where we can positively change will go a long way to keeping us happy and healthy.

Finding something you love and are passionate about has long been a great energizer. When you incorporate that passion into your daily life, you will find vitality. If you do not have something you are enthusiastic about, the process of searching for that something can in itself be a wonderful experience. Keep learning and developing interests in different things. You may find that passion, and you will definitely turn into a more interesting and well-rounded person.

> Live the lifestyle that suits you best; adjust areas that do not serve you. Make the effort to choose a lifestyle that enhances your well-being.

Indulgences. I've heard it said that there is more to life than just being comfortable, and while I agree, being comfortable (in comfort's most luxurious sense) is to me, about as good as it gets. A hot shower and putting on my favorite old clothes goes a long way toward maintaining my wellness.

The little ways we treat ourselves matter as much as the major life decisions we make. You may need to indulge yourself a bit while you are living on your own. Of course, I am not talking about negative indulgences here. I am talking about being nice to yourself. Do what it takes to keep yourself happy and content. Hopefully, when you're happy it will rub off on the other people in your life.

Stress may be an issue for you. Perhaps you are trying to excel and advance in your job. You may be carrying the additional responsibility of trying to get an education while working. You may feel stressed and overwhelmed by your new world of being an independent person. Being tender to yourself may help you keep the stress at bay and revitalize your spirit.

Indulge yourself once in awhile. Make sure, though, that it is not an indulgence that will *cause* stress in another area of your life. For example, don't rationalize indulging yourself with a major purchase you can't afford when you'll end up creating a stressful financial situation.

Be kind to yourself. Don't constantly push yourself too hard. Push yourself when you know you can handle the consequences. Now that you are on your own, do things you have always wanted to do. Find positive little ways to make life work for you, even if it's as simple as making your favorite cookies and taking a nice long nap.

Depression. Successfully living on your own requires responsibility in all areas of your life. If you start to feel overwhelmed with all your new responsibilities, seek out assistance. If loneliness becomes a constant feeling, get help. If you think you may be experiencing depression, not just a case of "the blues," see your doctor. Depression takes many forms, but a few of the symptoms include:

- Being sad, worried, irritable, and having little or no interest in the things that used to give you pleasure.

- Negative thoughts; difficulty concentrating and making decisions.

- Feelings of hopelessness, anxiety, or fear.

- Changes in sleep patterns, appetite, or weight.

- Thoughts of harming yourself or others.

We all go through periods when we are not operating at our best and can use some help. Please don't ever hesitate to ask for assistance.

The Doctor. Regardless of how attentive you are to your well-being, there will still be occasions when you will need to visit the doctor. The National Foundation for Cancer Research suggests a complete health examination for those between the ages of 18 and 20, with complete exams, at least every five years, until age 40. Having a regular doctor who tracks your history, a doctor that you are comfortable with and that you have confidence in, can be a real blessing.

There are referral agencies that will help you find a doctor. Look in the yellow pages under "Physicians." Here again, it may be a good idea to talk to your family, friends, and coworkers about their experiences with their physicians. Even if you have a medical plan that dictates which doctors you see, there may be several doctors available in the group.

Have you ever felt too sick to go to the doctor? While living on your own, there may come a time when you will need to determine carefully whether you are sick enough to see the doctor. Hopefully, you will see a doctor before you are so sick you can't get out of bed. Don't be reluctant to get a family member or a friend's opinion as to how sick you are. Often we tend to think we're not as ill as we really are and neglect getting timely treatment. Even a common illness like the flu can lead to secondary infections, such as bronchitis and life-threatening pneumonia. You need to take an illness seriously.

Know the difference between the flu and a cold. The flu usually hits you hard all at once, whereas you can feel a cold "coming on," with symptoms normally building up gradually. The flu usually includes a higher fever than a cold, more body aches, and possibly severe fatigue. Having over-the-counter medications like Ibuprofen on hand when the flu hits will prevent you from needing to shop when you feel awful.

Taking good care of yourself when you are sick will help reduce the chance of secondary infections. Your immune system needs all the help you can give. Get lots of rest and drink plenty of liquids. Do not hesitate to call the doctor.

- It is reasonable for you to expect your doctor to listen to all of your concerns.

- Ask direct questions and give direct and detailed answers to all questions your physician asks.

- Ask for detailed explanations of anything you do not understand.

- Do not be shy about taking notes. It's easy to forget what was said before you reach the parking lot.

If you cannot afford to see a private doctor, check your phone book for the location of the closest public health clinic.

Hint: Fortunately, one of the most effective ways to prevent getting sick is also one of the easiest things to do—wash your hands—often. When you pick up germs from infected surfaces, you infect yourself when you touch your mouth, nose, and eyes. According to the Centers for Disease

Control and Prevention, frequent hand washing goes a long way in preventing the spread of infectious diseases. Check out their Web site for additional helpful information: *www.cdc.gov.*

The Dentist. I know some people don't mind going to the dentist, but some of us put it off until we are in the throngs of a dental crisis. Don't we already have enough to do?

According to the American Dental Association we are supposed to visit the dentist regularly for an examination and professional cleaning. The dentist looks not only for cavities, but also for other dental and medical problems, such as oral cancer.

There are referral agencies specifically for dentists. Check the phone book, but also be sure to ask around for good referrals.

Your Time

Everyone's time is valuable. We've all had experiences in which we felt we were wasting our time, or worse, felt frustrated that someone else was wasting our time. Manage your time well and the benefits can be enormous.

Have you ever heard the adage that goes something like, "Ask a busy person to do something for you and it will get done; but ask someone who seems to have all the time in the world, and it will never get done"?

Some people have learned the skills involved with effective time management better than others. Some have learned time management skills, but are not time-integrated, and they are slaves to clocks, schedules, and a time-driven pace. When you have made peace with yourself regarding your use of your time, you will naturally set and be comfortable with your *own* pace, spending your time wisely.

One area that often trips us up is that we commit to things that we really do not want to do. We say "yes" instead of doing everyone a favor and saying "no." *Every commitment that you make is one that you should keep,* so use discretion when committing your time. Be in control of your time. For example, you may want to tell friends not to wake you up if they drop over, see your lights out, and know that you've gone to bed. You may want to discourage drop-by company altogether. The idea is for you to be in charge of exactly how you spend your time.

Procrastination. Some people need the pressure of a deadline to actually get a project accomplished; therefore, they wait until the last minute so they can catch that rush which fuels them to get the job done. Sound familiar? Putting things off until the last minute is not necessarily a bad thing. Sometimes it works. Yet, things are generally much easier and run smother when we face what we have to do and get it over with, dropping the excuses. There may never be the perfect time to make that phone call or write that letter.

Often the price of not doing the thing we are thinking about doing is so marginal we subconsciously think it doesn't matter anyway. If that is true in your case, if the cost of not doing it *truly* doesn't matter, maybe you are focusing your energy in the wrong direction to begin with.

Putting things off becomes a real problem when the task involved is one that gets bigger as time goes by. Leave the housecleaning for a couple of months and you will have a huge undertaking ahead of you. It's much easier to face a small task than an overwhelming one. It's easier to break a large task into manageable bits. It's also easier to spend the time it takes to do whatever you need to do, than to waste your time worrying about getting it done.

Errands. Running errands is one area in which a small amount of planning can save you a large amount of time. Thinking ahead, not only about what needs to be done, but also when and where, will really save you from time wasted dashing about.

- Remember that "cubby" area mentioned in Chapter 4? Pile up the library books, outgoing mail, film to be dropped off, and so forth into one space. This will prevent you from having to search around for items you need to have with you. Consider using a tote bag.

- Group your errands by location and do them in logical order. Zigzagging around takes additional time.

- If you are fortunate enough to live close to a facility that offers several services, try it out. Shopping for your groceries where you can drop off your film, dry cleaning, and medical prescriptions, as well as rent a movie, has got to be a time-saver.

- Anticipate your future needs. Are you low on, but not completely out of, stamps? If you are at the post office mailing a package anyway, buying stamps then will save you the additional trip. Buy some gas while you are out running errands, not when you are late for work.

- Keep slips from the dry cleaners and the photo drop in your car.

- Does something really require a special trip out or can you wait until you have an additional errand?

Free Time. It's wonderful to spend time as you genuinely desire. Even spending your free time doing nothing at all, on occasion, can be using it wisely. Do not let the demands of living on your own chew up all your free time. Become well-organized and a good manager of your time, even the small amounts. For example, find a way to make your lunch hour revitalizing. A change of scenery, a short nap, or a brisk walk may make a huge contribution to the rest of your day. Yes, you will need to keep up with maintaining your home, health, laundry, and car, but you also need to truly enjoy the time you call your own.

Chapter 6

Eating In And Dining Out

Managing Your Meals

We think about food every day. We need to earn the money to pay for it, and we need to shop for it, cook it, and clean up after it's prepared. Food is such a large and continuous part of a normal day that if we aren't careful, eating can turn into a big monotonous chore. So big, in fact, that supermarkets are full of ready-to-eat individual meal servings, cleaned and ready-to-use ingredients, and hundreds of packaged, processed shortcuts to preparing meals—all designed to make meal preparation easy for us. What could be less hassle than sticking a complete frozen dinner in the microwave?

Your lifestyle will influence your eating patterns. How much time and money you have to spend will affect the choices you make. Although some of your monthly expenses are fixed amounts, such as your rent, the amount you spend on food each month can vary. You may need to stick to some no-frills cooking at home when funds are tight and visit your favorite restaurant or buy the gourmet foods when you can better afford to do so. Fortunately, there is quite a range of options available to us when it comes to purchasing our food. This is one area where we can easily go financially overboard, or where we can eat well very reasonably.

Variety is important when it comes to food. Even your favorite meals will become tiring if you eat them too often. Have you ever ordered takeout pizza so much you got sick of it? It's also nice not to prepare all your own meals every single day. Going to a restaurant, to a friend's or relative's house for a meal, or cooking for someone else, can be a refreshing break. Try not to fall into a rut when it comes to your eating habits. If you give yourself an assortment of food options and make wise choices both in cooking at home and in eating out, you should have no problem managing your meals while living on your own.

Cooking at Home

Turning empty kitchen cupboards into a well-stocked, serviceable pantry is not difficult, but it can be expensive. You may need to spread the cost out over several pay periods. Buy basic items first and add to your supplies when you can afford to do so. For example, you will probably use salt and pepper before you'll use cloves or sage.

Always have back-up food available. A few standards, like peanut butter, pasta, canned tuna, or packaged soup, will get you through in a pinch. An extra loaf of bread in the freezer may save you a special trip to the store.

In addition to the fresh food that you like to eat, such as fruit, vegetables, meat, and bread, keep the basic provisions on hand. Adjust the following lists to fit your tastes:

Food Shopping List—The Basics

For the refrigerator:

- Milk

- Eggs

- Butter

- Cheese

- Yogurt

- Juice

For the freezer:

- Frozen vegetables

- Extra loaf of bread

For the pantry:

- Baking soda

- Bisquick all purpose baking mix

- Flour (store in an air-tight container, in a dark, dry place)

- Sugar (store in an air-tight container)

- Cooking oil—vegetable and/or olive (buy small containers—oil turns rancid in a couple of months)

- Pepper

- Salt

- Solid vegetable shortening (small)

- Vinegar

- Beans (canned or dry)

- Cereal (ready to eat or oatmeal, cream of wheat, etc.)

- Dried pasta and/or noodles

- Garlic

- Onions

- Peanut butter

- Potatoes

- Rice

- Soup (dry or canned)

- Catsup

- Mayonnaise

- Mustard

- Coffee and/or tea bags

- Syrup and/or honey

Canned:

- Pasta sauce

- Tomato sauce

- Tomatoes

- Tuna

Extras:

- Baking powder (small—keep tightly covered)

- Brown sugar (store in air-tight container or freeze)

- Cinnamon

- Cocoa

- Vanilla extract

- Bouillon cubes

- Dried herbs

- Paprika

- Soy sauce

- Tabasco sauce

- Crackers

- Jelly

- Nuts and/or raisins

- Soda

Shopping. If you plan to cook at home, you will spend some time in the supermarket. Since you will consistently spend your hard-earned money there, it only makes sense to take the time to learn how to be a savvy grocery shopper, whether you are shopping for food or nonfood items. You may already be familiar with some of the following suggestions. Just make sure you remember them as you do your marketing.

- Shop to control your diet. Not diet as in weight-loss; but diet, as in your daily food and nutrition intake. Every food you eat will affect you. You know what foods you are supposed to eat: fruits, vegetables, grains, and legumes. Simply put, these foods affect you positively. You also know that high-fat, high-sugar foods can affect you negatively and that they should be avoided or consumed in moderation. Buy the foods you need to maintain a healthy diet.

• Buy ingredients. If you look at an item and it doesn't look like anything you've ever seen in nature, chances are good you should buy something else instead. Heavily processed, convenience foods are more expensive and may not be the healthiest choice. Another thing to be aware of is that buying prewashed, peeled, and packaged food is going to be more expensive. That little convenience of buying preshredded cheese is going to cost you more money.

• Plan your trips to the market. Let as much time pass as possible between visits. Dashing to the store three nights a week is not only an ineffective use of your time, but you also run the risk of impulsively buying items you don't really need. It's common to go to the store to pick up one thing and walk out with a grocery bag full of things you had no intention of buying. Supermarket managers are well aware of consumers' inclinations. Look at how a supermarket is laid out. The milk is almost always way at the back of the store so you will have to pass just about everything to get that half gallon you need. The most expensive items are the ones that are the easiest to see and reach. The checkout is loaded with appealing little extras, like candy and magazines, that are just waiting to accompany you home. One long trip to the store is more effective than several smaller ones.

• Always shop for groceries when you are alone. You will shop more efficiently.

• Always shop from a well-thought-out list. Resist the temptation to add items that are not on your list, *except* for items that you regularly use which happen to be on sale that visit. For instance, if you see your favorite bath soap is substantially discounted, you should grab a few bars because you know you will eventually use it. Take advantage of special prices on the items that you normally use. When preparing your list, group items together that are in the same area of the store. This will make shopping easier by preventing time-consuming backtracking.

• Buy only the food you know you will eat. This sounds too obvious, yet most of us, at one time or another, have been guilty of throwing food away. If you know you have a demanding week ahead of you, buying the fresh ingredients to make complicated recipes may not be the right thing to do. The food can go bad before you have the time to prepare the meals. Also, don't buy anything you really don't like. Chances are good that you will end up throwing it away when you could have substituted it for something you do enjoy, that is just as nutritious.

• Consider trying store brands when they are cheaper. You may find you like them just as well. Experiment with a small size first to find out if you like the product. Do not buy a large box of Brand X breakfast cereal before you know whether or not you will eat it all.

• Pay attention to price, volume, and count. The larger size is often the most economical, but not always.

• If your Sunday paper has discount coupons, be sure to use them. Make it a point to always go through and save the coupons that are for items that you *normally* buy. Sure, try a different brand name if you have a coupon, but do not buy something you won't normally use just because it's a few cents off.

• If you have environmental concerns, buy products with the least amount of packaging. Look for flexible packaging, such as bags and pouches, and concentrated items that require less packaging.

• The grocery store is the place to buy your snacks and soda, not the convenience store. Nearly everything will cost more in a convenience store. Plan ahead. Buy snacks to keep in your car if it will prevent you from stopping at a convenience store when you are out driving around.

- Select the cold food last, go straight home, and put it away.

- Perhaps most importantly, don't shop for food when you are hungry. Eat before you go to the store. You'll save money.

Storage. Just as you made decisions on how to organize your kitchen items, you will also need to arrange your food to make cooking manageable. You are working against yourself if you have to hunt and dig for something you think you may have . . . somewhere. Unlike kitchen tools, food eventually spoils, so don't bury anything too deep.

- Whether it's dry groceries or cold stuff, group like things together.

Baking Supplies. Find a cool, dark, dry place to put flour, sugar, and so on. Once opened, these items need to be stored in an air-tight container such as a large Ziploc storage bag, plastic storage container, canister, or jar. This is also where you can store your pasta, rice, and grains. Keep them away from a heat source, like the dishwasher or oven.

Oil / Spices / Seasonings. Here again, it's important to keep these items away from heat. They will last longer and not lose their flavor as quickly. A little cupboard next to the stove or oven may be convenient, but not ideal if it gets hot when the oven is on. Check to see if the cupboard warms up when you use the oven. If you live alone, buy small quantities of oil as it can go rancid before you have a chance to use it all.

General Items. Organizing like foods together on the shelf will not only make getting to your food easier, but will also help in preparing your shopping list. You can see at a glance that you are out of pasta sauce if the spot where you normally store it is empty. If you buy multiples of any item, make sure you use the older one first.

Produce. Potatoes, onions, garlic, and anything else that does not need to be refrigerated should also be stored in a cool, dry spot away from sunlight.

Refrigerator. The refrigerator should be 40 degrees or less. Arrange items not only for your convenience, but also as to not interfere with air circulation. The refrigerator runs more efficiently when the air can circulate properly, so don't create a pile up or blockage.

- Keep eggs in the carton they came home from the store in. They will stay fresher longer in the carton than if stored in the egg compartment in the refrigerator door. Always check the carton for broken and cracked eggs before you buy them. Never use an egg that has even a hairline crack.

- Put items you use infrequently, such as cocktail onions, in the back. Leftovers should be up front where you won't forget about them.

- Keep uncooked meat and chicken in their original package *and* in a plastic bag or on a tray. Never let meat or poultry drip onto anything else.

- Make sure to eat the older items first and keep a watch out for food that is past its expiration date. When in doubt about any food still being good or not, throw it away.

- Consider getting into the habit of washing and drying your fresh fruit and vegetables when you get home from the store. You may find it makes cooking a meal or grabbing a nutritious snack much easier if that chore is already done.

Freezer. The temperature in your freezer should be zero or less. Food needs to be frozen in a way that protects it from freezer burn or drying out. Use plastic freezer bags or plastic containers with lids that seal tightly. Unless it is properly labeled, avoid wrapping anything in aluminum foil as it becomes hard to recognize the item without unwrapping. Keep a permanent marker close to the freezer and make it a habit to label and date what you store. Frozen vegetables and packaged foods can be frozen in their original containers. Don't wait too long to eat what you have in the freezer. Again, eat the older items first.

Snacks. When you are living on your own you may be inclined not to want to cook. I've often heard the remark, "I don't like cooking just for myself." If you let it, this notion is a direct path to snacking and little mini-meals (or frequent trips through your favorite drive-thru). While our bodies can handle reasonable amounts of junk food, be mindful to fill your home with healthy foods so you will not be having donuts, chips, ice cream, and soda for your dinner. Make it a point not to have high-fat, low-nutrition items sitting around your place to fill up on instead of eating something that's better for you. Enjoy those treats when you visit your friends!

Snack List. This list may remind you of snack time in kindergarten.

- Dried fruit
- Fresh fruit
- Granola
- Juice
- Nuts
- Raisins

- Rice cakes
- Sprouts
- Vegetables
- Popcorn
- Yogurt

Water. Don't underestimate the value of good plain water. Drink lots of it. Constantly buying bottled water can be expensive, so try to buy a water purifier or filter as soon as you can afford it. Remember never to use hot tap water for cooking or drinking. Hot water may contain impurities from the water heater. Also, never drink chlorinated water.

Food Safety. The U.S. Department of Agriculture, Food Safety and Inspection Service offers educational information on many food safety topics. The web address is *www.fsis.usda.gov*. The phone number is *800.535.4555*.

You should know how to handle and prepare food safely not only to protect yourself from foodborne illness, but also to protect anyone you may cook for, especially children or the elderly. Foodborne illness can be dangerous and knowing how to handle and prepare food correctly is critical.

- Shop for perishable items last, come straight home, and put them in the refrigerator or freezer.

- Items that are most likely to contain bacteria, such as meat, poultry, and seafood, should not be allowed to drip on other items in the refrigerator. Also, their packaging materials can cause crosscontamination.

- Wash your hands before you start cooking anything and after you handle raw meat, poultry, seafood, or eggs. Every time.

- Always clean kitchen surfaces with kitchen disinfectant or hot, soapy water, before, during, and after food preparation.

- Cooked food should not be handled with the same utensils that you used with raw food unless you have carefully washed them first. Wash anything that raw meat and poultry touch before you use it again.

- There are three safe ways to defrost frozen food. The refrigerator method requires you to put the frozen item in the refrigerator to bring it up from 0 degrees to 40 degrees. This will take at least a day. Cold water thawing is putting the food in a leak-proof plastic bag and submerging it in *cold* tap water. You have to change the water every 30 minutes until the food is thawed. A pound will take about an hour. The last method is defrosting in the microwave. Food defrosted in the microwave must be cooked as soon as it is thawed because some parts of it may have already become warm and reached the best temperature for bacteria to grow.

None of the safe defrosting methods involve taking food from the freezer and laying it on the counter until it is ready to be cooked. The center of the food may be frozen, but the outer layer will rise above 40 degrees and bacteria will start to multiply.

- Ground meat needs to be cooked until the inside reaches at least 160 degrees. This means the inside should be brown.

- Never eat undercooked or rare poultry. The internal temperature needs to reach 180 degrees. This means the inside should be white.

- The lowest setting to safely cook poultry or meat is 325 degrees.

- Never eat raw eggs or foods that contain raw or partially cooked eggs.

- Don't eat perishable food that has been sitting out for more than two hours.

- Put leftovers in the refrigerator immediately after your meal. Putting anything hot into your refrigerator can raise the temperature significantly, so wait until the food has cooled from hot to warm. Store food in shallow containers that allow the food to cool quickly and evenly.

- Use or throw away leftovers within three to five days.

- If you do not have a dishwasher, don't let your dirty dishes sit in water for a long time. The condition is just right for bacteria to grow. Rinse and stack if you want, but ideally all dirty dishes should be washed within two hours.

Dining Out

I love to eat out. I would rather eat at my favorite restaurant than cook. Yet, when you are just starting out on your own, dining out may not be practical. It certainly can be expensive. If you have limited resources yet still want to eat out occasionally, here are a few tips that may help:

- Check the paper for discount coupons. New restaurants often offer discounts to entice people to visit. The city where you live may have brochures for tourists that you can pick up free at the grocery store, library, and so on. These pamphlets are usually full of discount or "buy one, get one free" dining coupons.

- Lunch prices are usually less than dinner prices. Treat yourself to a big lunch and make yourself a light dinner.

- Avoid ordering drinks of any kind. Sticking with water will help keep your check total low.

- Share an entree with a friend and split the cost. This only works in restaurants that allow it and do not impose a per person charge.

- Don't worry if you are not financially able to eat at the restaurant you really want to try right now. You eventually will. If eating out means you must limit where you can visit, then that's the way it has to be, and good for you that you are not living beyond your means.

Dining Skills. Ideally we should all have only one set of dining skills that we use both in public and in private. Unfortunately, this is not the norm. People tend to be much more lax about the way they eat at home, alone, and with family, than when they eat out in public. The downside to this approach is that when they are out in public, it's much harder to use the correct skills because the skills are not automatic; the skills are rusty or nonexistent, and the person ends up feeling awkward. This is all easily avoided by learning basic dining skills and incorporating the skills into daily life until they become a well-developed habit. Buy *The Little Book of Etiquette* by Dorothea Johnson. The tiny book has all the correct and current information you need to know to become a savvy diner.

Napkin. The napkin has two functions. It's first use is to just sit unfolded in your lap and catch any drips or spills. Secondly, it is used to discreetly dab the corners of your mouth. It is not used to do major wiping of any other part of your face, particularly your nose. Carry a facial tissue with you or a handkerchief, but do not use your napkin to wipe or blow your nose. It is also not used to wipe crumbs off the table. Put your napkin on the seat of your chair if you temporarily leave the table during the meal and leave it directly in front of you when you leave the restaurant. If your plate is still there, leave your napkin to the left of the plate.

Posture. Yes, you should sit up straight and keep your elbows off the table. Unless you eat Continental-style, where it is appropriate to rest both wrists on the table edge, you should keep your arm and forearm off the table as well.

Silverware. This is an area of dining that a lot of people struggle with. It is the area that most reveals how much dining knowledge you possess.

- Do not worry too much about which piece of silverware to use. The outside pieces are used first. The pieces should be removed after every course, so you will easily figure out which piece to use next. If you see a fork and a spoon laying horizontally above the plate, they are to be used with your dessert.

- There is only one correct way to hold your silverware when cutting your food. It does not involve holding the knife or fork in your fists and sawing at your plate. Hold the knife in your right hand, blade turned down toward the plate. Put the tip of your index finger on the blade, where it meets the handle. Hold the handle with your thumb and middle finger about two inches away from the blade. These fingers hold the knife while the pressure from your index finger forces the blade to cut. Hold your fork in your left hand with the tines facing down. Put your left index finger on the center of the base of the tines. Your thumb should be below the handle, while your other fingers are curled around the bottom part of the handle. Cut with a forward stroking motion toward your body.

- If, after cutting, you secure a piece of food on the tines and directly bring the fork to your mouth with your left hand (tines still down), you are eating Continental-style. The knife stays in your right hand. This is the easiest, quietest, and most graceful style of eating. If you put your knife down and change the fork from left hand to right, you are eating American-style. As the name implies, it is mostly only Americans who still eat this way.

- Although it is very common for diners to prop their silverware up against their plate with half of it resting on the table, it is not correct. The rule is—once you pick up a piece of silverware, it should never rest on the table again.

  Rest your knife and fork over your plate when you are paused during your meal. Your knife should be pointed to about ten o'-clock on your plate and the blade should face inward. The fork tines should be turned down, cross the knife blade and face about two o'clock on your plate. They can extend over the plate about an inch, but do not rest them on the table.

- When you have finished eating, put both pieces of silverware side by side on the right side of your plate. The knife should be on the outside with the blade facing the fork.

- Do not leave your spoon in your soup bowl, cup, or sorbet dish when you have finished. Place it on the underlying plate.

- Don't be overly concerned if you drop a piece of silverware. You should not get up from your chair and pick it up off the floor. Just signal to the server. The server will get you a replacement and also pick up the dropped piece.

Offensive Behavior. You can easily guard against being unintentionally offensive at the table by keeping a few things in mind:

- When dining out, treat the wait staff with courtesy and respect. Remember to use the words "please" and "thank you" every now and then.

- Resist the urge to blow on any hot food.

- Make sure your mouth is completely closed while chewing and never, ever talk with food in your mouth.

- Avoid fiddling with your hair or scratching your head at the table. Never comb or brush your hair in a dining area.

- Don't stretch to reach something across someone's place setting. Ask the person to pass it.

- Keep your fingers out of your mouth. Fingers are not toothpicks, and even if they were, you do not use a toothpick at the table. Use a toothpick in the rest room.

- Watch your vocabulary at the table. Some things that should never be discussed during a meal are body functions, illness, diets, food preferences, and anything else that might offend someone.

Restaurants. When eating in a restaurant, remember to use all your dining skills and be familiar with the following:

- If you are the host or hostess (meaning you did the inviting) the responsibility of choosing where you are going to eat is yours. Sure, if you wish, you can say to your guest, "I'm thinking we'll go to 22nd Street Landing. How does that sound to you?," but try to avoid the conversation that goes:

"So, where do you want to eat?"

"I don't care. Where do you want to eat?"

"I don't care. Wherever you want."

"I don't know. What do you think?"

Does this sound familiar? It's very common for people to each pay their own way when they eat out and so the decision can be mutual, but if you are hosting don't be hesitant to take the lead.

- Try not to take the best seat at your table. The best seat is the one that has the best view of the restaurant. It should be given to your guest.

- Take off your baseball cap.

- Your personal items, such as keys, sunglasses, hats, and briefcases, do not belong on the table. A purse belongs on the floor near your feet, or if it is small, in your lap.

- If you sit down at a table that has a coffee cup already sitting there, do *not* turn it over to indicate that you do not want coffee. The server will ask you and if you decline, the server will remove the cup.

- When you have finished eating, leave your plate where it is. You shouldn't stack the dirty plates and push them to the edge of the table.

- Absolutely never withhold a tip because you are trying to economize! The average tip is between 15 and 20 percent of the total bill before taxes. If the service was really poor you may want to leave less; if the service was great feel free to leave more. Practice figuring out how to calculate tipping so you can determine the amount quickly. Don't get your dinner guest involved with discussing and calculating the tip.

Being a Dinner Guest. Remember not only to *use* your dining skills when you are invited to eat at a restaurant or in someone's home, but to keep in mind the following as well:

- Please don't be late.

- Wait to take your seat at the table until you are directed to do so. If the host or hostess tells you where to sit, don't suggest you sit somewhere else.

- Wait until your host or hostess picks up their napkin before you do.

- An invited guest is supposed to contribute something to the conversation. It is your responsibility to join in the conversation, yet to remember the things you should not talk about at the table. With those you do not know extremely well, you can pretty much add to the list of taboo subjects discussions about money, religion, and controversial matters of the day.

- Time the pacing of your eating to match the pace of others present. You shouldn't race to the finish or still be shoveling it in when everyone else is done.

- If the dinner was with someone you do not normally eat with (for example, not at your cousin's house where you regularly eat four nights a week), it is correct to send a thank you note.

Chapter 7

Becoming a Savvy Consumer

Consumer Know-How

You have been making choices about how to spend your money for many years. When you were younger, did you ever agonize over what to buy with the cash gift a relative gave you, when there were so many things you wanted? You did your best with the money you had and you learned some money management skills along the way. Well, now is the time to kick those skills into high gear. From here on out you've got to make the best decisions you possibly can to become a sharp and savvy **consumer.**

I am assuming that if you are young and just starting out, your income is not anywhere near what it will be in the future. Most likely your resources are limited, and your life is highly impacted by each financial choice you make. Yet, the need to be a savvy consumer does not disappear when you have greater resources. Later, you will make frequent decisions on more expensive expenditures. Regardless of your income, make it a point to be an intelligent and well-informed consumer.

Prioritize. Once you formulate what your goals are, you must prioritize your expenditures. For example, if your primary desire is to live on your own, obviously you are deciding that a top priority is to spend money for housing. You can decide if having one or more roommates is an option for you. Not everyone is cut out for sharing their living quarters, and you must make the decision that is right for you. You may decide that your housing costs are a higher priority than the year and model of the car you drive. The idea here is that your choices must meet your needs and you must finance those choices in the wisest possible way.

This brings us to the bottom line when it comes to consumer spending. Is what you're spending your money on something you really need, or only want, and is it a wise choice?

Before You Buy

Ask yourself these questions before you allow your money to flow away from you:

Purchase Checklist

- Am I purchasing something I really need?

- Does the item or service itself meet and fit my needs?

- Do I need to do any research before I buy?

- Have I done enough comparison shopping to make the purchase?

- Do I feel pressured to make this purchase?

- Can I truly afford this?

- Is there additional cost involved in this purchase?

- What's the worst thing that will happen if I don't buy this today?

Needs versus Wants. It's sometimes a pretty fuzzy line that separates your needs from your wants. Sure you want premium channel cable TV, but do you need it? These are the kinds of choices you are going to be up against. When you think about it, most of our purchases are for things we want all right, but not necessarily for goods and services that our survival or well-being depends upon. It's amazing how much we can do without if we have to. I don't want anyone to go without what he or she needs, but sometimes the habit of suspending our desires for *things* and *stuff,* until a better time, is the only practical option to exercise. Waiting may not be easy, but for some people, it certainly may be necessary.

Fitting the Need. On the surface a purchase may be just what you think you need, yet deeper examination proves that it doesn't exactly fit. For example, the cost of the used car you found may be just what you want to pay. It's in pretty good shape, but wait . . . what's this? It gets very, very poor gas mileage and your commute to work is forty-five miles each way! If you plan on driving the car to work, it would be in your best interest to keep looking.

You do not ever want to be sorry that you bought something you did. An example of this would be buying a desperately-needed winter coat only to realize the fabric should not be worn in the rain or snow, which is what you needed it for, and that it is dry-clean-only and will cost a mini-fortune to keep clean. Everyone has made thoughtless purchases at one time or another. Take the time to completely think through each purchase, and you'll find that your bad buys are few and far between.

Research. Today, we are fortunate to be able to take advantage of a tremendous amount of consumer research information. We have the benefit of consumer buying guides and consumer advocacy groups. There is information out there somewhere on just about every purchase you can think of making. Go to your local library or book store. Research online. For major purchases, check with the manufacture of the product you are considering to gain the knowledge you need to be able to compare it to similar products. There is an old saying: "Buyer beware." It's your responsibility to be aware of what you're buying.

Compare. Think about comparison shopping not only regarding the price of the product or service, but also with regard to the features of an item. For example, some small appliances have additional features for the same price of other models that do not.

Shopping around to get the best price is usually always worth it. Yet, keep in mind that the savings does have to be "worth it." By this I mean, it is not worth driving all over town the entire afternoon to save one or two dollars. First of all, your time is valuable and second, you are using up gas and incurring wear on your car. Not to mention that you will probably get hungry, go to a drive thru, and spend the few dollars you may have saved.

Don't forget that when you have decided on an exact item, you can call a store and ask the price for the item you want. This makes it easy to find the lowest possible price. Also check the paper for advertisements. This works especially well for seasonal items. Often you will spot the same item advertised at one store offered for less somewhere else.

Pressure. Pressure to make a purchase can come at you from several directions, not just from a salesperson who may be earning a commission and needs to make a sale. You may have time constraints. You may decide "just to get it," because it will be easier than thinking about it some more, shopping around some more, and returning back to the store again. You may have put off making a purchase for an upcoming event and now the pressure is on to buy something, anything close to what you need.

While operating under pressure in some circumstances may be appropriate, it is difficult to make the best consumer choices when you are under the gun. Resist feeling pressured into making a purchase that is not exactly what you need or can afford. If you do, learn from your mistakes and do what it takes; for example, planning ahead next time; to avoid the same situation in the future.

Remember all the talk of peer pressure in school? Well, for some people it never seems to go away, although it may change its form. Have you ever felt you wanted something because someone else had it? Don't get started in the "who has the most toys" game. It's a long trip to nowhere.

When I was in college I would rush to the bookstore at the start of every term to make sure I could pick a used textbook—at substantial savings. I had friends who would never buy a used textbook, with their big yellow stickers that didn't easily come off, because they felt it was a sign they didn't have money. I didn't care. I was not about to pressure myself into buying new when I was saving so much.

You may also be directly influenced by someone you know to buy something that *they* actually want. It's a good idea to ask for advice and information from friends and family before you make any major purchase. It's nice to run the idea by another person, perhaps hear something you haven't considered, or talk to someone who made a similar purchase in the past. Yet, keep in mind that the real user of the product or service is you, and your opinion is what ultimately should count the most. Do not let yourself be pressured or talked into buying something your gut feeling tells you is wrong for you, just because your best friend wants you to buy it. Trust yourself to figure out what is right for you.

Affordability. Are your finances going to be adversely affected in any way if you make this purchase? Can you make the purchase and still have funds left over to cover your other expenses? Do you have the cash? If you are putting a charge on your credit card, are you going to be able to pay the balance when your statement arrives or will you have to finance this purchase? Is this purchase worth incurring debt? Give yourself honest answers to these questions.

Additional Cost. It may not be a big deal if you need to buy batteries for the CD player you just bought. It may be a bigger deal if you realize the old motorcycle you just bought will be needing tires soon and a new battery. How much is registration and insurance? Title fees? Storage fees in the winter because you do not have a garage and the living room isn't all that practical? You get the idea. Think about additional costs that might come up, such as how much is that hard to fix item going to cost to get repaired? Go for the low maintenance items and items that will not require extraordinary servicing.

Worst Case Scenario. This question is particularity helpful for the times when you are undecided or feeling pressured. Sure the item may not be there if you come back looking for it later. What then? Is the item so special that you would *truly* regret not having bought it? Most likely you could track it down somewhere else.

Is your need for the item so great that it will truly impact your life if you don't buy it today? Try to resist feeling like "I've got to buy this right now." Take your time and think through every purchase.

Big Ticket Items. There is a lot to think about when you buy anything, but especially when you make major purchases. In particular, make sure you do the necessary research and price comparisons.

Learn when to buy quality goods. In some instances spending a few dollars more to purchase something well-made and long-lasting is the wisest way to go, that is, if the item is actually going to be genuinely useful to you. For instance, no matter how well made a dress may be, it won't be cost-effective if you only wear it once.

When you are just starting out, almost anything above the cost of food and shelter may seem like a major purchase. Anything over $500 is definitely a major expenditure. When you are satisfied that a major purchase, over $500, is right (you thought it through and did the necessary research and price comparisons), there is still one more thing you can do. You can haggle over the price. Nicely and firmly. You have nothing to lose and you may end up saving. Try it; you may be surprised.

Files. Keep a file that includes warranties, instruction manuals, and receipts for your purchases.

Hint. If you become tempted to rent furniture and/or appliances, carefully consider the idea. In certain circumstances, for instance, when you know you will need the items for only a very limited time, it may be a good idea to rent, but it generally is not to your advantage. Check the contract very carefully and make sure you know exactly what renting will actually cost.

After You Buy

It sounds really obvious, yet one of the smartest things you can do is take good care of the things you spend your hard earned money on. Take care of your clothes and you will need to replace them less frequently. Take good care of your car and you will decrease the chances of having to pour your cash into getting it repaired and yes, again, replacing it. Cars are now built better than ever and will last for many, many years with the right care. It only makes sense to want whatever you own to last as long as possible.

You have probably already developed rules concerning your belongings. If you are someone who has been careless in the past with your possessions; for instance, loaning things to friends who never seem to return them; you may want to start practicing a little more care now that you have so many financial responsibilities. Replacing an item because of carelessness is not cost-effective and will take you further away from reaching your financial goals.

Extended Warranties. When you purchase certain items, such as appliances, office equipment, and so forth, you will probably be asked if you would like to purchase an extended warranty. While you might think this coverage is not a bad idea, keep in mind that extended warranties are not used most of the time. This means the chances are good that you will never use the coverage you are paying for.

Buying Insurance

You've heard about insurance. You choose a policy, pay your **premium** (or payment for the coverage,) and hope you never need to file a claim. Auto insurance will probably be your first experience at purchasing insurance. It is only one of the many types of insurance you will need to acquire in your lifetime. You may need renter's insurance soon and home owner's insurance down the line. Whatever your needs are, this is one more area in which it is critical to do your homework.

Insurance is a big business. Always shop around for the best policy. This means the best coverage, with the lowest rate, on the benefits you are likely to use the most. The companies that issue insurance are rated by several agencies. Buy your policy from a company with a high rating.

Again, head back to the library. Ask friends and relatives. Call the free quote services. Do your research. The following are a few types of insurance you will need to consider now or in the very near future:

Insurance

Now:

- Auto

- Health

- Renter's

Later:

- Term Life

- Home Owner's

There are many large insurance companies that offer complete insurance coverage. This means you can obtain policies for different needs through the same company.

Auto. Auto coverage rates vary greatly from one company to another. Be sure to check with large national insurers. Buying direct without an insurance agent may save you money. The amount you pay for auto insurance will not only depend on the coverage you buy, but several other factors as well.

Your rates will be affected by the type of car you drive. If you have the hot car of the moment, your insurance rate will be higher. The type of vehicles that are most often stolen cost more to insure than others. Your age, sex, marital status, and driving record will be a consideration. Rates are usually more if you are under 25, a male, single, or worse, all three. Not having an accident or moving violation will help keep your rates low. The number of miles you normally drive are also a factor as well as whether or not you are a student.

While there are plenty of variables, one of the biggest factors is how high you set your **deductible.** (The amount you are required to pay before an insurance reimbursement is made.) A higher deductible will decrease your premium. Carefully consider how much coverage you actually need. Make sure you have adequate coverage without being overinsured. For instance, if you do not have assets to protect, you may not need $350,000 worth of **liability insurance.** Get quotes on several different coverage amounts, at different deductibles, before you decide.

Health. If you do not have health insurance, find a way to get coverage as soon as you reasonably can. Even a minor injury or illness could wipe out your savings and put you in debt. Look for a job that offers health benefits. Many universities and colleges require you to have health insurance. If you are a student taking nine hours or more, check into a student health plan. These plans offer limited coverage at reasonable rates.

If you cannot be on your parents' insurance policy, try to find a group policy of some sort. Generally, most group plans, such as those through an employer, alumni association, chamber of commerce, and so forth, will be less expensive than an individual policy.

Look at both indemnity care and managed care. An indemnity plan allows you greater freedom in choosing the services you may need, but you have more out-of-pocket expenses than with managed care. There is an annual deductible you must meet before the insurance kicks in, and you will also owe a portion of every bill (co-payment.) Policies differ as to what services are covered. Generally there is little or no coverage for preventative care, such as for getting a flu shot.

A managed care or Health Maintenance Organization (HMO) differs from an indemnity plan in that there is no deductible. You pay a flat periodic fee and a small co-payment every time you see a doctor or other practitioner. Your are limited to using the providers who have contracts with your HMO.

Be aware that short-term policies exist that will allow you to have coverage for up to six months. This may work for you until you can find an employer-sponsored health plan.

Renter's. You may think you do not have enough to insure, and in the very beginning you may be right. Yet, items add up quickly and soon you will accumulate enough to seriously consider renter's coverage. If you think it would cost close to $10,000 or more to replace what you have, it's time to purchase a renter's policy. Don't make the mistake of assuming your landlord's policy will cover your personal possessions. You need your own protection.

Understand what losses the policy covers. Typically, renter's insurance covers loss due to fire, smoke, theft, vandalism, and many other occurrences, but not losses due to earthquakes or flood, although you may be able to purchase the additional coverage with a **rider** or **floater** to your policy.

Renter's insurance involves personal property coverage and liability protection. If your guest gets hurt at your place and sues you for damages, your insurance covers your cost up to your **liability** limit.

You will need to make sure you understand the difference between a policy that pays **replacement cost** or **replacement value** and one that pays out **actual cash value.** If your old stereo system is stolen, actual cash value coverage pays out what the insurance company determines the old stereo was worth, and chances are the amount will be nowhere near the amount needed to replace it. A policy that pays replacement cost will pay what it costs to purchase the item again. Keep in mind that renter's insurance also has a deductible. That is, you will receive the amount owed you minus your deductible, or if the amount owed to you is not more than the deductible, the policy does not pay out.

Make sure you thoroughly understand the details and conditions regarding the company's procedure in paying your claim. For example, will you have to buy replacement items with your funds and submit receipts before you get a reimbursement?

Also, make sure you research what the policy covers on items such as electronics, jewelry, art, and antiques, which may only be covered up to a certain amount. If you have any of these items, make sure you discuss this with the insurance company so that you will be buying the correct coverage for your belongings. You may need to purchase an additional rider for these articles.

Remember the safe-deposit or strongbox suggestion from Chapter 1? Keep the receipts of all your purchases as well as a photographic inventory of your belongings in the box. The receipts may be used as proof that you bought an item in question. It is to your advantage to be as prepared as possible in the event you ever need to file a claim. Photograph possessions as you acquire them or videotape the entire contents of your place. Keep an up-to-date running inventory of your belongings. In the event of a disaster the last thing you will want to do is try to recall every item you owned. Here again, be prepared.

Hint: There are certain things an insurance company will give a discount on. No matter what type of policy you are checking into, ask the representative what discounts the company offers. For instance, you may receive a discount on your renter's insurance if you have smoke alarms and fire extinguishers. You may receive a discount on your auto policy if your car has an alarm. Don't forget to ask.

It is probably premature to worry about life insurance and home owner's coverage now when there are so many other things to get in place. Yet, you should know this very basic information:

Life Insurance. This type of insurance protects those who depend on you from the loss of your financial support in the event of your death. If you are not yet responsible for the financial support of someone else, and you do not own property, you probably do not need this type of insurance.

Life insurance is not necessarily a permanent need. You may need heavy coverage when you have the responsibility of a family and lots of debt obligations. In your later years, being lightly insured or having no coverage at all may be appropriate if your financial estate is in place.

When it is time to shop for life insurance, I recommend you seriously consider only term life. With a term policy you are covered for a specific amount of time, for instance 10, 20 or even 30 years. Term life insurance is generally the most cost-effective type of policy for providing a benefit for your loved ones.

If you are ever attempted to buy a whole-life policy (one in which you are covered your whole life) or a cash value policy, I suggest you go back and do some more research. Make sure you are not depending solely on the information provided by the insurance company or agent for the company. Making whole-life sound like a terrific deal is the agent's job. Do independent research.

Home Owner's. Similar to renter's insurance in that it provides personal property and personal liability coverage, home owner's insurance also provides protection against damage to, or loss of, the dwelling you own. When you finance your first home, the lender will require you to purchase this type of coverage. Again you will need to do the research, decide how much coverage you need in order to have sufficient protection, and decide which, if any, additional riders to the policy you need to purchase.

Buying a Car

You will probably always remember your first car and the independence and freedom it represented. If you haven't made the purchase yet, here are a few things to think about.

Before You Buy. While you may have an idea as to the kind of car you would like, what is probably more important is to have a very clear idea as to the price you are going to be able to afford to pay for the car. If you will be seeking a loan from a bank or credit union, shop for the loan first and get preapproved before you become too far involved with selecting your car. The loan amount that you qualify for will influence the options available to you, as will the amount that you have available for a down payment.

When deciding how much you can afford, be sure to factor in all expenses related to the purchase, such as taxes, fees, and registration; and to consider the monthly expenses involved, such as the monthly interest cost, maintenance costs, and the insurance premium.

Promise yourself that you will stick to the limit that you have set. It's easy to drift off and start looking at more car than you can afford. Stay within your limit amount and do not let yourself be talked into anything else.

Whether you buy your car from a dealer or a private party, have the car inspected by an expert. Make sure you know exactly what you are getting into. Ask yourself the questions from the "Purchase Check List" mentioned earlier. Be especially sure the car is the right one for you. It may be a while before you buy another one.

Your Test Drive. Take every car that you are seriously considering for a good, objective test drive. This is where you will see how well suited the two of you are. Keep in mind that the car that is most visually appealing to you may, in fact, not be the one that is exactly right for you. I've been in cars that no matter how I adjusted the seat, it never fit me correctly. Finding out how comfortable the car is, is one of the many questions you will need to find the answers to, so the longer the test drive, the better.

- How is the visibility? Check out the blind spots.
- How does the steering feel? Are you comfortable with it?
- How well does the car accelerate? Try to find an on-ramp to test acceleration. How well does it accelerate with the air conditioner on?
- Try to find a rough road to see how well the car rides.
- How does the car perform in tough traffic?
- Try the reverse gear. Do all gears work smoothly?
- Do you understand the instrument panel? Is it easy to use and read?
- What is your gut reaction to the car?

Try to have the least possible distractions. Don't hesitate to tell the salesperson (if he or she insists on going with you) that you would like quiet so you can concentrate. Check the radio when you get back to the lot, not during the drive.

The test drive is very important because the information you gain is critical to the final success of your search. Here again, take your time and trust yourself to make the right choice.

Protecting Yourself

You are accepting a lot of responsibilities when you live on your own. You'll spend time learning how to handle your finances; you'll make sound decisions. Crimes of financial and identity fraud are real in our society. You need to be aware of this so you will use your best judgment and exercise caution in your personal and financial life. Part of being a savvy consumer is being aware of potential fraud in your virtual surroundings and taking the steps you can to avoid it.

- I wrote in Chapter 2 that you should use discretion with regard to your Social Security number. The same applies to your credit card numbers. Do not ever give out either numbers over the phone to a business or service provider *who has called you.* Make sure you know to whom you are talking. Even if you are given a number to call back, check with the phone company to make sure the number matches the business.

- Take time to look at the itemized charges on your credit card statement. Call the card company immediately if you think there has been an unauthorized charge to your account. Check your phone bills, also.

- If you feel you must always carry a credit card with you, only carry one. Do not normally carry your Social Security card.

- If you have a personal identification number from you financial institution—do *keep it a secret!* Do not use the last four digits of your Social Security number, your birthday, your dog's name, and so on for the number and do not write it on anything you carry with you.

- Do not disclose personal information, such as your credit card number, Social Security number, mother's maiden name, and so forth in any e-mail message or over a cellular phone.

- Contact the Bureau of Motor Vehicles immediately if you think your driver's license number has been misused, for example, to write a bad check. You will need to get a new license and put a fraud alert on the old one.

- When you write a check to pay a bill by mail, drop the bill off at the post office or put it in a mail collection box. Never leave a check to be collected from your home mail box unless the box has a lock that can only be accessed by the postal carrier.

- Tear up or shred all offers for credit cards that you do not accept. If you receive checks from your credit card company (hopefully you will never need to use these) make sure you destroy them also.

- *Never* sign a blank check, blank contract, or blank sheet of paper!

- Most importantly—Trust your instincts. If your intuition tells you something is amiss, you may be right. While you do not need to live in fear of being a victim of financial or identity fraud, you will feel more empowered knowing you are taking steps to protect yourself.

Tipping

Somewhere along the line we learn that certain services performed for us by others require our tipping. While tipping in the United States is still voluntary for most services, it has become the accepted and correct thing to do.

Learn which services require tipping and the correct amount to give. The accepted amounts vary, depending on the area of the country where you live. Here are some general guidelines:

• Baggage Handlers:	$1 and up per bag
	The person who brings your bags to your room receives $5 or more, if there is a large amount of luggage.
• Beauty Operator—non owner:	10% to 20% of your bill
• Carwash Attendant:	$1
• Delivery Person:	$1 to $2 and up
• Golf Caddy:	15% to 20% of green fees
• Parking Attendant:	$1 to $3
• Taxi Drivers:	15% of the fare *Minimum is 50¢*
• Wait Staff:	20% of your check's total before taxes

It is appropriate to tip in accordance with the service provided. For example, if the valet ran through wind and rain to bring your car to the door for you, consider adjusting the tip upward, while if the wait staff neglected you and provided poor service, you are free to adjust the tip accordingly.

The day will come when you will successfully maneuver through enjoying the pleasure of up-scale restaurants. Here are the general tipping expectations:

• Coat Check:	$1 for one coat and 50¢ for each additional coat
• Maitre d':	$10 to $20 depending on the amount of service provided
• Pianist/Musician:	$1 per request
• Rest Room Attendant:	50¢ to $1 per visit
• Restaurant Wait Staff:	20% of the check total before taxes *5% for the person who took your order and 15% for the person who served your food*
• Wine Steward:	10% to 15% of your wine bill

$ **Watching Your Pennies** $

- If you are going shopping just for the fun of it, leave your money, checkbook and credit cards at home.

- Don't shop when you are feeling any mood extremes. Being too tired, sad, or even too happy may cause you to make an unwise purchase.

- Buy used. Not junk, but used items that still have plenty of life left in them. Be careful; going to garage sales and flea markets can become addicting.

- Check out your nearest beauty school. It may offer great savings not only on haircuts and nails, but also on spa services.

- If you or someone you know has a truck, pick up that new large purchase yourself and save delivery costs.

- Wait a day or two for your photos. One-hour service usually costs more.

- Set an amount limit on every gift you purchase and stick to it. If you give gifts during the holidays, try to spread your shopping throughout the entire year to avoid needing a large sum of money all at once.

✔ *Watching Your Pennies—Your Clothes*

- Avoid trendy fashions. This may be the last thing you want to hear, but buying something that is going to be out of date within six months is definitely not cost-effective. Stick to the classics.

- Buy on sale. Don't pay retail. Clothes do not set too long on the racks before being marked down.

- Make sure a retail outlet store is a true outlet and that the clothes really are cheaper.

- Avoid items that are "Dry Clean Only."

- There are several products available to help freshen and remove wrinkles from your "Dry Clean Only" garments. Using one may stretch out your trips to the cleaners.

- Buy items that can be worn with what you already have or that match other separates you buy. For example: Don't buy a top if it matches only one pair of pants.

- Consider taking a part-time job at a retail store that offers its employees a generous discount.

✔ *Watching Your Pennies—Your Car*

- Keep your driving record clean. Violations are expensive and your insurance rates will go up since you won't qualify for discounts.

- The most expensive time to buy a car from a dealer is March through June. Lots of people plan their summer vacations and purchase new cars. The weeks before Christmas and the first months of the new year are better times to negotiate a deal.

- Buying a preowned "new" car can save you thousands. Find one with 5,000 miles or less, that was a demo or rental.

✔ *Watching Your Pennies—Your Insurance*

- Shop around and around!!

- Find out what conditions qualify you for a discount.

- The higher the deductible, the lower the rates.

- Buying two or more policies from the same place may save you money, but only if it is insurance you were going to buy anyway.

Resources to contact for information and help:

Agency for Healthcare
Research and Quality: *www.ahcpr.gov/consumer*

Consumers' Checkbook: *www.checkbook.org*
A nonprofit consumer information and service center.

The Consumer Insurance Guide: *www.insure.com*

National Fraud
Information Center: *www.fraud.org* or *800.876.7060*

For comparison quotes on insurance policies:

InsuranceQuote Services: *www.iquote.com*   *800.972.1104*

Master Quote: *www.masterquote.com*   *800.337.5433*

Quote Smith: *www.quotesmith.com*   *800.556.9393*

Select Quote: *www.selectquote.com*   *800.343.1985*

Insurance rating services:

Standard and Poor's: *212.208.8000*

Moody's: *212.553.0377*

To report fraud to the credit reporting bureaus contact:

Equifax: *800.525.6285*

Experian: *800.301.7195*

Trans Union: *800.680.7289*

Chapter 8

Staying Connected

Positive Actions

I believe everyone should live alone for awhile before they take on the additional responsibilities of a life partner or starting a family. Living alone gives you the time to discover who you really are and how you truly want to spend your life. It's having your place in the sun. Yet, I have known many young people who, even though they had looked forward to living on their own, have ended up not enjoying the experience to its fullest. We are not all cut out to live alone, but the experience can give invaluable insight. It can be a time of great personal discovery and growth, and best of all—fun!

I think one of the contributing factors to how successful you feel about living on your own is how well you are able to feel engaged in, and connected to, life itself. Living on your own is *not* similar to solitary confinement. It's a wonderful opportunity to challenge yourself to expand and explore all the riches of our world and to make a productive contribution to society. Having your own place may mean that for the first time in your life, you are able to have the social life you want or to pursue areas of interest you have always wanted to try. It could be that for the first time in your life, you are free to truly express who you really are and what you are all about.

A pitfall of living on your own is that you can easily begin to feel lonely. Unfortunately, many jobs today also contribute to the feelings of loneliness and isolation. Some people spend the entire working day alone at a computer terminal. It can take an enormous amount of energy and will to combat the negative feeling of loneliness, yet you must make the effort.

Build a life for yourself that is comfortable, interesting, and productive and your experience with living on your own will be positive. I hope the following suggestions are helpful:

Create a Comfortable Home. Even if you think you live in a "dump," do whatever you can to make your *home* as physically and emotionally comfortable as possible. You have your own style—express it! Turn your place into an environment where you look forward to spending time and one that works for you. If you want to leave an ongoing project out so you can work on it whenever you feel like it—now is your chance. If you want a drum set, amplifiers, and sound equipment in the living room instead of furniture, it's your choice. You are a grown-up now and can live the way you please.

Make the effort to create surroundings that make you feel like you are home. Buy a plant. (A philodendron is hardy and will tolerate mild neglect.) Put out pictures of people you love. Unpack any boxes that are still sitting around since you moved in. The more you can do to make your home feel like home—a place you enjoy being—the better off you will feel.

Family and Friends. Not everyone chooses to be connected to his or her family, and very often today, families are spread out across the country. If you do not have close family ties, the relationships that you cultivate with friends and coworkers become that much more important. As you know by now, friendships do require a certain amount of cultivation and effort. Being a good friend does require your time and awareness, but having a good friend is a priceless experience.

You've heard the expression, "You can never have too many friends." Friends can enhance your life beyond measure. Don't limit yourself just to people whom you already know. Seek out friends from all areas of your life. Young or old—from your job, school, or where you do volunteer work. We tend to gravitate toward people we feel comfortable around and who we feel are like us and share the same interests. Yet, I hope you also cultivate relationships with those who are different from you. Everyone has something unique to offer.

- Always use sound judgment and trust your instincts when it comes to the people you include in your life. Remember a true friend is respectful of you. Someone who asks you to compromise your integrity or break the law is someone you should not include in your life.

- Learn the skills involved in dealing with difficult people. You may have to face someone who is hard to get along with every day at work or school. Turning a strained relationship with an acquaintance into a friendship may be too much of a reach, but having the skills to handle a difficult person without causing yourself undue stress can be a true blessing.

- Sooner or later you will find yourself being host or hostess to family and friends. With all entertaining, it is important to make your guests feel comfortable, but especially so when you have houseguests:
  - Clean your home.
  - Make room for your guests ahead of time. Clear an area where they can put their things. Make sure there is also space cleared in the bathroom to lay out items.
  - Lay out clean towels and show your guests where they are located.
  - Make sure your guests have enough bedding, and so forth.
  - Have food available and ready.
  - Anticipate your guests' needs and do your very best to make them feel at home.

Enrichment Classes. Taking a class just for the heck of it may be the last thing you think you want to do right now, but I encourage you to take every enrichment class that interests you or that you think you could benefit from. I have mentioned several subjects in this book that I think would be to your advantage to pursue and learn more about:

- Basic Real Estate: Learn as much as you can about buying and financing a home, so that when it comes time to purchase your own home, you will be a savvy buyer.

- Car Maintenance: Know how to handle routine tasks yourself as well as how to change a tire and jump-start your car.

- Cooking: A cooking class can be great fun and you (and your guests) can immediately reap the rewards of your learning a few different dishes.

- Dance: Be sure to learn the basic social dances.

- Dealing with People: Yes, there are even classes on dealing with difficult people.

- Dining and Etiquette Skills: Do not underestimate the importance of knowing the correct way to handle yourself in public, particularly if your career is one in which you are dealing directly with people.

- Disaster Preparedness: Learn how to be ready and how to deal with the types of disasters most common in your geographic area.

- Exercise: If taking an organized class is the only way you can get yourself to exercise, sign up! (If you are pursuing a business career, make sure you know how to play golf and tennis!)

- Money Management: Understanding the best ways to handle not only your day-to-day money decisions, but the different ways to invest safely and wisely, is a valuable addition to your financial knowledge.

- Public Speaking: Taking a speech class or attending Toastmasters International will help build your public communication skills.

- Relaxation: Consider massage, meditation, and stress reduction.

- Resumé Writing: Learn how to write the resume that is best for you and keep it current.

- Self-Defense: Learning the basics will help you feel more confident.

- Taxes: Obtain tips and advice and learn the tax laws so you can manage your money accordingly.

- Time Management: The more demands you have on your time, the more you need this knowledge.

- Being certified in the following areas is something that a potential employer may look at favorably:
  - American Sign Language
  - CPR
  - First Aid, including the Heimlich Maneuver.

Look for classes at adult education facilities, community and civic centers, churches, YMCA's, and so forth. Many bookstores now offer interesting classes free of charge. Our world is huge and brimming over with things to learn, and the returns of learning are enormous.

Volunteer. You are a unique individual and your community needs your contributions. Seek out ways to help others. If you had to do volunteer work or community service in high school, keep up the practice of offering your time to worthy causes and organizations. Not only does the organization that you help benefit from your time and effort, but few things are as personally rewarding as serving others.

Organizations and Clubs. If you have a particular area of interest, chances are good that there is a club or organization of people in your area who also share your enthusiasm. For example, if you love to go canoeing, joining a canoe team may be just what you need; not only to enjoy the sport, but also to stay connected with others.

Don't hesitate to try different clubs and groups. If you find something just isn't working for you, you can move on to something else. The point is to stay engaged in an active life and not to fall into the isolation of being alone.

Hint: Organizations, clubs, and communities often sponsor free events. Attending community events, activities, and concerts is a great way to economize on your entertainment expenses, meet a variety of people, and stay in touch with what is going on in your area.

Worship. I strongly encourage you to find a place of worship or a spiritual home. Some people know that organized worship is not for for them, while others instinctively know they need the fellowship experience that organized worship offers. If you are open to the idea of organized worship but have not yet found a place to attend that feels right to you, please keep looking until you do. Be open. Search for the place where you feel comfortable and spiritually nourished. Not only will positive fellowship enrich your life, but having a spiritual "family" can also give you the support base you may need.

Getting Help

When I started a small business, I was stunned at how many people went out of their way to offer help and assistance to make my business work. What surprised me the most was that other business people, people whom I had never met before, were offering me their expertise, lending me a hand, and doing what they could to help me get going. I will never forget their support.

My daughter had leukemia when she was nine years old. The disease caused her sternum to break, and caused several fractures in her back. For a while, she was unable to walk and had to be carried everywhere. Her low blood count made it impossible for her to be in public places. I couldn't leave her alone, and I couldn't take her anywhere except to her treatments. I was a single mother alone with all my family far away. A simple thing like getting to the store to buy food all of a sudden was a problem. I started to worry about how we were ever going to manage, but before I knew it, help arrived from the most *unexpected* people. I am telling you this because I want you to be sure you know and understand, that there are good, wonderful people in this world who love the opportunity to care for and help others who genuinely need a hand.

Don't ever feel too proud or embarrassed to ask someone for help. You can benefit greatly from other people's knowledge and life experience. Most people are flattered when asked to give an opinion or helpful advice. No one gets though life without the help of others, and we are all blessed when we are able to help each other.

A Final Word

Leaving your family home and moving out on your own is an important rite of passage. I hope it is a joyful, rewarding, and exciting time for you. You have the knowledge to make it a successful experience. You've been preparing for a long time . . . ever since you first heard the basics:

- Be nice.

- Pay attention.

- Wash up.

- Clean your room.

- Eat!

- Be careful.

- Go out and play!

You have my warmest wishes.

Glossary

Actual cash value: The current depreciated value of an item, usually less than what it costs to replace it.

Consumer: One who buys or uses a product or service.

Credit bureaus: Private agencies that collect information about an individual's credit worthiness and sell that information to authorized users, such as banks and credit card companies.

Credit report or credit rating: A formal record and evaluation of an individual's or business's history of credit responsibility.

Debit: The accounting of a debt. For example, to debit an amount from your account is to deduct that amount.

Deductible: Under your insurance policy, the amount that you must pay before the insurance company begins paying on your claim.

Deductions: The expenses or items used to offset the amount of gross income or adjusted gross income on a tax return.

Dividends: Payment of a share of the earnings or profits of a corporation to shareholders.

Full faith and credit: The unconditional commitment to pay interest and principle on a debt; for example, a federal, state, or local government's pledge.

Gross income: Your total income, excluding amounts not subject to tax. Amount before deductions are made.

Hold: When a financial institution does not immediately credit all or part of a deposit.

Interest: Money charged for the use of borrowing money or money paid for the use of money.

Liability: Money that you owe.

Liability insurance: Coverage to protect against claims of injury or damage to other people or their property.

Lien: A legal right to take another's property to satisfy a debt.

Networking: Being involved with an association of individuals who may have common interests or provide mutual assistance, such as the sharing of information or services.

Overdraft protection: Coverage that allows you to draw in excess of your account balance.

Period or statue of limitations: Period of time the Internal Revenue Service can assess additional tax, or in which you can amend or change your tax return.

Precedence: Priority of order based on rank or importance.

Premium: A periodic, regular payment you must pay for your insurance coverage. Premiums are usually paid in installments.

Prospectus: A document for prospective buyers describing the main features of a mutual fund, stock offering, business venture, and so forth.

Replacement cost or **replacement value:** Amount it will currently cost you to replace an item.

Resumé: A written summary of your work experience, education, and accomplishments used to obtain an employment interview.

Return: Annual percentage amount reflecting the gain or loss on a total amount invested.

Returned check: A check that your financial institution does not pay because you do not have enough money in your account to cover the amount of the check.

Rider or floater: An amendment or addition to a contract or insurance policy.

Securities: An investment instrument—usually stock and bond certificates.

Security deposit: Money held by your landlord during the term of your rental agreement to offset any damages incurred due to your actions.

Sublease: A lease granted by a person already leasing that property.

Surcharges: Charges in addition to another.

Tax return: Form used to provide the Internal Revenue Service with your taxable income information.

Tax schedule: Forms filed with your tax return to supply supporting information.

W-2 Form: The form you may receive from your employer that indicates the total amount of money earned in a calendar year and also the total amount of taxes withheld from those earnings. This form comes with several copies, one each to be filed with your federal, state, and local (if any) returns, as well as a copy for your records.

W-4 Form: The form your employer uses to determine the amount of taxes to be withheld from your wages. You fill out the form by indicating your Social Security number and how many personal exemptions or dependents you which to claim.

Withholding: The amount of your income that your employer sends to the federal, state, and local tax authorities as partial payment of your tax liability.

Bibliography

American Cancer Society. 1996. "Guidelines for Nutrition and Cancer Prevention."

Baldrige, Letitia. *Letitia Baldrige's New Complete Guide to Executive Manners.* New York: Rawson Associates, 1993.

Brody, Lora. *The Kitchen Survival Guide.* New York: William Morrow and Company, Inc., 1992.

The Car Care Council. "Signs of Impending Car Trouble You Should Know." Available from www.carecouncil.org/pk99tu.htm, accessed 12/15/99.

Eisenberg, Ronni with Kate Kelly. *Organize Yourself!* New York: Collier Books, 1998.

Friedman, Jack P. *Dictionary of Business Terms.* New York: Barrons, 1994.

Greist, John H. and James W. Jefferson. "Dealing With Depression: Taking Steps in the Right Direction." Roerig, Pfizer and Pratt, 1992.

Jhung, Paula. *How to Avoid Housework.* New York: Fireside/ Simon and Schuster, 1995.

Johnson, Dorothea. *The Little Book of Etiquette.* Philadelphia: Running Press, 1997.

Kiplinger's. "Smart Moves: Your Guide to Managing Your Money." *Kiplinger's Personal Finance Magazine,* 1996.

National Automotive Parts Association. "New Teen Drivers Learn ' Auto Care 101.'" The Car Care Council. Available from www.carecouncil.org/fw9c101.htm, accessed 12/15/99.

National Center for Infectious Diseases. 1999. "An Ounce of Prevention: Handle and Prepare Food Safely." Centers for Disease Control and Prevention. Available from www.cdc.gov/ ncidod/op/food.htm, accessed 12/20/99.

———. "An Ounce of Prevention: Wash Your Hands Often." Centers for Disease Control and Prevention. Available from www.cdc.gov/ncidod/op/handwashing.htm, accessed 12/20/99.

Nemeth, Maria. *The Energy of Money—A Spiritual Guide to Financial and Personal Fulfillment.* New York: Ballentine Wellspring, 1999.

Orman, Suzy. *The Nine Steps to Financial Freedom.* New York: Crown Publishers, Inc., 1997.

Social Security Administration. "Social Security: Your Number." SSA Publication No. 05–100002, February, 1998.

United States Department of Agriculture. "The Big Thaw." Food Safety and Inspection Service. Available from www.fsis.usda.gov/OA/pubs/bigthaw.htm, accessed 12/20/99.

Wall Street Journal. 1997. *Lifetime Guide to Money.* New York: Hyperion.

Weil, Andrew. *Eight Weeks to Optimum Health.* New York: Alfred A. Knopf, 1998.

Williams, Art. Common Sense—A Simple Plan for Financial Independence. Atlanta: Parklake Publishers, Inc., 1991.

Winston, Stephanie. *Stephanie Winston's Best Organizing Tips.* New York: Simon and Schuster, 1995.

Index

NOTES

NOTES

NOTES

Life Skills 101:
A Practical Guide to Leaving Home and Living on Your Own

CHECK YOUR LEADING BOOKSTORE OR ORDER HERE

Yes, I'd like _____ copies of Life Skills 101: A Practical Guide to Leaving Home and Living on Your Own @$14.95 each, plus $3.00 shipping for the first book and $2.00 for each additional book. Please add 83¢ per book for books shipped to Ohio addresses.

Name: _____

Address: _____

City: _____ State: _____ Zip: _____

Telephone: _____

Payment: ___Check/Money Order

Credit Card: ___Visa ___ MasterCard

Card # _____ Exp. Date ___ / ___

Signature _____

Please make your check payable and return to:

Stonewood Publications
P.O. Box Nine
Cortland, Ohio 44410

Call your credit card order to: 888.404.8310
Fax order to: 330.637.8315